"What's a little pain? At least you're alive, you lucky bastard, you."

— "Six Feet Under," 2004

"*LET us go then, you and I,*
When the evening is spread out against the sky
Like a patient etherised upon a table;

....

[Let us walk through]
Streets that follow like a tedious argument
Of insidious intent
To lead you to an overwhelming question …
Oh, do not ask, "What is it?"
Let us go and make our visit."

"The Love Song of J. Alfred Prufrock"
T.S. Eliot, 1917

Foreword

What you hold in your hands is a story about a hero named
Roger Madoff. I say this as someone who has known Roger and his
wonderful family—friends and supporters of Weill Cornell Medical
College—for many years.

When Roger was first diagnosed with leukemia at the age of 29, he
made a very conscious decision to fight his disease. As a patient at
NewYork-Presbyterian/Weill Cornell Medical Center, Roger was faced
with a dizzying array of treatment options designed to put his cancer
into remission. With the support of his loving family, he was able to
delay the progression of his leukemia for several months. When his
cancer recurred, he decided to write this book, hoping that it would
serve both as a form of personal therapy and as a guide for others who
might be traveling a similar path in the future.

What makes Roger's story so compelling is his ability to humanize his
treatment and his life during very trying times. With candor and
humor, Roger chronicles his illness up until a few months before he
courageously faced death in April 2006. A touching epilogue by his
wife, Jen, completes Roger's story and serves to remind us of the power
of faith and family in the face of extreme odds.

Leukemia for Chickens is a chronicle of a life well-lived. I invite you to
meet Roger Madoff and experience his journey for yourself on the
following pages.

Antonio M. Gotto

Dr. Antonio M. Gotto Jr.
Stephen and Suzanne Weiss Dean
Weill Cornell Medical College
Provost for Medical Affairs, Cornell University

To Jen, who promised always to stand by me.

I love you.

Part I: Auto

LEUKEMIA FOR CHICKENS

1

Earth

November 25, 2002, 5:50 PM

"Hold on, Mom. Call waiting, okay?"

"Okay."

Click.

"Hello?"

"Hey, it's Adam."

"Hey, what's up? Actually, hold on. Let me get off the other line."

Click.

"Mom, it's Adam, the doctor. I'll call back and let you know what he says."

Click.

"How goes it?"

"Okay. We got the results from your blood tests back. Normally we don't get them the same day, but the technician saw something he wants us to reconfirm."

"Okay. Like what?"

"Well, your white count was really high. Like 65,000."

"And normal is?"

"About 10,000."

"That sounds high."

"It is."

"So what does this mean?"

"Well, when something is this far out of line, you want to do the test again to make sure something didn't go wrong."

"How do we do that?"

"We need you to go to the Emergency Room and retake the test."

"Now?"

"Now."

"Which hospital?"

"NewYork-Presbyterian Hospital, on York."

"This can't wait until tomorrow?"

"No."

"What are we talking about here? What's so unusual?"

"Sometimes you can get these high white counts when you have a severe case of Mono. A case of Mono would explain why you feel so tired and lousy."

"Is there anything else it might be?

"Well, let's not go there yet. The important thing to do is to confirm these results. I'll meet you at the NewYork-Presbyterian Hospital Emergency Room."

"Um, okay. Jen's still in the subway on her way home from work. I'm supposed to feed Milo and take him for a walk. Should I do that first, or should I be going straight to the hospital?"

"Can Jen take care of the dog when she gets home?"

"Yeah."

"That would be better."

"Level with me, Adam. I won't freak out. What's the worst we're talking about here?"

"It could be leukemia."

Silence.

"You know my little cousin has leukemia. They found it in September. I just saw her last month in the hospital."

In addition to being my primary care physician, Adam had been best friends with another cousin of mine since elementary school. With this relationship came knowledge of the big and little medical problems of every member of our family.

"I know. It's weird. But let's not think about that now. Let's just redo the test."

"Okay. What are the chances it's leukemia?"

"I don't know."

"Let me just finish up some things here, and I'll head uptown."

"Not a problem. I'll meet you at the ER entrance at 68th Street and York. And bring a pair of sweatpants and a toothbrush, in case you have to stay overnight."

"Um, okay. Thanks."

"Bye."

"Bye."

Ring.

"Hello?"

"Hey Ma, it's me."

"So what did the doctor say?"

"Not great. They saw something funny in the blood test I took today. They want me to retake the test tonight to make sure it's right."

"Funny like what?"

"I don't know, something about a high white count. I need to go to NewYork-Presbyterian Hospital to retake the test. Can you meet me there?"

"Sure. What's the address?"

"68th and York, the ER entrance. You'll probably beat me there. I gotta leave a message for Jen to feed the dog and then come meet me, too."

"Well maybe now you'll find out what's been bugging you the past few weeks."

"Maybe. Bye, love you."

"Love you, bye."

Start recording your memo now. Beep.

"Hey Jen, it's me. You're probably wondering why I'm not home now. I got a call from Adam. He got the blood tests back and they looked bad. I'm not sure what's going on, but I have to go to the Emergency Room at NewYork-Presbyterian Hospital to retake the tests. I didn't get a chance to feed or walk Milo. You need to do that before you can meet me the hospital at 68th and York. (deep breath) Whatever this is, we'll get through it. I love you, and I'm really sorry."

Beep. *Memo recorded.*

Sweatpants and toothbrush stuffed in a D'Agostino bag in my right hand, I hailed a cab uptown with my left and was off. Maybe it was just a bad case of Mono.

On Saturday night, Jen and I had gone to a sitar concert at Columbia University. For more than a year, Jen and her co-workers at the Community Research Group at Columbia's School of Public Health had interrupted their usual agenda to focus on community-based recovery from 9/11. This sitar concert was one of a number of events aimed at helping people heal that her group sponsored. Though the music helped me relax more than I had in a while, Jen's boss, a physician with whom we sat during the performance, commented I looked tired, that work had run me down.

She was correct about that—work certainly hadn't been fun for a while. For the past three years, I had been spending my days doing an ill-defined job at a struggling financial software company. The mission of the company, Primex Trading, was to build an electronic auction for stocks. To get a traditional brokerage to join our network, we needed to persuade the firm that managed their current electronic system to get on board. They were in no rush, and it was my job to get them moving. On Friday, I had threatened the CEO of one firm that I would sit outside his office all day until he agreed to meet with me. The childish prank worked. I got my meeting. Except when we met, he offered no excuse for ignoring my requests to meet. Basically, we were just at the bottom of his priority list and had fallen through the cracks. With no apologies he said to me, "You guys were collateral damage."

And a big, fat, wet, sloppy kiss to you, too. Today, Monday, I had written an email to Anthony, my main contact at the company: *Can't make it to work today. Feel like hell. This job is killing me. I'm reachable at home or by email. Cheers, Roger.*

A case of Mono might be just the break I was looking for. Leukemia might do the trick, too. Then again, leukemia could be fatal. Of course, living in New York in 2002 seemed like a death wish in itself. More than a year after the attacks of September 11, I was not yet inured to the constant alerts—headlines about stolen ambulances, threats of nuclear-laden cargo, reports of suspicious bulk purchases of teddy bears. Not to mention the actual horrors that were occurring overseas, which seemed inevitable to occur here as well.

I was more paranoid than most. I couldn't step into a subway car without considering, even if only fleetingly, whether someone might blow it up. During the previous year I had talked weekly with a therapist about my worries. More than once in the recent past I had found myself thinking that if I became ill and had to consider my own health first, those concerns might overshadow my fears for the world at large and actually lessen my anxiety. Those who have never struggled against illness can envision the challenge of doing so as a relief as well as a curse. Be careful what you wish for.

LEUKEMIA FOR CHICKENS

2

Water

November 25, 2002, 7:30 PM

The triage nurse moved me from the Emergency Room waiting area to a small room where the doctors were working with patients. Adam, my internist, who had met me at the hospital, was quickly joined by my wife, Jen, Jen's parents, my parents, and my sister, Shana. I was lying on a gurney, my head and torso raised up on an angle. My coterie arranged themselves in a semicircle behind me.

Though I couldn't see them arrayed behind me, I could guess how everyone was reacting: My mother had been mostly silent since I had first met her in the waiting room; my dad shook off his fear of the unknown by rambling on about his workday; Shana was on her phone, organizing the care of her daughter and other details of her life; Jen's dad, who worked in medical education, sporadically threw out whatever facts he knew about treating leukemia. Occasionally someone would put a hand on my shoulder; I assumed it was one of the moms. Jen and Adam were the only two people I could see. Jen had come in after the others, distraught and feeling uninformed. I assured her that we didn't know much more than what I had left on the machine at this point.

As we waited for a doctor from the hospital to enter, we as a group did our best to keep conversation light and off-topic. The plan for our two families to fly to Palm Beach on Wednesday for Thanksgiving was obviously not going to happen. Someone needed to call a local butcher and reserve a turkey for Thursday, three days away. The families divvied up responsibility for making sides: Lois, Jen's mom, said she would make her famous squash soufflé and cranberry sauce; my mom took responsibility for chicken soup and chopped liver. It was still up for grabs who would cook the turkey. A lot depended on where we would eat. Everyone agreed my pop would carve the bird.

We all fell silent as Dr. Gail Roboz entered the room and introduced herself as the "on-call" doctor for the leukemia unit. She was in her mid-thirties, petite and very put-together. Though it was 6 p.m. and probably the end of a 12-hour shift, she looked as fresh as if I were her first patient of the day. She was clearly the Type A, top-of-her-class overachiever—a necessity for ranking as high as she did at her age. She quickly listed what would happen next, with the firmness of a pro: She would repeat the blood test taken earlier today, look at the slides in the lab, and be back in about twenty to thirty minutes. With that, a nurse was summoned to draw blood from my arm for the test. Dr. Roboz said she would have more to discuss with us once they looked at the test results. She and the nurse departed together.

My fate, to be delivered in under a half hour. Preparing for Thanksgiving seemed less compelling all of a sudden. Groping for topics of conversation, I figured now was as good a time as any to unveil My Plan.

"Dad?"

"Yeah?"

"You know how things have been a little slow at work the past few months?"

"They haven't been that slow."

"Well, it's been slow enough that I've had time to work on other things."

"Like what?"

"You know how Jen and I went to Lake Placid for Memorial Day? You all saw the pictures. We loved it. It was beautiful. The mountains, the space."

"Okay."

"Pretty as it was, there ain't much to do up there other than walk, talk and eat. Jen and I spent a lot of time thinking, 'What could we do here to make enough money so that we could earn a living?'"

Jen: "Roger, are you sure you want to get into this now?"

"Why not? Got anything better to talk about?"

It wasn't out of character for me to talk with my dad about harebrained schemes. Some background: My father is an entrepreneur and always looking for new ideas. He and his older brother had built together a successful stock-trading firm. Five years ago, Dad and a few outside partners founded Primex, my employer. The idea behind the struggling financial software company was to build a "virtual" New York Stock Exchange—a computerized version of the traditional trading floor. Everything was going digital, and the NYSE was a relic of an age of face-to-face business. The trick would be to simulate and speed up the intricate auction process that happens on the Exchange floor.

My father had become enamored with this concept and had laid the groundwork for the project while I was abroad in Italy, working as a reporter for the Bloomberg newswire. After a year, my family and Jen grew antsy about my extended absence. At the same time, I was becoming physically weary of my ex-pat existence: aimlessly bar-hopping til the wee hours, riding my scooter along the narrow cobblestone streets home to my lonely bed. When the number of *apertivi* began to correspond with the number of typos I was making in the stories I wrote, I knew it was time to call it quits. And with Primex, my dad's pet project, looking as if it might actually take off, I came home, becoming the last of my generation of Madoffs to succumb to joining the family firm.

But my role at Primex was never really defined. For a year or so it didn't matter much. I needed the transition time and didn't mind the slow days. When slow became stagnant and my feeling of being aimless at the company dragged on for months, then years, I distracted myself with my own pet project. Until this moment, I had not discussed it with my family. Jen was staring at me with a look that said this might not be the most appropriate time to spring it on them.

Jen, warily, sing-song-y: "Okay."

"One favor. Let me walk you through the whole idea. Try not to interrupt. Thanks."

My audience murmured its assent.

I continued with my spiel, which I had rehearsed informally in talks with friends.

"As I was saying, Jen and I went through the usual list of tourist-town ideas—ski shop, B&B, clothing store, deli, pizza joint, newspaper stand, trinket hustler, coffee shop. All covered. You could do a Starbucks and run the local coffee house out of business, but it doesn't seem like the best way to make friends. Not that they don't have a McDonald's and Ben and Jerry's already, but you get the idea.

"There's no bagel shop, but I'm not about to get up at 3 a.m. and bake for a living. So it wasn't so easy to find a niche. But the night before we left, I noticed a bottle of Adirondack Natural Spring Water at the bedside. Damn! Another idea taken, I'm thinking. Then I read the label on the bottle closely. The source of the water was in Red Hook, NY. Red Hook! In the Hudson Valley. Not even within the Adirondack Park. Hundreds of miles from Lake Placid. So I made a note to look into the Adirondack Beverage Co. and the market for bottling water in the Adirondacks in general.

"And you know what? There's no major bottling company within Park borders. Now you're thinking, 'That's because it's a park.' Fair enough, but it's an unusual park. Half the land is owned by the state and is inviolate. The other half is owned privately, with varying restrictions on development. There are small-scale bottling programs dotted around. Nobody's invested the capital and gone through the hoops set up by the Park Agency to do a medium to large-scale project. Part of the reason is that it's almost impossible to build a structure bigger than 10,000 square feet in the Park. And you pretty much need that much space to bottle at the source."

Dad: "You got a name for this, this venture?"

"High Peaks Water Company. The High Peaks region is the area of the Park where Lake Placid is located. But I've got more than that. I've got properties in mind with list prices of about $1,000 an acre. I've got geologic surveys from the state showing me the location of sand and gravel aquifers within Park boundaries. Truth is, you'd probably rather drill a borehole and extract spring water from deeper underground. The trick to that is to make sure the water doesn't contain a lot of manganese, which gives it an orange-y color and not-so-great taste. Also, you have to find a renewable source, meaning one that collects a lot of water. But it's generally a rainy place. We're not talking about the desert southwest here.

"I've found companies that have drilled boreholes for local municipalities, studies detailing the cost of extraction and bottling equipment. You can get prefab bottles from Ball Corp. or you can buy your own bottle press from a manufacturer in Indonesia. You're probably talking a start-up investment of a million dollars, max two million, maybe breaking even on an operating level in three years."

Dad: "Who's going to buy this water? There are no people up there."

I wasn't thrown by my dad's skeptical questions. In fact, I knew they would be coming and maybe that was why I was subconsciously using the hospital room and my impending diagnosis as a buffer. But I had confidence in the research I had done on this alternate life plan. As for the others in the room, they mostly kept quiet, except for some giggles—probably from nervousness about the whole situation, possibly from disbelief at the timing of my pitch.

"You're right. The key to making it work is getting people to buy your brand rather than the Coke brand, Pepsi brand, or Nestle brand. They are the dominant bottlers, although they call themselves Dasani, Aquafina, and Poland Spring. You'll never beat them on price or volume. That's where the Park tie-in comes in.

"You play on people's perceptions of the Park. That it's bigger than Vermont and still unspoiled. You set aside 10% of the proceeds to buy more land for state preservation. The state designates the land 'forever wild'. That's the clause in New York State's constitution that forbids any development. Catchy, huh?

"Your gross margins before marketing are still almost 65 percent, based on what I've seen in the financials of publicly traded water companies. Of course, Pepsi and Coke could eventually drive those margins close to zero, because they're overwhelming competition for a small operation. So there's always a risk. But it's an idea."

Pop was about to give his two cents on the scheme, starting with, 'I'm glad you've been busy, at least,' when Dr. Roboz knocked on the door again and let herself in. Saved by the bell. I was relieved to have let my secret out and to be spared the need to explain myself any further.

LEUKEMIA FOR CHICKENS

3

Fire

November 25, 2002, about 8 PM

"It's leukemia. I looked at the slides, and it is unmistakable."

In giving her diagnosis, Dr. Roboz wasn't mincing words or wasting time.

"We still need to do some more blood tests to determine what kind of leukemia you have, but it won't affect your initial treatment, which is a standard protocol that's been used for the last fifteen to twenty years."

Dr. Roboz's words stunned me. It's not that the signs hadn't pointed to this, but all my life I had escaped worst-case scenarios. This was worse than any worst-case I had previously imagined. But any effort to grasp how my life was about to change was secondary to keeping up with the information being fed to me. The first thing I learned from Dr. Roboz about leukemia, other than that the disease was a cancer of the blood, was the fact that it can be cured. That was a relief. The next thing I was told was that I wasn't going to leave the hospital again for about four weeks. Yikes.

"If you agree to be treated here, we're going to start you on chemotherapy immediately."

Me: "How immediately?"

"Within 24 hours."

"Ah."

"The first round of treatment lasts about twenty-eight days. Some patients stay longer. Some stay a little less. I've seen some patients fly through this induction process in as few as eighteen days. Your first round is designed to get you into remission, and we achieve remission in about 70 percent of cases. After your first round, you'll rest at home for about ten days. You'll then check back into the hospital for a second round of chemo, which is called consolidation. That stage of treatment usually lasts a few weeks. If you continue to remain in remission following that treatment, you'll undergo a third round. What happens in that stage depends on whether we determine your cytogenetics to be good, bad, or average."

Me: "Cyto-?"

"It's a measure of your body's likely response to treatment. Most people have average cytogenetics. Those patients receive an infusion of their own stem cells during their third round of treatment. We extract stem cells from your bone marrow and freeze them after the second round. Then we put you through another round of chemo before giving you back those stem cells, which will regenerate as normal bone marrow cells, optimally."

The terms and time frames flew by me, barely registering. Mercifully, Dr. Roboz paused at that point to give us a chance to breathe and to ask questions.

Me: "Not to be rude, but should we be talking to other doctors?"

Dr. Roboz: "Of course you can. The treatment for leukemia is a standard protocol that does not vary much from hospital to hospital. NewYork-Presbyterian Hospital has the largest leukemia program in the Metropolitan area. We're also a teaching and research hospital, which means we participate in clinical trials that may improve your chances of being cured. In fact, we are the only hospital in the area that is now offering a promising drug that is in its final trial stage. You could be randomized into that study, if you choose to participate.

"Another benefit of being at NewYork-Presbyterian Hospital is that you have the resources of the entire hospital available to you. We're not just a cancer center, like Sloan Kettering across the street. As a circulatory disease, leukemia affects many parts of the body, and we often call on specialists from other areas to assist in treatment."

For a guy who had spent the previous six months looking into the minutest details of a pipe dream of owning a water company, it might seem strange for me not to want to further investigate Dr. Roboz's claims. But I had put my faith in Adam: He would send me to capable doctors, and he should know who was capable, having been at this hospital from his residency forward. From the urgency Dr. Roboz was conveying, it seemed as though my diagnosis wouldn't allow time for comparison-shopping for oncologists, anyway.

This cemented a precedent of trusting in my doctors' advice and counsel throughout my treatment. Jen and I found comfort in the prospect of being able to leave the details of managing my disease to the experts. We wouldn't even google "leukemia" for the first year of the ordeal. Blind trust was out of character for Jen as well, given that she was a public health researcher by trade. But were we going to discover something for ourselves that wasn't already known by someone in the field? It didn't seem likely. And managing the emotional aspect of all of this seemed task enough for both of us.

Furthermore, Dr. Roboz exuded confidence. As for her aside that I would need the services of the many specialists who could be found in a general hospital as opposed to a dedicated cancer center, there would prove to be more truth to that statement than I could have imagined.

I struggled to think of a way to say, 'What are my chances of survival?' without appearing to be morbid.

"Where am I now? Am I coming late or early to treatment?"

"We're right where we want to be. It's not too late. A few weeks from now it might have been too late. Once we start treatment, the chemo will bring down your white count. You're probably going to feel better in the next few days than you've felt in a while. After we've knocked down your immune system, you're going to get sick again. Everybody does. Your body won't be able to fight infection. We'll treat you then with antibiotics."

"Is it strange for someone who's 29 to be getting leukemia?"

"It tends to affect older people, but it can strike at any age, as you'll see when you get up to the ward."

"What causes leukemia?"

"The truth is we don't know. It's not considered a genetically transmitted disease."

"What happens now? I mean from this point. Assuming we go forward."

"First we need to get you X-rayed, get a baseline of your lungs and GI-tract. Then we'll find you a room on 5 North, the leukemia ward. I don't think we have any private rooms available tonight. We can work on that in the days ahead."

"How long are we talking here? What's the time frame for all this?"

"This disease will be your first priority for the next six months, at least. You will be very busy with this."

"Thanksgiving in the hospital room, then."

"Yes. I'll be right here with you. Why don't I give you guys some time alone? You probably want to talk things over."

When Dr. Roboz walked out of the room, I checked Jen's reaction. She didn't seem ready to comment on what lay ahead. I then looked over at Adam. "So, I guess this wasn't the flu after all."

Jen: "And when Milo bit Roger yesterday, this has nothing to do with it."

Adam: " I'm 'fraid not."

"What do you make of what Dr. Roboz said?"

Adam went on to express his confidence in Dr. Roboz and reiterated that the treatment regimen she described was the "industry standard." He continued by saying that we wouldn't hear much different from other hospitals, omitting the reality that there wasn't time to seek alternatives.

With reassuring pats on the back and strained optimism that we would get through this, our family left Jen and me to mull it over alone for a few hours. The bureaucracy of moving into the hospital for a month ate up the time. We checked into a double room on 5 North, and squeezed ourselves into a twin bed. A guy from Egypt about my age was my roommate. Intermittently above the Arabic coming from his television, he shared snippets of what he had been through. He had finished his first round of chemo and other than his hair changing to a redder shade, he seemed okay. This was encouraging.

I don't recall crying until I called my friends Noah and Nancy to tell them I had cancer. I remembered a few years back when they called me to tell me Nancy had thyroid cancer. I had been devastated.

I saw their life grinding to a halt and could only imagine what they must have felt. She was healthy now and moving past that chapter in her life. Now I was on the other side, experiencing what they must have gone through.

A nurse, Rita, came in shortly after Jen and I got settled on the leukemia floor to do an initial patient interview. From her first entrance, I could tell Rita was savvy and tough, with a big heart. Her manner was friendly, not clinical. Her charm, not to mention her strong abilities, won her many fans. Recounting my brief history of feeling sick put me on firmer ground, placing me in the here and now of being ill and getting better. After the interview she took my temperature, which was more than 40 degrees Celsius, or 104 degrees Fahrenheit. Rita stuffed ice packs under my armpits, behind my neck and between my legs to cool me down.

Me, to Jen: "I'd love to talk about this, but I feel like I don't even know what to say. And I'm burning up. All I can think of is, 'I'm sorry.'"

"I know. Try to sleep. Tomorrow will be even crazier. I love you."

"I love you, too."

Jen moved to the high-backed chair next to the bed and bunched up her fleece as a pillow, leaving me to spread out in my new accommodations. It wasn't a good night's sleep for either of us.

LEUKEMIA FOR CHICKENS

4

Air

November 26, 2002

There was a carnival-like quality to the next day. News of my illness traveled fast. Some three dozen people came to the hospital: aunts, uncles, cousins, and friends. It felt like an impromptu going-away party, down to the silly, last-minute gifts. The twist was that my visitors would be the ones going away. I would stay put for a month. In between the time I visited with people, my doctors prepared for me a full schedule of procedures to complete before I began my chemotherapy regimen that night. The commotion was a distraction from my fever. I would have time to be exhausted later.

The day began when Dr. Roboz entered my room around the time that nurses served me breakfast, 9 o'clock or so. Actually, the end of the previous day and the beginning of this one were not very distinct—nurses and aides came in regularly throughout the night to check vital signs and take bloods, not to mention the noises that came from my neighbor, which would take some getting used to. Jen was still there, having slept in the upright chair next to me and washed up in the visitor's bathroom.

Dr. Roboz's visits were part of the daily routine conducted by doctors and residents to "round with the patients."

"How are you feeling today?"

"Wasn't an easy sleep, as you can imagine."

"Yes. Sit up, please."

Dr. Roboz placed a stethoscope to each of my lungs, put her pointer finger to the underside of my wrist, and palmed my neck, where she detected swollen lymph nodes.

"Those will go down once the chemo starts," she said, referring to the nodes. "There's a few things we need to go over today before we begin: You must decide whether you wish to participate in the clinical trial. Like I told you last night, one of the advantages you have being in a research hospital is that we conduct trials of new therapies that can augment the standard treatment."

"What does this experimental drug do?"

"What it does is concentrate the chemo and focus its attack on cancerous cells in your blood. Sometimes cancer cells reject the chemo. This drug tries to prevent that. It's in its final stage of testing. You can read more about it here."

Dr. Roboz handed Jen and me a packet of photocopied sheets.

"Should you decide to participate, we need to have your consent on this six hours before your chemo starts. We will contact the CALGB [Cancer and Leukemia Group B], which runs the trial. They'll do a randomization to see if you qualify to receive the test drug. If you don't qualify, you'll still get the standard leukemia treatment protocol, which consists of three chemotherapies: daunorubicin, cytarabine and etoposide."

Me: "There are risk factors in agreeing to the study?"

"Yes, of course. I'm not going to get into side effects of any of the drugs we are planning to give to you. We'll address them as they come up. It's better you don't think about what could go wrong. Just about anything can go wrong. Something will, for sure. You can read about some of the issues that have come up in previous tests for this drug in the sheets I just gave you. I will be happy to show you reports by other doctors about results that they have seen. They're very optimistic."

"We also need to do a bone marrow biopsy to get a baseline of your leukemia. Honestly, many patients think getting the biopsy is the worst part of leukemia treatment. Even though it takes only about five minutes to do, and some people sail through it. One patient fell asleep on me."

"What happens?"

"We do it right here. We put you on your stomach and sort of drill into your hip to extract bone marrow. Then we chip off a few pieces of bone from your hip. I won't describe it any more than that. I already talked with your doctor, Adam, about this. He said he would be there for support during the procedure if you want. Jen, you can be there too, but I don't recommend it if you're at all squeamish."

"Okay, what else?"

"You're going to get a catheter put in you today. It will be inserted into your chest and through the principal vein to your heart."

"The vena cava." (I felt smart when that bit of 10th grade biology came out.)

"Yes, the vena cava. We use the catheter to deliver the chemo and also to take bloods. Interventional radiology does the surgery."

"And that is?"

"It's a fancy name for the unit of surgeons who use X-rays to guide them in inserting catheters and doing other minimally invasive procedures."

"Okay."

"Obviously, you have a lot to talk about. And a lot of visitors here, too, my God. I'll leave you guys alone now. If you need me, just have the nurse page me."

As if finding out you had leukemia and that you're going to start chemotherapy within 24 hours wasn't enough, I took a quick glance at the clinical trial document. Though just a few pages long, the tightly packed text was full of jargon. I didn't read past the first sentence. Fortunately for me, my friend Rich dropped in just then. Rich was a resident at Columbia Presbyterian Hospital, which made him far more qualified than I to make a medical decision about entering a clinical trial. I asked him to read over the documents and give me his opinion. I realized that it was presumptuous of me to ask Rich to decide whether I should take an experimental drug in a life-threatening situation, regardless of his educational background. I assured him that I trusted him and would never question his decision. Jen seconded me. He agreed to help and took to the assignment with his usual thoroughness.

Dr. Roboz came back in with Adam and told me she was ready to conduct the bone marrow biopsy. She prepped my backside with iodine and numbed the area by injecting lidocane. As the sting from the lidocane faded, she asked me silly questions about my favorite Thanksgiving dishes to distract me. We continued talking as she began the procedure. I couldn't see what she was doing. I only felt a sensation as if somebody were chiseling into my bone. After a few moments of knocking around, Dr. Roboz inserted a needle of indeterminate length into my hip. Based on what I was feeling, I envisioned that the needle was the size of a dipstick.

Dr. Roboz drew through that needle sticky fluid from my marrow—fluid that my marrow appeared reluctant to part with, given the intensity of my pain. I made a wail that sounded like a cross between a howl and a quack during each of three extractions. Dr. Roboz said my cry was unique among her experiences.

Outside, Jen played host to the parade of guests and well-wishers. She had no interest in doing this, but not much of a choice, considering the throng. When some of her own friends arrived, she took a time-out and escaped with them to a more private place to let out her emotions. At the time, the crowd didn't seem over the top to me. I felt like I was about to begin a monumental journey, and I welcomed their support. For the time being, my fever was down and my adrenaline was up. But to the ward, which had 20 or so leukemia patients in various stages of recovery, it probably looked closer to a "final days" gathering than a first day affair. My visitors blocked the hallway and talked loudly. Each time the clamor reached a certain threshold, a nurse would kindly ask the crowd to keep it down or move away from the other patients' rooms. I cried and hugged old friends. Had I been a 5 North veteran at that point, looking at me I would have thought, "Heck, you ain't seen nothing yet, boy," or something less polite.

One in-patient stopped by to give advice. Mike was 20 years old, 9 years younger than me, and suffering from the childhood form of leukemia—the same disease my 8-year-old cousin had contracted just two months before. The standard treatment for this kind of leukemia was two years in length—four times the duration of my regimen, less intense, more frequent rounds of chemotherapy, and shorter hospital stays.

Mike was the first to tell me about some of the spooky side effects I would be experiencing, like losing my sense of taste, big weight swings, intense mood swings, and balding.

"You better shave that hair before it looks like a moth-eaten quilt," he advised.

Then he left to smoke a cigarette with his mom.

Dr. Roboz, clearly concerned that I may have been tainted by Mike's leukemia tales, came back soon after.

"He has a different form of leukemia than you. Do not expect to go through the same things he has. If you feel you're losing your taste, you could get some Lemon Drops or Red Hots." Apparently the sourness and spiciness of the candy would stimulate saliva and help the sensation return.

After lunch, Dr. Roboz's head nurse, Sandy, checked in on me.

"Has anyone talked to you about sperm banking?"

"No. What about it?"

"Well, this treatment can leave you sterile. Even if you aren't sterilized, there's a possibility the chemo will damage your sperm. So it's a good idea to bank at least some sperm before we begin.

"I know this is short notice, and you're running a fever, and you're probably extremely stressed by everything that's happening, but you should definitely do the best you can. Your top priority is getting better, but you don't want to neglect other things."

"How do we do this?"

"We'll give you a sterile cup. Someone will need to bring it to a sperm bank. We send patients to one on 30th street. They're open until three today."

"There's nothing in the hospital for this?"

"No, sorry."

"I assume you don't keep handy any 'paraphernalia' for aiding sperm deposit, if you know what I mean."

"I know what you mean. You need to get that on your own."

A resident entered my room and told me the doctors had reserved a time slot for the catheter procedure. Someone would come by with a wheelchair in about forty-five minutes to take me down to Interventional Radiology, the resident said.

That gave Jen and me a short window to work on banking sperm. I told Jen I could manage this alone, as long as I had the right reading material. I interrupted Rich, engrossed in analyzing my research trial material, to help me with something more pedestrian. With all the noise around us, I could speak freely with Rich.

Me: "Bring me, I don't know, *Penthouse*, *Hustler*, whatever looks smutty."

Having lived with Rich for three years in college, I knew he was the man for the job. After visiting a local magazine shop between York and First Avenue, Rich returned with the booty I'd requested.

I offered an awkward thanks and stepped into my semi-private patient's bathroom, quietly closing the door behind me. The patient's bathroom did little to enhance my mood, clad as it was in yellow tile with fluorescent lighting. I could hear my visitors chattering loudly through the walls. Reality was all too present. I skimmed the magazine titles and settled on tales of sexual good fortune, as related to the editor of *Penthouse Forum*. One woman wrote about her fantasy when her boss helped her refasten a garter. But the stories rang hollow. My efforts were complicated by the fact that I had no lubricant. I also still felt weak from my lingering fever and last night's poor sleep.

After a few minutes of fumbling, I heard a knock on the door. Jen wanted to know if she could do anything. I invited her in. We stood together in the stall and groped awkwardly, somehow finding a way to make a deposit in the sterile cup the nurses had provided.

There was no time to snuggle afterwards. Jen bagged my sample in a Ziploc and hurriedly left the fifth floor so as to get to Repro Lab on 30th Street before the 3 p.m. deadline. She just made it, arriving ten minutes before the office closed. In our haste, nobody suggested to Jen that she tell the lab technicians to store my sperm in multiple vials. Instead, a single specimen was frozen. Months later we learned that because it would all be thawed in one shot, it could only be used for one round of IVF treatment. That donation remains our sole hope for rearing a child of our own creation one day down the road.

In the cab ride home from Repro Lab, Jen found herself alone with her thoughts for the first time in the twenty or so hours since this all began. She broke down in tears. The cabbie asked her what was wrong, and Jen explained what had happened, as best she could.

Cabbie: "You must stay strong. My sister killed herself two weeks ago. You must stay strong."

Jen expressed her condolences to the man. She couldn't spare much sympathy though. She felt bad enough for herself.

Meanwhile, back at the zoo that was 5 North, Dr. Roboz sought my consent to participate in the clinical trial and go ahead with randomizing me to either the standard or the experimental treatment regimen. After going over the materials Dr. Roboz provided, Rich told me he believed that joining the trial was a good idea. In fact, Rich's biggest concern was that he had offended Dr. Roboz by asking so many questions of her and by requesting to read the comments posted by other doctors whose patients had participated in the trial. I thanked Rich and told him I would wait for Jen to come back from the lab before we gave our okay. She returned soon after and we signed the consent form.

The gurney that the nurses had ordered to transport me to Interventional Radiology was waiting. I climbed aboard and wheeled past the friends and family who were still chatting in the hallway. I was waving goodbye as if I were pulling out of port on a cruise ship. Jen followed on foot behind me during the short trip to an adjacent wing of the hospital. As we waited in a hallway outside IR to be rolled into the operating room, I became nauseous, probably due to a combination of my brewing illness and anxiety. Jen screamed for a garbage pail to the doctors and nurses milling around, but was met with blank stares. I threw up over the edge of the gurney. That finally prompted a response and a nurse called Environmental Services, whose job it was to clean up after such messes. The stench lingered as we continued to wait in the hall.

At the start of my catheter procedure, the doctors injected into me an anesthetic called Versed. The drug put me into a twilight state of semi-consciousness. I remember about 15 seconds of what happened during surgery. An hour later I was back on 5 North, with a matching set of white tubes dangling from my right pectoral.

The crowd had thinned by the time I returned. I was told that while I was in surgery, I had, in fact, been selected to receive the experimental drug in the clinical trial. I would receive the drug via my new chest port, along with the other chemotherapy medications that were called for in the standard treatment protocol.

For the next few hours, I could relax and eat dinner. The nurses would begin to administer the chemo later that night. I might have used the time of relative peace and quiet to reflect on all that had happened in the previous 24 hours, but I felt vacant. The day had whooshed by. The practical necessities of prepping for chemo, along with the distractions of my visitors, had overwhelmed everything else.

Yet the constant motion of the day gave me confidence that there was a method to this madness, a path that I could follow to somehow get through this ordeal. I would remain focused on the daily grind. Although my life was about to change entirely, a routine still existed: bloods taken at 6 a.m., breakfast at 8, morning visitors, afternoon visitors, doctors, nurses, Oprah at 4. I didn't realize then how much remained to chance, how often we would need to improvise in the weeks that followed.

I would still dream about my bottled water company, and at times cling to the possibility of a simple life in Lake Placid ever more so. I would read books about things that had absolutely nothing to do with my life at the moment, like *Dark Star Safari*, Paul Theroux's tome on trekking across the African desert. I would think, this isn't so bad, I only have to work on getting better. Until it became really awful.

5

Chicken

My life as a wimp, in a nutshell:

As a seven-year-old, my biggest fear was that I would forget to turn off the toaster oven. This seemingly small mistake had the potential for calamitous consequences, like my house burning down. Not that we'd ever had a fire, or that I'd known anyone else whose house had burned down, especially from a toaster oven being left on all night. My imagination, or maybe my fear of being blamed, often trumped common sense.

There was no risk of forgetting if I made Wonder bread toast in the toaster oven. For that I used the timer button. If I wanted to warm a Pop-Tart or bake an Ellio's Pizza however, that required me to use the oven dial, which had no timer. Sometimes I would forget to turn the dial back to zero. I usually realized my error after I'd gone to bed for the night. To clear my conscience, I would get up and go to the kitchen to check on the toaster. Sometimes checking took more effort, like the time my family was on its way to the airport for a vacation. In that case, my older sister Shana called our neighbor Blake to ask him to check on the toaster, both for my sake, and for the house's sake. Shana and I had shown Blake how to open the garage without a key, enter the house through the laundry room and turn off the alarm without raising undue attention from others. Blake unplugged the toaster and called us back in 20 minutes to tell us everything was okay. According to my mom, he didn't say whether it was on or off when he unplugged it.

When I was an eight-year-old, in my second year of sleep-away camp, my counselors devised a prank called "the snipe hunt." This adventure involved waking up their campers, including me, and telling us it was after midnight. (It was probably closer to 10 p.m., which left plenty of time for the counselors to go to the local bar afterward to laugh about their "hunt.") The counselors instructed us to dress in our underwear and flip-flops and follow them out to the far softball fields. A lot of activities at our unreconstructed hippie camp were conducted in our underwear, or sometimes even naked. No one thought anything of it at the time.

Once we campers made it to the ball fields, guided by flashlight, we were instructed by our counselors to remain quiet while they searched for snipes—the vicious, nocturnal birds that lived in the woods surrounding the fields, according to camp lore. We fell silent and listened to spooky noises that sounded like large animals stomping on branches. We also heard hoots that we were told were the war calls of the menacing snipes. Next, our counselors emerged from the woods bearing "Grade A" eggs from the cafeteria that they had flecked with spots of watercolor paint.

In the dark, these eggs became convincing fresh evidence that flesh-eating snipes were nesting in the woods, just as the counselors told us. Who were we to argue? Even John, the nature counselor, agreed with my counselors' assessment. When John warned us to watch out for snipes, I ran for my bunk at full speed, terrified I would be attacked.

My parents later told me (and anyone else who would listen in the 25 years that followed) how they roared with laughter when they read the letters I wrote to them describing our bunk's snipe hunts, as well as the box scores from the camp softball league, with stats like "doobles" and "turples." When camp ended for the summer, my parents came to pick up my sister and me. That year, on our way back to Long Island we stopped to look at vacation homes in the Berkshires. Roaming the backyard of an old mill house that was for sale, I found an oversized green feather alongside a creek bed. Ack! The dreaded Emerald Snipe had escaped its Camp Scatico lair! Those treacherous birds were now infesting Massachusetts, as well. I ran for the safety of our red Volvo station wagon, locking myself into the back seat.

Convinced by that incident that my snipe phobia wasn't as harmlessly funny as the stories I told in my letters had led them to believe, my parents called Camp Scatico's owner, Irwin "Flick" Fleischner, and asked him to help rid me of it. That fall, Flick visited our house on Long Island and told me that man-eating snipes did not really exist, regardless of the information I'd found in *World Book Encyclopedia*, which briefly described snipes and showed a picture of a cute-looking long-beaked example.

During my elementary school years, I sometimes accompanied my father to his office when we had days off from school for holidays. Going to work with my dad was an adventure, even if I spent most of the day rocking in the armchair that sat unused in his corner office. Dad spent his time with his associates in a separate room that was wired to trade stocks electronically, early 1980s style.

On those days, we both woke up early, around sunrise. Dad drove his Porsche 911 west on the Long Island Expressway towards Manhattan. When we reached the final leg of the LIE—an elevated section of road that bisected gritty Long Island City and led to the Midtown Tunnel—I would estimate that we were halfway to our destination. From the crest of the elevated highway, looking southwest I could see to the horizon. There, I would spot two beacons that I would use as guideposts for the remainder of our journey to my dad's office.

I named the first of these beacons the "Pencil-Top Building." Officially, the edifice was the headquarters for the New York Life Insurance Company, which was located on Madison Square. That marble building had a distinctive cone-shaped crown, which was made of glimmering copper. To me, the building's top looked like the sharpened end of a No. 2 Ticonderoga pencil, just like the one I used in school. Beyond the New York Life building, directly southwest, I could spot my far beacon, which marked our destination.

Actually, what I saw was two beacons. They were the Twin Towers, matching monoliths that loomed over Manhattan's southern tip. My dad and I were headed to Wall Street, an invisible narrow path that wound its way from World Trade Center's plaza, home of the Twin Towers, to the East River. While the name 'Wall Street' may be synonymous with American commerce, the street itself is not the first image that comes to peoples' minds.

I would guess I was like most people, and when asked to conjure an image of Wall Street, I envisioned one of two icons: either the New York Stock Exchange (actually on Broad Street), or the Twin Towers. Though the Twin Towers were completed early in my lifetime, I regarded them as somehow eternal. I imagined that five hundred years hence space-age kids, little Elroy Jetsons, would regard the Towers as I regarded the Coliseum in Rome, as monuments to an empire. The fact that Rome's Coliseum lay in ruins foreshadowed nothing to me as to the ultimate legacy of the Towers.

When I was 11, our neighbor Blake gave me a preview of what to expect in Junior High. Of the different things he told me, what I remembered most was that boys and girls kissed each other in the hallways. Ack! Here I was, a fifth-grader who knew nothing about sex but what he'd seen on MTV.

I made many circles around our Long Island cul-de-sac on my ten-speed, contemplating how I would survive the pre-teen social jungle. A year later, with some prodding from my parents, I asked Fara, one of the popular girls in my class, to be my first girlfriend. Since I was in sixth grade, I defined a girlfriend as the female with whom I had the best conversations. She agreed, and as a token of our platonic affection, she and I saved seats for each other in the cafeteria at lunchtime. This commitment cut into the time I could spend playing Dungeons & Dragons with my nerdy friends, but I felt it was probably time to move on anyway. That spring, our class took a field trip to Washington, D.C. It was there, standing atop the steps leading to the Lincoln Memorial, that Fara and I ended our relationship. Just moments before, I had challenged her to a race up the steps from the reflecting pool located in the plaza below. She won the race. However we defined our relationship, the bond couldn't withstand the fact that Fara was a superior athlete.

At 14, I often fell asleep at night listening to WCBS News Radio 88. The half hour loop of headlines droned on until the clock's sleep timer silenced the broadcast. Before I drifted off, I would hear the radio announcer review the day's events, including reports on military skirmishes in which the United States was involved. Often the announcer reported news of rebel attacks against pro-Western forces in Nicaragua, a country in the middle of civil war at the time. I became obsessed with the fear that in a few years' time, the army would draft me and send me to that banana republic to fight communist-backed Sandinistas. Fortunately for me, the pro-Russia Ortega-led government fell to a new regime. Thereafter, all was quiet in Central America for a while.

For all of my childhood fears that something terrible would disturb my safe and sheltered world, I can only remember one real tragedy. A friend got into an awful car accident just before my senior year in high school that left him paralyzed from the waist down. We weren't close at the time, but had been when we were younger. Anyone in my position would have joined the rest of our small community in offering support through visits and calls. Not me. In retrospect, I realized that I didn't want to face the fact that a single, awful event had turned his life upside down. If this could happen to Ross, maybe something equally horrifying could happen to me.

Later that fall, when it came time to choose a college, I leaned towards Stanford, way across the country. This was a bit out of character for someone who had always preferred the confines of what was known and secure. But after the '88 earthquake in San Francisco, I, with the input of my family, settled on Duke, still outside the more usual options my peers were choosing and much farther from home. For my application essay on the most influential person in my life, I chose Bugs Bunny. The raffish clown who always got away with everything was my exact opposite and thus my idol.

Those of us in high school who applied to colleges under the early acceptance program learned our fates in November, while attending a Model Congress meet in Washington, D.C. It turned out that almost everyone at the meet had been accepted by their first-choice college, including me. To celebrate, we underage students bought cheap Popov vodka from a bodega and partied in our hotel rooms. Our chaperone, Dr. Leitner, who was also my Latin teacher, heard our loud celebration and sensed something verboten. He called me in to his room to ask what was happening, trusting that the wimpy honor student wouldn't be able to lie. Though I could hardly feign complete innocence, I appeared sober enough to calm his concern. We got away with it. Maybe there was more of Bugs in me than I thought.

Also in my senior year, Mr. Piorkowski, my English teacher, asked if I was leaning towards English as a major in college. I was the teacher's pet, always managing to contribute in class even with the crossword in my lap, but English as a major seemed anathema to me. In my town, being successful in life meant making money, and one thing I learned early on was that there wasn't much money in studying English. When my family met at the kitchen table to eat dinner, conversation revolved mostly around two topics: the New York Mets and the New York Stock Exchange. Lame athletic ability ruled out my choosing baseball as a career, so that left business as a vocation. It didn't hurt that my dad and uncle had their own financial company, where a position as trader lay waiting for me.

Before I graduated that year, I would, however, learn that the written word could be powerful and could help you achieve your goals. On an otherwise unexceptional morning, I drove to school in my mom's black Jaguar sedan. Knowing the car stood out in the student parking lot, I parked it at the opposite end of the campus. The car nonetheless drew the attention of one student, Tom, who bet his friend that he could set off the alarm it didn't have with a good kick to the rear bumper. When Tom missed the car's rear bumper and instead hit its fender, the result was a dent behind the rear wheel well.

Tom didn't confess to me what he had done. I learned the story's details as it traveled through the student grapevine in the following days. As I said, Jericho is a small town, and there were few secrets. I didn't know how I should respond. I was afraid to confront Tom face-to-face. If our confrontation escalated into a fight, I would lose and then be even more ashamed. So, I came up with another way to avenge Tom's dirty deed.

Here's what did: I knew the senior class yearbook included a section at the end where students could write each other personal notes, classified ad-style. No one edited these notes; they were sent raw to the publisher. As a fluke, my submission ended up as the first note on the first of these pages, and thus was the first one every student would read when they opened their yearbooks to this section. For ten cents a word, I wrote a note to Tom saying, in effect, "No one can see the damage to the car anymore, but everyone will see this note."

Yuck! What a lame-o I was. Too wimpy to confront the guy face-to-face, I blindsided him with a printed low blow. Still, however artless and juvenile my stunt, people actually gossiped about my reprisal. It's not as if the entire cafeteria was abuzz, but word spread wide enough to rattle Tom, who threatened to respond, but ended up doing nothing. He and I were even.

If I learned from this incident that words can deliver retribution, I nonetheless can't say it played a significant role in my decision to become a journalist. I didn't have many adversaries whom I personally wished to avenge, nor did I have the mindset that leads one to muckrake on society's behalf. I credit my interest in becoming a journalist to my early childhood passion for reading *The New York Times*. Our high school newspaper was weak and I don't recall seeing more than two issues in three years. So, I had little experience as a reporter when I started attending Duke University. I responded to an open call by the school's student newspaper, *The Chronicle*, to volunteer as a reporter. My first assignment was to cover a speech by Richard Gephardt, who was then a member of the U.S. House of Representatives and considered a potential candidate for President. The following day, my story appeared at the top of the newspaper's front page. What a rush! I could shove a notepad or a tape recorder in front of somebody's face, and that person would feel compelled to talk to me on almost any subject. The kid from the suburbs suddenly had instant authority.

In subsequent years, I climbed up the paper's hierarchy, rising eventually to the position of editor of *The Chronicle*'s monthly magazine. I never considered myself a creative writer. As I viewed it, the job of a reporter was to give the details of somebody else's story. After graduating from college in 1995, I returned to New York and met with Matt Winkler, editor-in-chief of *Bloomberg News*, a business newswire. During that interview, he hired me to sort mail, starting at 7 a.m. Mr. Winkler promised me that I would soon be assigned stories. One night, the editors asked me to cover a speech on the phenomenon of the Internet being given by Bill Gates at the 92nd St. Y. Gates said he was skeptical; some of the hype was overblown. The following morning,

Gates' hometown paper, *The Seattle Times*, printed my story. I was on my way.

Early 1996 also marked the beginning of a significant relationship, and the end of a short but frustrating stint as a bachelor. On President's Day weekend, my friend, Lauren, asked me to meet her and Tom, this new guy she was dating. Lauren and Stacy were my two close friends from high school who had gone to Cornell together. I often met them out with their crew of college friends, especially when they made the rounds of the bar scene near my apartment on the Upper West Side. Normally, I would wander in and out of small talk with them while hanging at the bar, but that night I stuck close by with the intent of getting to know Tom. After a short while, most of the crew moved on.

Not in any rush, I lingered and got into conversation with Lauren's one remaining friend, Jen. We both admitted that we hadn't yet found the New York scene to be too interesting or meaningful. We had ourselves to blame, as plans to go out south of 14th Street seemed as radical as crossing the Mason-Dixon line. I found Jen's candor and self-criticism appealing, and as we continued to talk it became clear that she had diverse interests, interests that might even fit someone who hung out downtown. I had dismissed the idea of dating any of Stacy and Lauren's friends, because I figured I had already met all of them and no sparks had flown. But I hadn't had the chance to single Jen out until now. By evening's end I had resolved to ask her on a date. She agreed and we made a plan for the next Sunday.

She met my friend Russell and me at a bar where we had been watching a Duke basketball game and from there we walked to a theater a few blocks away to see *Sense and Sensibility*. Afterwards, I took her to the local café on my corner and convinced her to try a Frangelico with our tiramisu. In my pitch, I erroneously described it as tasting like peppermint. She recoiled when she sipped the hazelnut-flavored liquor, assuming it had gone bad, but of course it was I who had flubbed the description. It was then that she confessed that Lauren and Stacy were "surprised" by our date and thought it was an odd match. Fortunately for me, Jen seemed to find my goofiness charming.

Jen was distinct from other girls I had dated, but still fit comfortably in my world. She loved music, but was more grounded than your typical "Deadhead" or "Phish-kid." She could make fun of life growing up in suburban New York without getting overly ideological. Jen cared deeply about her friends and invested serious time and energy nurturing her relationships. She took an interest in learning about her new city, mostly by sampling new and noteworthy restaurants, but also by walking the streets and exploring neighborhoods. At heart, we were both urbanists, and we whiled away many early Saturdays of our courtship wandering aimlessly. Our first "day-date" was a trip to the Central Park Zoo, and already we were comfortable enough to act juvenile together, laughing at the stench of the monkeys and the penguins vomiting. We went straight from that date to being a couple, though it would be more than five years before we got engaged to marry.

With a new girlfriend and a handful of good news stories under my belt, I was a middling success for a twenty-four-year-old, though still consumed with fear that the sky might fall. Later in 1996, the editors requested that reporters assume a topic in addition to their primary beat—mine being stocks—about which they would write occasional stories. I chose the Year 2000 Millenium bug. Cutting-edge paranoia would become my specialty. My investigating uncovered more people looking to make a quick buck than anything very interesting about an actual problem. My stories were full of technical details and my fact-checking abilities weren't up to snuff. Most of my mistakes were flubbed names or small math errors, but *Bloomberg* considered all errors heinous. My years there became a humbling education in contrition. Owning up to mistakes was never one of my strengths, so I often projected an overly confident air as a protective shield.

Even with my sloppy proofing, I managed to get placed on the stocks desk within six months, an accomplishment for which I owed no small thanks to the years spent in my kitchen table finance classroom. I rose to the securities firm beat two years later and soon after received an offer to transfer to *Bloomberg*'s Milan office. My job there was described as beat reporter for Italian transportation companies. While the title wasn't glamorous, the beat included the carmaker Fiat, owner of Ferrari. I had loved cars since the days of reading out license plates and car names from the back seat during family road trips. Who cared how many stories I would have to write about Alitalia or Aeroporti di

Roma? Italian transportation reporter was a dream assignment, in my opinion.

I rented an apartment in Milan's old city center, bought an Aprilia scooter, and made it to Maranello, home of Ferrari, on two separate occasions. During one visit, I was given the keys to a F360 coupe and a map of the surrounding hillside. An intersection near the factory was marked with an 'X'. The mark designated where I would meet Ferrari's head of press relations for lunch. On my circuitous route to the restaurant, I passed an eighteen-wheeler filled with ceramic tile at 120 miles-per-hour, checking one more thing off my personal "must complete before I die" list.

While in Italy, I managed to hold together a cross-Atlantic relationship with Jen, seeing her about every six weeks: for a two-week jaunt through the south of France or sometimes for as little as a weekend at home to go to a friend's wedding. As exciting as meeting up halfway in Australia was, we knew we wouldn't be able keep up the long-distance relationship indefinitely. I felt like I was living a double life. Not in the sense of anything underhanded, mind you; just one life more than I could manage comfortably. My Italian life was fun, if a little dangerous when I scooted to work on my Aprilia still blurry from a hangover. But to stay safe, I needed to choose one life to live. I would either commit to going native in Italy or return home.

So in the fall of 1999, I chose my New York life. I joined the family firm to help them build their newly created virtual New York Stock Exchange. After a brief period of hesitation, I moved into Jen's alcove studio and after almost a year of adjusting back to reality, we got engaged. Jen and I married on August 30, 2001, in the soaring atrium of the old Bowery Savings Bank on 42nd street. We had no idea how much overcoming the challenges our relationship had encountered so far would provide us with the strength we would need in the future.

Twelve days after our wedding, while Jen and I watched cheetahs stroll in the South African bush on our honeymoon, two planes flew into the Twin Towers, killing thousands and shattering my benign worldview, honed over 15 years of taking small risks and generally achieving my goals. A week after the attack, Jen and I flew home. As we descended into Kennedy Airport heading west over Long Island, we followed the same route with a view of Downtown that I remembered taking as a child riding into work with my father. Only this time I had a bird's-eye view and in place of the twin beacons, which I had used to mark our destination then, I saw a single grey plume of smoke rising above Manhattan's skyline.

Me: "They're really not there anymore."

Jen: "No, they're gone."

Our apartment was located just a mile north of Ground Zero. That fall, I would often direct tourists to take Greenwich Street, my street, to find their way to the site of the disaster. I myself never ventured down to see the rubble. For months when the wind blew up from the south, Jen and I could smell the stench from smoldering I-beams (in addition to other unfathomable things) as it wafted through our neighborhood.

I struggled to find my bearings that following year, the same year that our fledgling company, dedicated to building a "stock exchange in a box," ran into one of life's great counter-forces: inertia. Getting clients to embrace new ideas meant forcing them to learn new things. After the attacks of 9/11, people didn't feel compelled to overturn existing institutions or stray from the status quo.

Two tenets in which I had put much faith, change and progress, no longer seemed certain. I was adrift: spiritually lost, then physically ill, and eventually diagnosed with leukemia.

LEUKEMIA FOR CHICKENS

6

Coop de Grace

November 26, 2002

At the end of my first full day in the hospital, my nurses moved me
into a private room. Hard as it was for me to imagine that I would
spend the following month in a single room, I knew most leukemia
patients had it worse. They had to share a room with another patient.
The two patients' lives were separated only by a wispy sheet hung
between their beds. During their hospital stay, one patient or the other
is bound to cough through the night or get violently ill and maybe
vomit in his or her bed. This, at the same time the doctor is cautioning
patients to avoid contact with anyone who may be carrying something
contagious. Fortunately for me, my family had the means to pay for a
private room, which is the only way to get one unless the doctors deem
you "a contact precaution," thereby giving you the right to be moved to
an insurance-approved "isolation unit."

Around 1 a.m., Rita, the nurse who had done my initial
patient interview, began administering my first round of chemotherapy. First she checked my ID number, 299-7511, against the ID
printed on the plastic bag that contained the chemo—that is, the
poison—to ensure that it was indeed prescribed for me. Then she set
up a pump to administer the chemo through tubes attached to the port
in my chest. I was nervous, as any cancer patient would be, while Rita
was getting ready to start the pump. She assured me this was not the

part to be frightened of. For all of the destruction the chemo would supposedly cause, taking it in was a non-event.

During the following five nights, nurses, both men and women, would hang plastic bags and glass containers of chemo from the metal pole holding the pumps, which looked somewhat like a tall coat rack on wheels. The medicine would drip in painlessly as I drifted in and out of sleep.

Some two hours after Rita began my first treatment, I found myself awake, alone, and soaked with sweat. I canvassed the walls of my private room and noticed they were bare, save for a faded poster print of San Francisco's Bay Bridge. By tomorrow I'd have a host of other decorations to look at. Meantime, I wondered what I was supposed to be doing in the middle of the night as the chemo dripped. Then I realized I was supposed to do nothing. Tied to an IV, I wasn't even supposed to get out of bed. If I had to urinate, I had to do it into a plastic bottle.

Soon after I woke early Wednesday morning, Rita came in to change me out of my soaked clothes and to replace my drenched sheets. She had quickly become my buddy, always entering with a smile or a joke. We talked about what was to come: I would be on a constant drip at night until December 1, a total of five days, Rita said. Slowly my white cell count would drop, followed by my platelets and my red blood cells. I would feel better, then worse, as my white count approached zero. It would take a couple of weeks for my counts to rebound, at which point my bone marrow would be free of leukemic cells. That was the hope, at least.

As an aside, Rita commented that I had a good family; that my wife Jen was wonderful.

"I knew you were a good person when I saw all the people who came to see you," she said.

I held back tears. But for the odd hour, I felt good. Rita gave me confidence as she moved purposefully around the room, switching bags as they ran out, describing plainly what I should expect in coming weeks. Could I already be feeling the positive effects promised by Dr. Roboz? I felt my head clear, my fever come down.

Finally I found it in me to look ahead. I recognized that my hospital room would be no refuge; it would be an epicenter. In addition

to functioning as my home for the next month, it would become the
central meeting place for my family and friends. That much was clear
from just my first day here.

Up to this point, I hadn't had much experience with illness.
My grandparents died before I was ten years old. When my father was
diagnosed with bladder cancer in 2000, my parents kept matters
mostly to themselves. Discussion was restricted to immediate family
members and rarely embraced topics beyond the logistics of treatment
and the markers of getting better. No one broached the idea of
mortality or how my father or our family's life might change going
forward. Instead they asked questions like "How soon can Peter get
back to work?"

That method of coping wouldn't suit my situation or me. I
would be in the hospital for such a long time that I couldn't hide my
illness from people. Nor did I want to. This would be my life now; I
was going to live it in full view of everyone around me. Maybe by living
openly with leukemia, I would make this disease less frightening.
Here's the logic: When a person witnesses something, that person gains
some understanding of it. Whereas, a person who remains in the dark
about what is going on usually envisions the worst possible scenario. Or
turns a blind eye. Either way, a lack of understanding can cause small
misunderstandings that can, in turn, fester under pressure.

It wasn't long before my moment to reflect had passed, and my
second day began. My friend Rich came by again at 7:30 a.m., before
he conducted rounds with his own patients at Columbia Presbyterian.
NewYork-Presbyterian Hospital's doctors and residents stopped by
soon after on their rounds. My dad arrived before 9 a.m. with a dozen
bagels, the *New York Post*, and *The Wall Street Journal*. Rich
recommended to my father that he leave the leftover bagels at the
nurses' station. It would be the surest way to their heart, he said. Thus
my dad began his ritual of bringing bagels to the nurses every day that
I remained in the hospital.

By mid-morning, Adam, my internist, and my sister, Shana,
came to visit. Shana brought Scrabble and "Get Well" pictures from
Rebecca, her two-year-old daughter, too young to visit anyone staying
on the leukemia floor. Shana could take her time visiting—it wasn't
hard to convince her boss, my dad, that she needed to spend time with

me. She and Rebecca lived just 15 blocks south of the hospital. Rebecca's pre-school arts and crafts projects would often be dedicated to her uncle Roger and delivered promptly. Jen and I were her godparents, and since Shana's separation two years earlier, we had made an effort to spend a lot of time with her and Rebecca.

Mom arrived a short while later with juices, milk, water, and cheese to fill the mini-fridge. My appetite was still strong and I wanted to pack in the calories while I could. Jen brought a bag full of comfortable clothes—sweats, underwear, socks—and toiletries from home.

Jen's parents and my mom hung family photos and spread around items collected from strong-willed relatives: a Sears portrait of Grandpa Lee, taken on his 80th birthday; a photograph of Jen's younger brother, Evan, the mountain man, skipping through verdant New Zealand woods; a hand-knit yellow wool blanket, made by Great Aunt Esther and given to us for our wedding. These family members were beacons of vitality and I needed to channel their energy. Following a summer of teaching rock climbing in British Columbia, Evan was spending the winter in Utah, forecasting avalanches. The snow season had officially started the week before and he was trying to juggle his duties so he could get back and be with us. More than his strength, we needed his clownish humor to bring some levity to our days.

These personal touches made a home of my hospital room. As we further outfitted my room with hospital furniture, we found our bagels had already paid dividends when the nurses looked the other way as Jen raided the supply closet for extra pillows. Someone must also have turned a blind eye when her father and mine wheeled in a table from the visitors' room. That table would allow us to eat Thanksgiving dinner in a somewhat civilized fashion. We reasoned that if we used our own tablecloth, no one would recognize the table underneath it as hospital-issue.

It wasn't yet noon. The visitors cleared out while a nurse's aide gave me my first hospital sponge bath. I couldn't use the shower until the wound healed around the area where the surgeons had inserted my chest tubes. By the time I finished my "bath in a chair," I needed to nap. An hour later, the phone woke me, sweaty again. So much for that bath.

The call was from my friend Justin, whose family lives in Florida. Justin had flown home from Los Angeles for the holiday. I had been planning to see him when we flew down to Florida for Thanksgiving. Now, instead, Justin would come visit me in New York during the New Year's break. I told Justin I should be out of the hospital by then, though it remained to be seen what I would be capable of doing.

Following my nap, I found I had some extra energy, which I used to wrap up some loose ends at work. I called Liz, a colleague, and asked her to take on some of my responsibilities while I was in the hospital. I also told her that she could pass on word to people in the office that I was in good spirits. I reprogrammed the outgoing message on my voice mail: *I am out of the office. In my absence, please contact…*

As my second day in the hospital progressed, I received a steady stream of new guests. My friends Noah and Nancy visited and left behind a picture of flowers for me to put up on my wall. Visitors couldn't bring real flowers into my room, doctors said, so Noah, a professional photographer, had improvised by making a life-size color portrait of a bouquet of sunflowers and tulips.

Shana returned for the second time that day, this time carrying a laptop computer and a pair of small speakers that I could use to listen to music. With some friends I discussed my bottled-water dreams, expanding on the conversation that I had begun the previous night in the Emergency Room. I became hoarse from the chatter.

As the evening approached, Dr. Roboz visited. I told her that my biggest complaint so far was that I'd lost my voice by talking so much. Dr. Roboz replied that, actually, hoarseness was a common side effect of the steroids that I had taken the previous night, prescribed to counteract side effects caused by the chemotherapy. She assured me that my normal voice should return when I stopped receiving chemo in a few days.

As she left, she commented, "I haven't thought about you since this morning during rounds. You're already responding to chemo. The white blood cell levels are dropping. You're a boring patient."

After dinner, I shivered with exhaustion. Jen and I asked everyone to leave. It was difficult for me to ask people to leave, because

I wanted to show strength. I realized, though, that it was more important for me to give my body a chance to rest.

Me, to Jen: "Things will calm down in a few days. You'll see. People will have their own Thanksgiving events to attend."

• • •

The following morning, I slept through my first visitor: Rich, again. I woke to find him being entertained by Jen. I looked out the window of my room and saw that it was a gloomy Thanksgiving Day. Stray snowflakes trickled down the airshaft that sent dismal light into my room.

My second visitor on my third day in the hospital was Shana, who had taken Rebecca to watch the Macy's Thanksgiving Day parade earlier. Soon after, two of my childhood buddies, Russell and David, visited, their wives in tow. Both Elyse, Russell's wife, and Stephanie, David's wife, had baked cookies for me. Elyse presented hers first. She had made simple chocolate chip cookies, which she served out of a reusable Ziploc container. I tasted one with a few sips of milk. A few minutes later, I reached for one of Stephanie's cookies. They were presented in a small, crisp white shopping bag labeled with a personalized sticker reading, "Simon's Sweets," Simon being her last name. In the shopping bag, I found two stacks of crispy, almost lacy, chocolate chip cookies wrapped in cellophane and tied tightly with purple ribbon. Stephanie worked for Martha Stewart Living and it showed.

Washing this cookie down with milk, too, I sensed my friends' desire to have me offer a judgment in favor of one wife's baking over the other. I smiled, milk moustache intact, and announced that I was smart enough not to pick a favorite.

"Let the nurses decide."

With that, Jen brought a portion of each batch to the nurses' station. While there, Jen overheard a nurse say that the nicest private room on the leukemia floor, a room on the opposite side of the ward facing the East River, might become available in the days ahead.

Jen: "If it does become available, don't forget about us."

Though I never heard the nurses' opinion on the cookies we offered, I suspected that they preferred Elyse's down-home preparation, which was also my favorite, since I am partial to tradition. But more importantly, the cookie contest put me in a position to barter for better living quarters.

Later in the morning, I received a call from my friend and former college roommate, Ben, who offered to give me the crew cut I was told I needed, using his electric clippers. We arranged for him to set up a makeshift barbershop in my hospital room on the following evening.

Over lunch, we as a family finalized our plans for that evening's Thanksgiving dinner. Dad's U.K.-born assistant, Elaine, offered to prepare for us a home-cooked turkey that could be reheated in the microwave in the unit's waiting room. Lois, Jen's mom, would make squash soufflé and some vegetables as side dishes. Her friend Evelyn, a phenomenal baker, would prepare pumpkin bread. We thought it was better to keep the feast simple and contained. We presented our dinner plans to Dr. Roboz to ensure they met her standards for food safety. She approved, reminding us to make sure Elaine cooked the turkey thoroughly. Between the overcooking and the microwave reheating, I was not optimistic about the juiciness of that evening's drumsticks.

My range of meals would continue to narrow as the chemotherapy depleted my white count. The lower my counts fell, the more vulnerable I became to infection, the doctors said. Among my restrictions, I was told not to eat food prepared by "unknown hands." Nor could I eat anything that contained uncooked ingredients. The banned food list included most fruits. In addition, I was told to avoid eating anything that might inhibit my bowel movements or that might irritate my stomach.

At the mention of those final two restrictions, I recalled that I had last pooped on Tuesday, three days ago. I had burped a lot since that time, and experienced some gas pains, but there had been no bowel movements.

Considering its hasty preparation, Thanksgiving dinner went well enough. We split the evening into two shifts, eating the first part of the meal with Jen's parents and grandfather and the rest with my parents. It wasn't the perfect picture of togetherness one would expect from our tight-knit clan at Thanksgiving, but our "dining table" could only seat four at a time and we had to compromise. I tired from eating all the food. After dessert, Jen and I did laps up and down the hallways in the hope of stimulating my digestive juices.

Mom and Dad had spent the earlier half of Thanksgiving dinner at Shana's apartment with Shana and Rebecca. After their meal, Shana called to say that Rebecca now understood what my illness meant. The two of them had watched "Snoopy Come Home." In that Peanuts cartoon special, Snoopy visits his former owner, who had had to give Snoopy to Charlie Brown because she became sick and was therefore unable to take care of a dog. In Rebecca's two-year-old mind, I had become Snoopy's former owner, Shana explained.

At that point I thought of my own dog, Milo, who was staying at Jen's parents' house in Rockland County, northwest of Manhattan. Her parents had taken Milo home to Pomona on the night that I was diagnosed, because taking care of him would have been too much for Jen while she was spending nearly all her time at the hospital with me. Milo would remain with Jen's parents until I left the hospital. Jen's dad took pictures of him playing in the snow at their house to assure us he was happy in his temporary home. These pictures came to line the walls of my room and became easy conversations starters with doctors and visitors. When doctors and nurses asked if we had any children, we answered, "Only Milo."

Before going to sleep, Jen and I played a game of Scrabble, a favorite pastime for us, especially when we traveled. Though Jen is an expert Scrabble player, I won that evening for the first time since I could remember. Her loss at Scrabble was my first clue that Jen was under enormous stress. Even so, Jen and I reveled in our quiet time alone. Already, we realized how hard it would be to find privacy in the weeks that would follow. We hugged each other and sobbed.

The following morning, Shana brought in the requisite dozen bagels, most of which were given, as usual, to the nurses' station. I knew that day was probably the last time I would be able to eat one of those bagels for a while. With my blood counts falling, any day now I would drop below a threshold that would cause the doctors to restrict me from eating food prepared outside the hospital or brought from home. The doctors also said that my platelets, which helped form blood clots, had fallen to a point where I should avoid blowing my nose.

That day I talked to my therapist for the first time since I had been diagnosed with leukemia. I had been seeing Dr. Curcio since my anxiety peaked following 9/11. We had a comfortable relationship, mixing in our mutual love of all things Italian with psychotherapy. Jen had called Dr. Curcio to let her know about my illness and she had offered to be available to me in any way she could. On the phone, we discussed many of the things that I had talked about already with the friends who had come to visit. I confided to her my lingering concern that I had brought this illness on myself through my persistent brooding about my job and my dread for the future of the world. At the same time, I told her I felt some relief, odd as it seemed, at no longer feeling I had to worry about those problems that were beyond my control.

Isn't it true that dealing with such a horrible sickness will relieve me from the stress of work and the horrors happening in the world, I asked my therapist? I sensed that she didn't want to agree with me and thereby reinforce any notion that I was better off being possibly fatally ill than being stressed at work. Still, she was glad I felt able to channel my strength into fighting my disease.

During my phone conversation with her, a nurse came by to tell Jen that the "suite" rumored on Jen's cookie contest foray to soon become available could be ours for the taking. Were we interested in switching rooms, the nurse asked? Jen jumped at the chance for us to move. Earlier, she had peeked inside room 211 and had seen that it was a true recovery room. The view from the bed was a wall of windows overlooking Roosevelt Island and the massive power station that lay across the river. To the south was the 59th Street Bridge; north was Hell's Gate, Randall's Island and the Triboro Bridge. Only a full set of blinds, half-drawn to cut the glare, would keep a person from taking in the entire panorama at once.

To add color to the scene, boats of all shapes and sizes zipped up and down the river. Among them I saw tugs, tall-mast cargo ships, mini oil tankers, yachts, Circle Lines, and Waterway ferries. The oversized room included a chair that reclined like a La-Z-Boy. A few weeks into my stay in room 211-A, I learned that those chairs were "chemo chairs" used by patients while they received infusions, so they wouldn't always have to sit in bed. My coterie switched me from one room to the other, remounting the decorations and even carrying the furniture taken from the common area from my old room to the new one.

At 5 p.m., Ben became the first visitor to my new suite, arriving with his clippers to shave my nappy hair. I wanted to play the music from *The Barber of Seville*, but, not surprisingly, we didn't have the classical title on hand. I felt Ben might need inspiration, because he had a lot of hair to work through. We started with a simple buzz around the edges. Trying to cut deeper, the motor on Ben's clipper began to wane. Army-grade, this Wahl was not. Undaunted, Ben switched to scissors. Some 30 minutes later, he had trimmed, kneaded and chopped my hair down to a more clippable level, at which point, he returned to the electric shears, whose motor had since regained strength.

Jen stayed overnight in my new room, some ten feet away from me on a rollaway cot, after two nights at home attempting to get some real sleep. Though this time she was in her own bed, and not attempting to squeeze next to me in my twin or sleep upright in a chair, as she did the first night, the next morning she woke with a debilitating throb in her neck. It was clearly from stress. We asked Adam to help Jen with her pain. He prescribed migraine medication and told her he would find her a neurologist if the pain continued.

Our friend Lauren called early that morning, and asked if she could bring anything. Jen remembered that I still hadn't had a bowel movement and had an epiphany. Lauren could bring Go-Lean, a high-fiber cereal that works for humans like Liquid Plumr works for clogged sinks. Our last-ditch effort to bring on a bowel movement worked almost instantly. All of a sudden, my belly bulge disappeared. But the end result was not as we hoped. The Go-Lean had set things in motion and I now had the opposite problem.

Soon after, I began to writhe with cramps in my abdomen. We called for a doctor. One soon came, placing a stethoscope to my stomach.

"Awfully quiet down there."

Me: "Good or bad?"

"Not good."

7

Stoppage Time

The doctors said I should wait a day to see if my stomach cramps would subside on their own. The pains persisted, however, making that Sunday the most difficult day yet for me in the hospital. Weekends are bad times to get sick, because the more senior doctors generally do not work on those days. And the staff in charge on weekends often is hesitant to change the direction of a patient's care. So I had to wait until Monday morning, when Dr. Roboz and her colleagues made their morning rounds, to find out what was going wrong in my bowel tract.

By 10 a.m., Dr. Roboz had called in a team of doctors from the gastro-intestinal unit to examine me. The GI doctors conferred with Dr. Roboz, who delivered my diagnosis:

"You have an ileus."

Ileus (pronounced ill-e-as). I fished around in my head for where I had heard that term before, then remembered it was when my father had completed surgery to remove the cancerous growths in his bladder. In the days that followed, my father's stomach blew up as if someone had slowly inflated a beach ball inside of him. I recalled that my father seemed to be in terrible pain at the time. We pleaded with his doctor to do something, but the doctor simply said that the condition would pass eventually. It did.

Like father, like son.

Dr. Roboz continued with a more technical explanation of an ileus, trying her best to use laymen's terms.

"Your intestines have stopped working. Until they start functioning, any bowel movements that you have will consist of undigested food. There's probably a lot of food still blocked up in your stomach, because peristalsis has stopped."

(Peristalsis moves digested food through the intestinal tract.)

Me: "Why did this happen?"

"The chemo we gave you targets the fastest-growing cells in your body. Which are cancer cells, primarily. Fast-growing cells also include those that regulate hair growth and digestion. In your case, the chemo killed the cells in your GI tract."

"What can we do about it?"

"Nothing, really. You've finished your first round of chemo. Now we wait until your cells begin to grow back, including those in your GI tract. The bad news is you will have to stop eating, if you sense your stomach is beginning to swell."

I rolled my eyes. At about 160 pounds, I had always found it easier to lose weight than to gain it. If I stopped eating, I might waste away.

"How long are we talking here, without eating?"

"Could be a few days, could be a week, perhaps."

"That's awful."

"You can take it. You'll be on IV the whole time. Your body has a lot of stored energy to work with."

"Eating is one of the few things I look forward to in a day."

"I can imagine. I'm sorry about that."

"There's really nothing I can do to make this re-growth faster?"

"No, sorry. You'll just have to wait it out."

This was depressing. I looked to change the topic.

"Anything else we need to talk about?"

"Actually, we received your cytogenetic test results. You have an average chance of beating leukemia."

"That's good?"

"Average is fine. Most people are average. It means for the third part of your treatment, we will give you an autologous stem cell transplant, sometime around February-March. For the stem cell transplant, we will give you back your own stem cells. It's safer than giving you cells from a donor, because the body can reject a donor's cells.

"I have some more good news. If you ever do need a donor transplant, your sister is a perfect match, based on her test results."

In the previous week, Shana had given a sample of blood for a test to see if her immune system "matched" mine, and could thus serve as a replacement. Siblings who are matches are preferred as donors, because there is less chance for rejection.

Me: "We're not anticipating the need for a donor transplant, are we?"

"No. But it's good to know, nonetheless."

"Okay, all good, I suppose."

"Yes."

"Doesn't really change the fact I probably can't eat, though."

"No."

"What if the bloating and cramps persist, eating or not?"

"We'll have to put in an NG tube."

A nasogastric tube. That was bad news. If I had a vision in my head of a typical hospital patient, it would be a person lying on a twin bed, with his or her head raised. A clear plastic tube would protrude from the patient's nose, snaking alongside the cheek and hooking behind the ears, running to someplace hidden behind the bed. Usually those tubes provided patients with additional oxygen. The part of the tube that entered the nose would end just inside the nostrils. An NG tube looked and felt much worse. Rather than stopping at the nostril, an NG tube continued up through the nasal passage, down the esophagus, and into the stomach—hence the name, nasogastric tube. The tube was attached to a source of suction on the wall that pulled fluid out of the stomach into a bucket stuck to the wall behind the bed.

My dad had told me terrible things about NG tubes.

"Do you really think we'll have to put in an NG tube?"

"We'll just wait to see if your stomach gas goes away naturally. But don't get your hopes up. It's not likely. We'll probably have to put one in eventually."

"So this is what you warned me about when I was diagnosed. When you said something will go wrong. And you deal with the problem as it happens."

"Buck up, kid."

• • •

It was pretty much down hill from there. My stomach swelled. I decided to stop eating a day later. I held off on allowing the doctor to insert the NG tube in the hope that my bowels would start pumping again. Since I was no longer able to digest food, the doctors converted my medications from pill form to IV fluid. When medications are delivered intravenously, the medicine flows into the body over long stretches, often two hours or more. I was taking many medications at that point, to inhibit infection. Some medications couldn't be sent down the same tube at the same time. The doctors ordered nurses to insert temporary intravenous ports. On occasion I would have a temporary port in each forearm in addition to the central line emanating from my chest.

Phlebotomy nurses changed my temporary ports every three days. Soon my arms resembled a Dalmatian's coat, riddled with deep blue spots formed from small pools of blood that had collected under my skin. The wounds didn't heal properly, because my low platelet count hampered my body's ability to clot its blood.

As my condition deteriorated, Jen told me that her head and neck aches were getting worse as well. Initially we had assumed her pains were related to spending those first few nights sleeping on a flimsy cot in the hospital. Jen went to a chiropractor, who pressed and pulled on her back and neck. That only alleviated the pain temporarily; the aches returned soon after. The migraine medication that Adam gave her didn't work for long. So, as promised, he called a neurologist colleague of his. That doctor prescribed Elavil, a medication that is used to treat tension headaches, but also helps symptoms of anxiety and depression. Jen agreed with the neurologist that this added benefit would probably come in handy. After a few days on the pills, the pain subsided.

At some point during my second week in the hospital, my white blood cell count declined to zero, or at least to an undetectable level. That was just what the doctors predicted would occur. With no white blood cells in my body, I had no ability to defend myself against infection. This is the most fragile moment in a leukemia patient's recovery, and my physical state had my doctors concerned. At nights, my temperature spiked, declining during the day. I did have some bowel movements, but they were loose and watery. The bloating in my stomach did not abate. I was losing about a pound a day. My energy level had dropped, too. It took longer to complete my turn at Scrabble.

Jen: "Let's go, Roger. Make a word."

Me: "Where are we going? What's the rush?"

A lot of the trouble I was experiencing was typical for a patient who had received five days of intense chemotherapy, as I just had. The fact that I couldn't eat was unusual, but I dealt with that setback better than I thought I would have. Sometimes I had cravings, like when I heard my Mom crunch the turkey salad that she ordered daily from Café Luka, or when I caught the aroma of stir-fried veggies delivered by Evergreen Chinese. Still, I told my friends and family that they could eat in my room. Asking them to leave would have been even more frustrating than seeing them eat. I distracted myself at those moments by watching television or reading a magazine. And if I had been given a painkiller or an anti-anxiety medication, like Ativan, I didn't feel any urge to eat. Both drugs made me sleepy and suppressed my appetite.

Weekends always seemed to bring bad news. As at any office, Friday afternoons at the hospital saw doctors scrambling to finish their work and get out of Dodge. That's not meant as criticism. My doctors generally spent more hours at the hospital, and worked harder during those hours, than anyone I'd ever encountered, short of a junior investment banker. On Fridays, the doctors handed over responsibility to the weekend staff, which I dubbed the "B Team."

It was probably a coincidence that things always seemed to go wrong on weekends, but my anxiety rose on Fridays all the same. The previous weekend had brought word of my ileus. The next Saturday, we inserted the NG tube. I had delayed this action, preferring to suffer continuing abdominal cramps to having a vacuum tube up my nose. But the pain was becoming all too present, so I gave in and allowed the doctors to put it in.

The experience was as bad as I had feared. To begin, a doctor threaded the tube up my nose and then down my throat. As the doctor slid the tube lower down my esophagus, she instructed me to make swallowing motions in my throat. Doing that would limit the sensation of being choked, she said, and it did help a little.

The doctor made three separate attempts to plunge the tube into my stomach. After the third insertion, she was confident that she had found her destination. The staff then rolled in a portable X-ray to take a picture of my stomach and the tube that now resided inside of it. Specifically, the doctors looked for the metal tip at the end of the tube to see that it was positioned squarely in the middle of my stomach; it was.

Spinning a dial on the back wall of my hospital room, the doctor turned on the suction power for the NG tube. I felt a jolt inside me. Seconds later a stream of red-brown fluid shot upward through the tube, out my nose, and behind me into a plastic bucket mounted on the wall. It was gross, for sure, but I felt the pressure in my stomach release. That made putting in the tube worth the effort. The doctors had the tact to place the waste receptacle behind my head, so that to see what was in the bucket, I had to turn my body around.

The doctors promised they would take out my tube once my stomach had drained, maybe in as little as forty-eight hours. That was a promise easier made than kept. For one thing, there was no set definition of an empty stomach. Two, the doctors preferred not to reinsert an NG tube a second time. Given how it feels to have an NG tube inserted, many patients willingly agree to just let it be until everyone is certain the tube is no longer necessary.

My stomach felt better, but everything else felt worse. My diarrhea became "explosive." That was the doctors' characterization, and an unusually colorful one at that. Having such trouble holding in my bowels, I no longer trusted myself to make it to the toilet in time. The nurses brought a portable commode into my room and placed it next to the bed. The tube from my nose to the wall was just long enough to allow me to move to it from the bed. Every time I had a bowel movement, we had to call a nurse's aide to clean out the commode.

To add insult to injury, I soon stopped peeing. A new doctor came to figure out why that had occurred. Dr. Weinstein was a kidney specialist. Each day, he checked the level of my creatinine and my calcium. He would come to my room, once or even twice a day, and give anyone in attendance a lengthy technical explanation of my bodily functions. Based on the way Dr. Weinstein spoke to me—using lots of technical terms and speaking about my organs as if they were separate from my being—I felt as if I were a mathematical equation that the doctor was trying to solve, as opposed to a patient. But I enjoyed his visits, in part because it gave me a chance to think of my body's inner workings as separate from my situation.

Apart from my kidney issues, my nightly fevers persisted. The doctors theorized that the fevers were a signal of an as-yet-undetected fungal infection that they hadn't been able to eliminate with standard medications. Dr. Roboz called in a specialist in infectious diseases, Dr. Helfgott, to assess me. Dr. Helfgott recommended that I take Abelcet, an extremely strong antifungal medicine, which could be administered overnight via IV. He warned that the drug could have serious side effects, such as rigors, or extreme convulsions.

The first night I received Abelcet, I shook violently and was calmed only when the nurses administered a dose of Demerol, a strong narcotic. From then on, the nurses gave me a preventive shot of Demerol before my nightly dose of Abelcet. Sweet Demerol. It produced a warm, cozy sensation in me the moment after it was injected. I would revel in that state for about five minutes before passing out. And when I woke up, I would feel and remember nothing.

Until I began taking Abelcet, I had relied on the regular nursing staff and my visitors to assist me in the small but difficult things I needed to do during the day, such as going to the bathroom, retrieving tissues, or applying moisturizing lotion. At night, I relied on the nursing staff or Jen to take care of me, even though those nights Jen stayed left her exhausted.

But the strain on everyone was becoming too great. My parents hired a private nurse, Avril, to stay at my bedside from 8 p.m. to 8 a.m. She was a talkative, spiritual Jamaican woman who was very determined in her duties. Avril helped me with basic activities and sang me to sleep with gospel, transporting me to a more peaceful state—something I needed. In the morning, she would give me cold water baths to reduce my fever. I dreaded these morning wash-downs, which chilled me to the bone, as intended.

Having more assistance made things easier for me and my family, but it didn't improve my health, which was still deteriorating almost two weeks after I stopped receiving chemotherapy. During the second weekend, the "B Team" staff became concerned I was not taking in enough oxygen. They feared I might have a lung infection or, worse, a pulmonary embolism, a potentially fatal clot in my lungs. They recommended that I be moved to the intensive care unit where I'd be under continuous observation.

I protested.

"I'm okay. The reason you think I can't breathe is because of this stupid NG tube. My nose is stuffed with it and with boogers. Take it out and I'll breathe fine."

Adam came in to calm me and tell me the Intensive Care unit might not be so bad. He reasoned that it was what I needed and promised that he would help me get the NG tube out as soon as I improved. Still, I protested.

Me: "The doctors on call are just being overly cautious. They're worried something might go wrong, and they don't want it to happen on their watch."

It was to no avail. All the doctors agreed that I should be transferred to the "MIC-U" (Medical Intensive Care Unit). Though at that point I probably had no choice in the matter, I also finally agreed to the change. The nurses promised they would hold my suite on 5 North until I returned.

They say you don't remember what happens in Intensive Care. I remember lots of things, but what I recall makes no sense.

8

Bananas

For music: Cue "Lucy in the Sky with Diamonds." For stage props:
Bring in walls of electric blinking lights turning on and off in a vertical
progression. The room is dark, like a Sci-Fi vision of a spaceship control
center. I am one of four patients. We are seated two abreast, stadium-
style.

My chest and arm ports connect via tubes to bags of medicine
hitched to metal poles. I have on an oxygen mask to boost my air
intake. Doctors monitor my heart rate and other functions via stickers
taped to my body. It is quiet, save for the plinking of machines and the
scurrying of nurses.

My recollection of the room and what happened that night is
spotty. As I reached for ice chips that were in a cup on a tray next to
the bed, I was certain that I rolled off my Craftmatic-style ICU bed to
the floor. No nurses were present at that moment, though they came in
when I called for help. They righted me, although apparently I was
much less contorted than I believed. I was concerned that my "fall"
had caused my Broviac—that is, my chest tubes—to dislodge. The
nurses ran some saline through the tubes and pronounced everything
okay. I remember something about staple guns and being wheeled to
surgery, but everyone says that that memory is crazy.

My next memory was of a dream in which my dad wheeled me
around outside the hospital in an oversized baby carriage. I had on a
heavy jacket and felt warm.

"Look at my son. He is healthy."

The dream ended quickly, and I woke up knowing I was not healthy. My overnight fever had not gone down sufficiently. The first person I saw when I woke was Avril, who was finishing her night shift. My recollection of the night's events was becoming even more worrisome.

"You were there. You saw they dropped me."

She nodded.

Avril reinforced my suspicion that being in Intensive Care did not feel as much helpful as frightening. By that point, I could not control my bowel functions at all, and nurses had to wipe me clean constantly. I felt increasingly weak and distressed.

Although she probably had them already, I insisted on giving Avril my home telephone number, then my parents' home number. I had difficulty recalling both of them and had to rewrite them many times before they were legible.

"If anything happens today, and you don't see me tonight, call Jen or my parents and tell them about the dropping incident. I trust you."

Adam came in. I told him I believed that the Intensive Care doctors had dropped me. He looked stunned and a little incredulous. He said he would talk to them about what had happened. When he returned, he said simply that the doctors had no idea what I was talking about. Later I learned he had gone so far as to check overnight hospital records to refute my claim that I had been wheeled to surgery after the "fall."

"Of course they're saying that. They don't want to be held responsible. You can ask Avril. She was there. You've got to get me out of here, Adam. This is only hurting me. I am okay. Just let me prove it to you. There must be some way I can show you I don't need to be in Intensive Care. You've got to get this NG tube out of me. With it in, I can't breathe, and I'm only getting worse."

Adam looked sympathetic. "I'll see what I can do."

Next the doctors rounded. I didn't bring up the drop, but I repeated my belief that being in Intensive Care was not helping me. I pleaded with them to let me leave the ICU. The doctors nodded but did not offer support. To them, the fact that I was getting weaker and that my fever had not gone down was evidence that I needed to stay in Intensive Care, not leave it.

"But I won't get better in here. I will get weaker and sicker. We need to change our strategy."

Arguing my point drained me of any strength I'd gained from the previous night's sleep. Jen and my parents came into the room and listened, though I knew they were powerless to help me, even if they believed me, which I don't think they did. At that point, Adam came back.

"We've devised a series of tests with the staff doctors that will determine if you are fit to leave the intensive care unit."

"Really?"

"Really."

"And what are these tests?"

"First, they will shut off the suction on your NG tube and give you some water to drink. If you can keep the water down, then they will do other tests."

Adam explained those tests, too. I didn't understand them, but I did understand that if I could complete them successfully, they would let me return to my room on 5 North.

"Don't assume you will be able to complete these tests. I don't want you to be too discouraged if you have to stay in Intensive Care."

It seemed like a dream, or some cornball reality TV challenge, but this was the real deal.

The doctors turned off the suction and brought me water to drink. I took my first sips of liquid since they had placed the NG tube in me more than a week ago. I needed to hold down the water for six hours, so there would be no immediate yea or nay. The initial signs were good. I did not throw up.

"Don't drink too quickly. Your body needs time to adjust."

I didn't need much cautioning. The experience was upsetting for my stomach. I fought to keep things from ending badly.

Later, the doctors attached me to a device that measured my lung capacity. I don't recall what it looked like, though the piece they attached to my mouth felt like an oversized pacifier. The machine made sounds like a cornet and blew bursts of air into me at high force.

I was told to "breathe normally," as these bursts of air waxed and waned.

I did not do well at this exercise. The inside of my mouth was extremely dry. The whooshing air felt like it would blow chunks of skin off the roof of my mouth, if not dislodge my teeth altogether. My lungs pulsated inward and outward, but I could not keep pace with the airflow. I raised my hand often to ask them to stop the test, take a break, and start over. I was not helping my cause. We took an extended break and agreed to try again later.

The second attempt went little better than the first. We moved on to the final test. The nurse placed a confining apparatus over my mouth and nose; exactly what it looked like I couldn't say. She said that the key to this test was to see if I could maintain my sense of balance, but I didn't know what that meant. I felt like my head was being spun in one of those metal crates that are used to mix raffle prize tickets. My interpretation of my task was to keep my head from banging against the sides of the crate, which would signal that I was out of balance.

I didn't bother to find out what actually was happening. The important thing for me was that I passed whatever test they gave me and that I felt someone was looking out for me and what I thought were my best interests. We completed the three tests. I drank more water and held it down. That was perhaps the most surprising feat of all, according to the doctors.

Adam returned with the verdict: I had passed. I would return to 5 North after one more night's observation by the nurses in Intensive Care.

Glory me! I had done it. I had willed my way out of the valley of the shadow of death. Jen and my family rejoiced in my relief, though they were more cautious about my readiness to leave Intensive Care. In hindsight, we saw this moment as marking the upward turn from the nadir of my "induction stage" of treatment for leukemia, though I was far from basking in the sunlight of good health.

That night in my room in Intensive Care, a nurse checked to see if I was delusional.

"What is your name? Where do you live? Where are you now? Who is the President of the United States?"

"George Herbert Walker Bush," I said with complete conviction.

"George W. Bush is the President," the nurse corrected.

"Right."

"What year is it? Why are you in the hospital?"

I made it through the rest of the Q&A without any further slip-ups. Nonetheless I was delusional, only my delusions were even grander than the doctors could imagine. I suddenly understood how I had contracted leukemia. The problem was that I was "out of phase" with the rest of the people on the planet. I could feel particles in the air pelting my body. These particles were altering my DNA and making me sick. Most people did not feel these particles. These particles passed them by harmlessly, because they were "in sync" with the flow of the universe. If I could just slip back into the mainstream...

I told the nurse I could feel the TV emitting beams that were endangering me. She told me that there was nothing to be concerned about. I should go to sleep. The nurses wrapped me in a bunch of sheets in my bed, perhaps to create a makeshift straightjacket so that I would not claim I had fallen to the floor again. I spent much of the night unraveling myself.

The next morning, calamities receding into the past, I entertained my usual retinue of guests and one new visitor: Rabbi Carnie Rose, who had officiated at my marriage to Jen. Rabbi Rose was not the stereotypical rabbi of my youth: authoritative, white-haired, drab. In fact, he was only about two years older than I. My parents likened him to a camp counselor. Rabbi Rose was not above egging on the congregation to perk up when their chanting sounded lugubrious. For one of our pre-wedding consultations, Jen and I met Rabbi Rose at a sushi restaurant. I liked Rabbi Rose.

I had some questions for the Rabbi, in light of my recent experience in the hospital. To understand my questions it might help to know a little of my religious beliefs. Bear with me.

I learned in my Western philosophy review course in college that people understood the universe using one of two methodologies. They were the Aristotelian way, named for the oracle Aristotle; and the Platonic way, named for Aristotle's teacher, Plato. Dividing the world into two opposing camps was a facile dichotomy, but I found a lot to like in that breakdown.

To wit: Aristotle believed that a person could understand everything in the world through scientific analysis. For example, consider the sunrise. It is possible to measure the time when the sun first appears on the horizon, as well its location on that horizon, and through these measurements, along with others, define a sunrise as something that is true, or real.

Platonists, on the other hand, believe that things that happen in the physical world cannot be considered true. Consider again the sunrise. Each sunrise differs from the sunrise that precedes it. One sunrise might appear later in the day, or its position on the horizon could shift. In other words, each sunrise is a distinct phenomenon. Yet all are called sunrises. That is because, in Plato's world, all the phenomena share a quality that is immeasurable: that of an ideal sunrise. It is only the concept of a sunrise, which is intangible, that can be considered true, or real.

Still with me? I hope so. While I was taught that these two philosophies existed in opposition, I found them quite complementary. The Aristotelian way suited my yearning to understand the physical world—such as trees, plants and animals—in scientific terms. The Platonic method was best for understanding such intangible human qualities as honor, love, and God. To believe in those qualities, all I needed was to have faith that they existed. And my faith was tested every day of my life. For example, if I encountered people who were honorable, then my faith in honor was justified.

The point of my digression is this: I understand Judaism as a romantic attempt by Aristotelians to describe, in tangible terms, those things that lie within Plato's realm. Take the Torah, which is the principal text of the Jewish faith. It describes in physical terms the most inconceivable things: the mystery of creation is described as six days of work and a day of rest. The Torah also posits a code of ethics and a basis for a well-functioning society in ten easy steps: Respect thy mother and father, do not kill—a.k.a. the Ten Commandments.

In terms of depth of analysis, the Torah is a mere paperback novel when compared with a lesser-known Jewish tome, the Talmud. That 2.5 million-word treatise answers all sorts of impossible questions, such as which family member should be saved first in the event of a catastrophe. I have never seen an actual Talmud. Nor have many other Jews, I would venture. Many Jewish households do possess what I believe to be a popularized summation of the Talmud, a book called "Why Bad Things Happen to Good People."

I have never read this book either. I don't think I need to go any further than the title to understand its message: God is good, but shit happens, and here's how to deal with the consequences.

That—the whole shebang of using faith as a foundation for religious belief—was what I wanted to talk about with the Rabbi. I told him that I didn't expect prayer alone to save me. That would be too much of a leap of faith. But now that I was in the dumps, I wanted to know, "Where are the more spiritual elements of Judaism, the gospel-like hymns that can elevate a person beyond the matters of the world and can inspire faith?"

If any rabbi could point me in that direction, it would be "camp counselor" Carnie. But the Rabbi basically agreed with my premise. Judaism didn't offer many ideals in which a person could simply put his trust. The religion was, indeed, grounded in reality, which discouraged understanding the world in terms of faith and ideals.

If I was looking for spiritual comfort, Carnie recommended I read a book by an Israeli friend of his who had written a memoir about raising a child amid the rash of suicide bombings that had taken place throughout Israel in recent years. Strength through adversity, so to speak.

I decided I preferred to escape my world from time to time, and put my faith in the hope that things were meant to work out for the best, in the end. In those moments, as if on cue, my private nurse Avril would sing me her gospel hymns. It was as if she could sense my need for spiritual soothing, and she was at the ready with her brand of faith.

• • •

Now that I had proved to the doctors that I could keep water down, it became harder and harder not to think about eating again. Soon they would remove my NG tube, and I could take my first bites

in more than a week. That last morning I, along with my guests in
Intensive Care, steered the conversation to food and my all-time great
meals. One feast I recalled vividly was a 12-course mushroom lunch I
had had in a small restaurant in Piedmonte, Italy. The mushrooms
were handpicked in the local *bosco*, or forest, as was customary in the
early fall. The chef made all sorts of mushroom-infused dishes, from
mushroom pasta, to risotto, sautéed dishes, purees, and simple *misti*
(mixed salads). Another tasty meal I remembered was at a '50s-era
greasy spoon, The Varsity, on the edge of Georgia Tech University in
Downtown Atlanta. Actually, the atmosphere was the most
memorable aspect of that meal. A sign that had been posted at the
time of the first Gulf War declared, "There may be a shortage of oil,
but not here." What I also remember about The Varsity was the
restaurant across the street, a classic Southern Fried Chicken shack. Its
yellow neon-lit banner stated, "Chicken is Chicken, but the Wing is
the Thing." Try getting that ditty out of your head after you've had a
few bong hits, or a few days in Intensive Care, for that matter. The
Wang is the Thang. The Wang is the Thang. Heh. Heh.

But what I craved most at that moment was no unique
concoction. Oddly, it was a banana smoothie. I couldn't explain why I
found something so pedestrian my definition of a slice of heaven. I
never really had a thing for smoothies—had I even ever had a banana
smoothie? Yet I was certain there could be no greater satisfaction than
the cool icy flow of a smoothie down my throat. I knew the experience
would have to wait until the doctors removed my NG tube, something
that probably would happen only after I left Intensive Care.

Dr. Roboz said strange cravings weren't uncommon among her
patients in Intensive Care.

"All one guy wanted was one of those hot dogs you get from a
street cart."

"A dirty-water dog?"

"Uh-huh."

"You didn't let him have it, did you?"

"He begged and swore that it was the only thing that would
make him feel better, get him out of Intensive Care."

"So you gave in?"

"Eventually, yes."

"And?"

"He got out of Intensive Care, and made it through the rest of his treatment—thanks to a nasty hot dog."

"There is hope for us, after all."

In hindsight, I could offer a possible explanation for my craving. While I was in the Intensive Care unit, my constant diarrhea severely depleted my electrolytes, including my level of potassium. Eating bananas is one of the best methods for ingesting copious amounts of potassium quickly. Perhaps my yearning for bananas was merely a subconscious cry for more potassium and increased electrolytes. An explanation for everything. I guess I'll always be Aristotelian at my core.

LEUKEMIA FOR CHICKENS

9

Sit. Stand. Release.

December 16, 2002

Following my successful test-taking in the Intensive Care unit, the doctors gave the okay for me to return to 5 North. A nurses' aide wheeled me out of the ICU on a gurney as Jen and my family trailed close behind. I waved to the staff behind the nurses' station as I glided by them. Jen warned me not to hoot, because other patients were not so lucky as I. It was a quick trip back to 5 North, which was located on the same floor as Intensive Care, at the far end of a long hallway. I ate my first "meal" in almost ten days. It was not a banana smoothie, the libation of my recent dreams. Instead, I drank clear chicken broth. It is said that hunger is the best sauce, so it was no surprise that I found the simple broth sumptuous.

It was close to bedtime when I was released. Jen and Avril, my private nurse, prepped me for bed with a quick sponge bath, dressing me in a fresh hospital gown and rubbing lotion on my chafed skin. In the background I heard the song, "Dead in the Water" by David Gray, as it played through speakers on my laptop computer. The lyrics were grim, but the melody not nearly so. Refreshed from my washdown, I felt an urge to write down my thoughts. Jen handed me the computer and I tried to put my experience in Intensive Care into words. I didn't write much about how I had felt, surprisingly. I was thinking more about something I called the "life force," an energy that had propelled me through my darkest hours. In the notebook where I had been keeping sporadic, diary-like entries, I later found the following ramble:

> *Maybe if I tried an easier medium ... like pen and paper ... you might have heard some of the rawness that you hear from heroin diarists, like Kurt Cobain ... I don't think I still could have taken time to reflect on paper. To find the will to write, or do anything therapeutic, when the life force is so weak. Those people are spiritual giants.*

I am pretty sure that in that mildly coherent passage I was describing how impressed I was by other people's ability to describe their emotional state at moments of physical weakness. Months before I became ill, I read an excerpt of the diary of Kurt Cobain, the former front man for Nirvana who eventually killed himself after a short, tormented life. The excerpt concerned his experience of going through drug rehab. Based on his description, the symptoms of withdrawal felt similar to what I experienced when leaving the ICU: a physical emptiness.

It was no surprise that I felt weak spiritually and emotionally. Having been sedentary for so long, I could no longer walk without the aid of a nurse or walker. When I went to the bathroom, Jen and my parents would take turns wiping my behind. By the hospital's measure, I had lost almost 30 pounds in the three weeks since I was admitted. Worse, Dr. Weinstein, my kidney specialist, had just determined that I required an immediate boost of electrolytes.

He ordered a bolus, a massive infusion of fluid given over a very short amount of time. The nurses attached oversized bags of liquid to poles beside my bed and threaded the lines through pumps to regulate my body's intake. Those tubes were then connected to the port in my chest tube and to temporary IVs in my arms.

Once the drip began, it felt like an internal flood. Though nothing was given to me orally, I remember sensing drops falling down the back of my throat. I awoke the next morning with massively fat legs. My weight rose 20 pounds overnight. The doctors called the phenomenon an edema. My family restrained themselves from laughing at my "cankles." I had to cut through the elastic on my extra-large hospital socks just to fit them around my ankles. Moving around my room became a chore. The excess fluid would drain away in the next week or so, the doctors assured me. And they seemed glad that at least my testicles hadn't swollen, which could have been painful.

The following morning I tried to resume my normal hospital routine: Eat, talk to doctors, host guests, etc. Dr. Roboz, cheerleader that she was, encouraged me to talk to my body, even kiss my own arms—anything to encourage my bone marrow to produce white blood cells. The chemo had stunned my bone marrow, by design. Now we were waiting for cell reproduction to begin. This time, hopefully, the cells would be normal and not cancerous.

"You're a little behind schedule on your induction treatment. When things start growing again, we'll still need to watch you for a little while before you can be released."

Dr. Helfgott, the infectious disease specialist, gave me counsel on eating again.

"Don't push it. It will take a while to recover your appetite, and you don't want to do anything that would make us put the tube back in."

Me: "You can't imagine what sorts of bland food passes for tasty right now."

Everything but a banana smoothie, strangely enough. What a disappointment. Whatever flavor sensation I had built up in my head, it far surpassed what a smoothie could deliver. After I few sips, I began to feel full, no doubt because my stomach had shrunk.

Jen, Jen's parents and my parents experimented with a variety of easy-to-digest meals. I quickly tired of chicken broth. We moved on to Jell-O, noodles and butter, then more complex soups. Jen's mom made her sweet squash soufflé, a staple of family meals, with the consistency of pudding. Sometimes after eating, I would throw up, ruining my calorie intake.

I started training sessions with a physical therapist to build strength, such as shoulder lifts using cans of ginger ale as weights. I could only manage a few repetitions before tiring.

After a few days out of Intensive Care, I gained strength enough to read the papers. The big story at the time was Mayor Bloomberg's plan to build an Olympic Village on the Queens shoreline across from Manhattan. The industrial zone in question corresponded with my view facing southeast. I looked at the faded shipping docks and in my stupor thought I had the answer to exactly what Bloomberg should build: an American West-style encampment of cottages for people who work and recreate outdoors—climbers, hikers, and the like. People like Jen's brother, Evan, who lived an adventurous outdoor life in Southern Utah.

I tried a sample pitch on my captive audience in the hospital room: "There aren't enough 'outdoorsy' people in New York. Everyone is inside too much. New York needs to reach out to these people. You could build this kind of village on the cheap. Campers don't need fancy digs. And the city could provide bus service north to places like New Paltz and the Adirondacks. We'll call the development 'Evan-ville' (after my brother-in-law, my inspiration for this plan). I know Mayor Mike. I used to work for him. I can contact him and tell him my idea."

My audience gave me the silent nod I often saw when I expounded on some harebrained scheme. True, any armchair psychologist could have interpreted my rants as a cry for fresh air by a stir-crazy, quarantined hospital patient. But I pressed on with my idea.

"Climbers have lots of gear. They need space for bikes and tents and stuff."

I had shakily sketched a street layout and prototype house designs with small rooms and big storage closets on a large pad of paper the night before. The drawings would have made a six-year-old proud, though they wouldn't have impressed many people older than that. There were talking points for my "presentation" scratched on the following pages as well. My delusion killed time, at least.

A couple of days later the doctors saw signs of cell growth. Blood tests showed my white count had risen to 100 from zero, or undetectable levels. We all cheered, though Dr. Roboz cautioned that they needed to see three consecutive days of rising counts before they could be confident that my body was rebuilding. Only when my counts rose above 1,000 would I have sufficient immunity to be exposed to the outside world. At that point, Dr. Roboz said, I could be released from the hospital, assuming I was otherwise healthy.

For every step forward, there was a step back. My diet of neutral-flavored liquid and mush still managed to irritate and bloat my stomach, and induce gas pains. After a day or two of discomfort, the doctors said they would have to put the NG tube back in temporarily. I didn't even fight them this time. Fortunately, the gas pressure eased quickly, and two days later they were able to remove the tube. Meantime, my counts continued to rise. First by 100 a day, then by 200 and 300 a day. I added a new activity to my morning routine: walking out to the nurses' desk around 7:30 a.m. to ask if the lab had posted my morning test results. A female doctor from Eastern Europe who wore heavy makeup would usually know the answer off-hand; if not, she would bring the numbers up on the computer for me.

This was the good news. The bad news was my night fevers persisted. My private nurse, Avril, tried different methods to reduce my temperature, such as cooling blankets at night and those frigid sponge baths in the morning. They worked to a degree, but the doctors said they would not send me home until they knew what was making me sick. Speculation centered on my chest tube. Perhaps it was infected internally. The doctors weighed the pros and cons of removing the tube. If they removed the tube, and it proved infected, then the fevers would likely stop. On the other hand, I still required medications via IV, daily blood draws for tests, and occasional transfusions. These could be handled through temporary IVs, but those kinds of ports were less reliable. As it was, my veins were pretty beat up, so inserting new IVs might be difficult.

Christmas approached. The TV ran endless ads for Macy's, encouraging people to come in at 7 a.m. for "door-buster" savings. I never lacked for gift ideas, thanks to the seemingly repetitive segments on the Today show about what to buy. Shopping may have been the opiate of the mobile masses, but I couldn't get out to the stores and was grateful to receive genuine opiates to pass sleepless nights and mute lingering pains.

Not that I received these balms daily. Jen was always watching in case I had managed to smooth-talk a nurse into over-medicating me. My family members found their own ways to divert themselves from the tedium of sitting in the hospital room. Some activities were healthier than others. We devoured crossword puzzles and held marathon Scrabble sessions. We gossiped and discussed terror threats, an airborne microbe (abbreviated as SARS) that could cause pneumonia, especially among people with weak immune systems. My parents chatted about going to Florida and about looking for a new apartment in the city, since the one they were renting was being sold. My sister's boyfriend went to Canal Street and bought bootleg copies of movies that were then playing in the theaters. I felt guilty as I popped those pirated films into a portable DVD player, but the poor film quality, combined with the tiny screen, prompted me to turn them off within minutes, my conscience still clear.

My mom and sister smoked discreetly outside the hospital, though they weren't discreet enough to close their pocketbooks, which revealed packs of cigarettes. I recognize people smoke to relieve stress, but I am puritanical about that addiction. It amazes me that anyone would willingly increase his or her risk of cancer, especially when looking directly at the potential consequences daily. I have heard the argument that since I did nothing to encourage my cancer and contracted it anyway, why try so hard to be healthy? If bad things happen to good people, why bother being good? But I regard those arguments as a weak justification for risking a similar fate.

After the doctors pondered for a couple of days about what to do with my port, they decided to remove it to see if my fevers would abate. Removing the tube required less effort than putting it in. While I was lying in bed, a doctor injected Novocain around the port. Using a scissor, he cut through fibrous skin that held the tube in place. He pulled the device out slowly from my chest. Amazingly, the inner part of the tube was almost twice as long as the exposed end. The whole process took about ten minutes. The doctor then placed the tube in a sterile bag for tests to see if any bacteria would grow. As nothing grew in the following days, the root cause of my night fevers remained a mystery.

I approached the four-week mark, the average length of stay in the hospital for an induction treatment. The doctors began talking about sending me home. I could get out of the hospital around Christmas, in less than a week. I would have ten days to rest at home before my next treatment, a less intense round of chemo, designed to kill off any lingering cancer cells.

Before being released, I would need to undergo another bone marrow biopsy to show my cancer was in remission, defined as a very low or undetectable amount of cancerous cells present in my marrow.

Since my white count had risen to more than 1,000 by that point, I had cleared the hurdle of no longer needing to be quarantined. (A normal white cell count is anywhere from 5,000 to 14,000.)

Me: "What will I be able to do once I'm home?"

Dr. Roboz: "Pretty much what you want. Though you'll be much more exhausted than you realize. It will simply feel good to get out of here."

After Dr. Roboz left, I said to Jen that maybe we could go back to Lake Placid for a few days.

"What could be more refreshing than that? I know it's far, but we could take my dad's plane."

My dad and his older brother had purchased a fractional share of a small jet, which they used to visit clients and to fly back and forth to their houses in Palm Beach. I knew it was an extravagance to use the plane to go to Lake Placid, but I doubted my father would refuse me. I certainly couldn't make the five-hour trip by car in my state.

Jen: "Roger. I think we need to be reasonable here. Let's just worry about getting out of the hospital."

"Well, it shouldn't be hard to book a room in the winter last minute."

Once the doctors started talking about sending me home, it became a regular topic of conversation in my hospital room.

Nurse: "What will be the first thing you'll do when you are out of here?"

Me: "Cry, probably."

If I was going to adjust to life at home again, I would need to cut down on my dependence on others. I told the night nurse that I should probably try to be on my own. A week before, I had considered Avril, who sang me to sleep at night, my spiritual rock. I vowed to involve her in my recovery long after this hospital stay was over. But Avril quickly faded from my life as I grew tired of the early morning sponge baths and craved some sleep and privacy in those hours. Later on, when I returned to the hospital, she visited me only occasionally when she worked for other patients on the ward. I was okay with that.

In the morning, Dr. Roboz said she wanted to do the biopsy to test for remission. I winced, recalling the pain. Also, I knew that if the results were not favorable, I wouldn't get my ten-day break. Instead, I would have to go through another round of chemotherapy immediately. That had been the fate of another patient who was two doors down from me on the unit.

Dr. Roboz drew the marrow in three agonizing pulls. I gave my signature howl with each needle extraction.

"We should know the results by tomorrow."

I didn't have to wait that long. Dr. Roboz came back eight hours later, smiling widely.

"We got everything back. You're clean. You're in remission!"

I was truly excited. Bizarrely, I heard in my head the chorus line of the song "Tradition" from *Fiddler on the Roof*. Instead of hearing the word "Tradition" sung four times over, I heard "Remission" in choral concert, trumpets blaring.

Jen and I hugged and kissed. I now knew for certain I would go home soon, though it took a few more drawn-out days to finally get out of the hospital. I had a fever one night, which delayed my release. Then the doctors said they needed to put in another port (this one in my forearm) to administer medications and transfusions at home. That required jockeying for an appointment with Interventional Radiology, no small feat on Christmas Day.

Once the line was slotted, the doctors threaded it into my arm just below my right bicep. This setup was easier to keep clean than a chest port. Covering up for showers required just placing some Saran Wrap over the end and sealing the edges with tape.

We started unpacking my room, sending home bags of books and magazines, clothes and trinkets. I received the final okay to leave on December 26, some 31 days after I had been admitted. Though I still had a runny nose, the doctors thought it best for me to recoup at home. Jen wheeled me off 5 North in a chair and we headed out to the visitors' elevators bank. I had tissues in one hand and a canvas tote bag full of stuff in my lap. I held my breath in the elevator, fearful of others' germs. My family and I exited as a group.

We passed through the marble-laden front entrance of the hospital. I had never seen this grand entrance. On my first visit, I had entered via the whitewashed Emergency Room. That was way back on November 25.

Once past the front door, I breathed in the brisk air on that quiet winter morning. Slowly I rose from the chair and shuffled sideways into the back seat of my Dad's black Mercedes sedan. At the helm was my father's driver, Sankey. He pulled out from the curb. The motion felt fast, startling me. Sankey headed down the FDR, passing alongside the portion of the East River that was my view from the hospital. Absorbing how still I had been for the past month, I bawled onto Jen's shoulder.

We met Jen's parents at our apartment. They brought Milo back to us from the suburbs. Our two families exchanged gifts in a belated Chanukah celebration. I received lots of lounging attire—sweatpants, long-sleeve t-shirts, thermal underwear and the like—perfect for sitting on the couch in my apartment. My sister, Shana, wrote me a long holiday card. I made it about halfway through, to the point where she told me I was her hero. She was applauding my courage, but I didn't feel so courageous and started crying again.

"I didn't do anything. I just sat there."

My family left the next day for Florida. Jen and I stayed in New York, planning to relax at home during our 10-day break. But I was back in the Emergency Room within 48 hours.

LEUKEMIA FOR CHICKENS

10

Interlude

It's never easy to break free from something on which you've come to depend. As soon as the doctors released me from the hospital, I began to long for its secure confines, to worry whether my blood pressure and temperature were normal. In the hospital, nurses checked my vitals every six hours. Now how would I learn these things? I slept fitfully my first night in my apartment, half-expecting to be awakened by Jen for a medicine bag change or a pulse check. Years later, I still couldn't sleep through the night.

My first morning home, Jen began taking on the responsibilities previously left to nurses and doctors. The hospital had provided us with medical supplies to last a few days, which was essential, because many of the medications I required had to be special-ordered by the local pharmacist. The hospital had also arranged for a home healthcare provider to visit our apartment three times a week to flush saline and heparin through the port in my arm, as well as to administer medications via IV that weren't available in pill form.

Arthur was our visiting nurse. He gradually taught Jen how to tend to my health needs. This was better than having to rely on him, as his idea of a scheduled appointment meant arriving at our apartment sometime "in the morning" or "in the afternoon."

My second night at home, I tried to relax and not worry about things like my blood-oxygen level. I rolled over on my stomach to sleep, something I rarely did in the hospital, for fear that it would kink the lines delivering medications. I reveled momentarily in the prone position until I felt a thump in my chest. I rose with a start and immediately felt short of breath. Jen asked what was wrong, and I said I didn't know. I felt like I'd just had the wind knocked out of me. Would she take my pulse?

It was more than 140 beats per minute. In the hospital, I usually had a high pulse rate, but 140 was elevated even for me.

Me: "What should we do?"

Jen: "Call Adam?"

Calling Adam, our regular doctor, seemed an easier, faster way to get an answer than calling the leukemia unit answering service and waiting for a call back from an on-call doctor. Over the past month-plus, we'd grown close to Adam, who had come to visit me in the hospital almost daily. It didn't seem an imposition to call his cell phone at 10:30 p.m. We caught Adam as he was coming out of a movie.

"Roger says he's not breathing well, and his pulse is really high."

"He's feeling tightness in his chest?"

"He says he is."

"It's probably anxiety, but I think you have to go to the Emergency Room to be sure. I know it's a pain, but lots of people go back to the hospital right after they're released, especially if they've been in for a long time. Don't be too concerned. The ER shouldn't be that busy the day after Christmas. I'll meet you there."

Click.

"Adam says we should go to the hospital."

Me: "Good. I don't feel comfortable letting this slide. I'm sorry."

"My parents will have come into the city to take care of Milo."

As we left for the hospital in a taxi, I concentrated on breathing deeply. At the Emergency Room, the triage nurse took my temperature and blood pressure. Though those readings were normal, my pulse still raced at 140 beats per minute. The nurse moved me to an isolation room in the ER, out of concern that I would be vulnerable to infection. Once in the room, a different ER nurse attached a saline drip to my port, in case I was dehydrated.

Dehydration was likely. Newly released hospital patients often get dehydrated, because they are used to receiving fluid through a saline drip and forget to take in enough fluid orally. A little later, someone took an electrocardiogram. Another nurse drew blood to measure my white count, red count, and platelet levels. This was much the same procedure I had undergone whenever something had gone wrong on 5 North.

Adam came by to make sure things ran smoothly and to insure we weren't left unattended. An average visit to the ER could last eight hours. Adam had worked as a resident at the hospital years ago, and he knew many people in various units—far more people than doctors on staff who had been hired later in their career. As an example, later in my treatment I needed to take a Pulmonary Function Test so that my insurance would agree to fund my stem cell transplant. Adam sent us to a far corner of the hospital to knock on an unmarked door. Inside, Jen and I found two technicians surrounded by lots of breathing measurement equipment.

"We only do PFT's in the morning," George, one of the technicians, told us, "but since you're a friend of Adam's…"

Lying on a gurney in the Emergency Room, I felt my heart rate slow down. I began to nod off. Jen sat in a chair beside me and waited to hear from the doctor. Adam left. Hours passed. Finally, a nurse told us the doctor had the results of the electrocardiogram and the blood tests. He would talk to us when he had a free moment. We had no TV and struggled to kill time. After another few hours and multiple pleadings by Jen to see a doctor, any doctor, one came by. He wanted to take a stool sample.

Me: "What for?"

"We don't have a good explanation for your high pulse. We would like to do more tests."

Jen: "What about the explanation that this was simply an anxiety attack? Doesn't that seem logical?"

Me: "How long would it take to analyze a stool sample?"

"At least a few more hours."

"I gave a stool sample a couple of days ago, when I left the hospital. Will we really find anything different so soon? I'm feeling better now than when I came in."

The doctor left the room and returned a half hour later to say that we could go home. He said if anything further arose, I should call the leukemia unit answering service.

As it turned out, there was an explanation in the doctor's hands for my strange condition. The electrocardiogram taken that night in the ER showed an abnormal heart rhythm that a doctor might not notice if he wasn't looking for a particular pattern. Though serious, the arrhythmia would remain undiagnosed for another three months. In that time, I would experience three or four more similar episodes, each of which was life-threatening, according to the cardiologist who eventually "fixed" the problem. More on that later.

Jen and I returned to our apartment where her parents, Lois and Marty, were taking care of Milo. We had called them in a hurry when we were leaving for the ER, and, not knowing how long we'd be gone or if I'd be admitted, told them they could take care of Milo when they asked if there was anything they could do to help. I was exhausted but afraid to fall asleep for fear I would feel that thud in my chest again. We told Jen's parents they could leave, but they insisted on staying the night. I lay down on the couch on my back, watched a bad movie, and tried to doze. Jen's dad lounged uncomfortably in one of our armchairs. I caught the sunrise over Greenwich Village through our loft apartment's east-facing window.

Jen and I didn't do much in the ensuing days, other than acclimate to life at home. Jen took primary responsibility for walking Milo and cooking meals, among all of the other daily chores and errands. For New Year's, we did laundry and watched Dick Clark count down the final seconds of 2002.

Me, as the ball dropped: "To a better 2003."

We ate caviar and sipped champagne. The chemo had reduced my alcohol tolerance to almost nothing. I fell asleep instantly.

A week into my interlude between treatments, I made my first hospital visit as an outpatient. I wore a mask over my face to avoid contracting an infection from others who were waiting in the clinic. Dr. Roboz ordered a transfusion of platelets for me, something I received every few days while in the hospital. She told us my blood tests showed elevated liver enzymes. This was common, though my levels would need to drop before I could begin another round of chemotherapy.

"You will have more time at home to gain strength. At least a week."

Me: "This is okay? I'm not putting myself in jeopardy?"

"The treatment protocol is just a guideline, not a strict regimen. You're in remission right now. We don't want to wait until we see signs of leukemia again, but it's okay to hold out a little longer, so that you can better withstand the next round."

My next round, dubbed "consolidation," involved two steps. First I would have a round of chemo, sans the experimental drug I'd received in the first round. This regimen was expected to be less intense than the first round, in part because it lacked the experimental drug, which was designed to concentrate the effect of the chemo. The second step was intended to eliminate lingering leukemia cells. I would stay in the hospital as my white cell count fell and then rose again above the 1,000 mark, the threshold that signaled I had a minimally functioning immune system. When I reached the minimum threshold, I would receive a drug that would induce my white cell count to grow more rapidly and to a level much higher than normal.

This same medication would prompt stem cells to circulate in my blood stream. Once those stem cells reached a critical mass, a machine would harvest them, using a process called aphaeresis. The hospital would freeze the harvested stem cells and re-infuse me with them during my third round of treatment, the stem cell transplant.

Though all this was important to know, my mind now was fixated on the fact that I had extra time off before going back to the hospital.

"Does this delay mean Jen and I can go to Lake Placid?"

"That might be a little farther than I would prefer you to be."

"We wouldn't drive there. We'd fly. It's less than an hour by plane. If something goes wrong we could order a plane on short notice and be back in the city the same day."

Jen: "Roger, have you even discussed flying with your father?"

"Not officially, no."

Dr. Roboz: "If you can really fly there, you can go. Jen, will you be comfortable with this?"

"I think we need to talk about it alone."

"Let me know either way."

Jen's major concern was that she wouldn't be able to call on someone else to help her take care of me in the event something went wrong. Her reasonable concern lost out to her desire to get far, far away from the hospital. Lake Placid had taken on a magical aura for us since I was diagnosed with leukemia. Even before I was diagnosed, I had envisioned Lake Placid as a refuge, a place where I could build my eco-friendly bottled-water company.

Now Lake Placid represented peace and tranquility of another sort, a place that lacked a history of my illness. We knew we weren't going to be on our own up there. Hotel staff would be available if a serious problem arose. We booked a room at the Lake Placid Lodge, where we had stayed the previous Memorial Day weekend. I explained to the concierge that we required extra attention. They assured us they understood.

My dad said it would be no problem for us to take the plane. We flew from the airport in Teterboro, New Jersey, in a six-seat Cessna jet. On our approach to Lake Placid, low clouds obscured our view of the snow-covered "High Peaks," but we saw glimpses of a winter paradise as we touched down at Adirondack Regional Airport in Saranac Lake—little more than two hangars, a barn and a windsock, about fifteen miles from Lake Placid.

Everything was white, from the snow-packed runway to the roadsides, which bore two feet of fluff. On our ride to the Lodge, we passed stoic ice-fishermen waiting for tugs on lines sunk below the frozen surface. The Lodge set us up in their wheelchair-accessible room, even though I was capable of climbing stairs, if slowly. Our first night's meal was my first meal outside my apartment since we had left the hospital. We ate in the Lodge dining room, and I ordered lamb chops over white sweet potato mash. When the waiter brought out the plate, I lifted one of the chops and shook it, noting it wobbled. I told the waiter that I had never seen a chop that flexed. My mom's lamb preparation tended toward burnt edges.

"Look at the middle of this rib! It's pink. Amazing."

Thrilling over a fattening meal was refreshing. Though Jen's cooking efforts were admirable, since leaving the hospital meals at home were not nearly as exciting as this, and I had often struggled to finish my portion. Not that night.

In the morning I awoke and went alone to the main lodge for breakfast. I read the *Times Digest*, a faxed, abridged version of *The New York Times*. The physical paper wouldn't arrive in Lake Placid until 9 a.m. I sat on the porch under heat lamps and behind a see-through cellophane curtain, looking out at frozen and snow-covered Lake Placid. I watched trucks drive over the lake to make repairs on summer homes that lacked road access. As I ate my pancakes, the waiter told me that workmen preferred to move heavy objects back and forth from the houses in the winter. In the summer, they would need to use boats, which were less stable. Lake Placid was living up to its billing as another world.

Jen came over a little later. I ordered a second helping of cereal and a yogurt smoothie. After our lazy breakfast, we went for massages in town. The masseuse tried not to look surprised when I showed her my arm port. Our first three days in Lake Placid passed slowly. We often just sat by the fire and read stray magazines and books. I made short entries in my journal.

On the third night, we caught a movie at the 1930s-era State Theater on Main St., the only movie house within fifty miles. Afterwards, at a restaurant in town, we overheard the host say that the first real cold spell of the season was coming tomorrow.

"Might get to 10 below."

We flew back to the city before we had a chance to feel what the locals called "a real winter chill."

Our brief getaway made it easier to accept my next round of chemo, though I still cried the night before my scheduled return. For all the doctors' assurances that my body would handle the toxins better this time around, I remembered their claim that some people "sailed through" the previous round as well. Clearly I was not among the lucky ones. I printed lots of pictures from Lake Placid to adorn my hospital room. Milo and I cuddled on our last night together before he would return to his country home. Even at fifty pounds, he curled up with me as if he were a big stuffed animal and seemed to know how special and fleeting our time was.

We arrived at the hospital on a Monday, a little more than two weeks after my release. The nurse took blood for yet another round of tests from my arm port. An hour later she returned and said that my liver enzymes were still too high for the doctors to start chemotherapy treatment. They wanted to wait another week. I could go home.

"That's it? I should just pack up?"

"It seems strange, but yes."

"Don't the doctors want to come by and talk to me first?"

"I don't know. I'll put in a call."

Dr. Roboz did come by, though she didn't offer much explanation beyond the fact that the protocol called for my liver enzymes to be below a certain level, and the tests showed them to be slightly above that level. Waiting a week would provide time for the enzymes to drop into the acceptable range.

"You probably have mixed emotions about waiting. Let me tell you it's better not to start the treatment than to have to cut back on the chemo dosage once we've begun because your body can't take it. The best chance we have for success is if we give you the full dose of chemo."

Another week at home. Come to think of it, this wasn't so bad. When people hear they have cancer the first reaction is often, "Get it out of me. Now. Whatever you have to do." Leukemia isn't like that. It circulates in your blood, so it's everywhere in your system at the same time. There's no quick and dirty way to "cut it out," as if it were a tumor.

The waiting process was teaching me patience, something needed in large amounts, not only to endure treatment, but the lengthy recovery period that follows.

11

My Tiger Woods Moment

On my second attempt to begin my second round of chemotherapy, the doctors gave me the okay to enter the hospital. They based their approval on a blood test showing a decline in my liver enzymes to "acceptable" levels. These levels suggested I would be able to tolerate the full dose of chemotherapy prescribed by the leukemia treatment protocol drawn up by specialists in the field years ago.

To review leukemia treatment protocol: The chemotherapy portion of the consolidation round (the second round) lasts five days, during which a patient receives via IV the drugs cytarabyne, etoposide and danarubicin. This toxic cocktail kills fast-growing cells, like cancer cells, and stuns the bone marrow, stopping its production of white blood cells. Slowly, the bone marrow recovers and begins to produce white blood cells. It is hoped that these cells will be normal, healthy cells, not abnormal leukemic ones. The best chance of seeing normal cells usually occurs when doctors administer the highest possible dose in as short a period as possible following completion of the first round, known as induction. This is so the leukemia cells, if they're there, don't have a chance to proliferate.

Doctors have tried to explain to me the science behind this process. But it is beyond me. I find it easier to understand in philosophical terms. Chemo is like punitive behavior modification. To wit: If a person does something wrong, beat him or her senseless. The traumatized person, it is hoped, will think twice before misbehaving in the future. Though not popular as a social engineering tool, this method of treatment is alive and well in oncology. Researchers have even found that the more times a patient receives high-dose chemo—that is, the more a patient is beaten senseless—the less likely it is that the patient will experience a recurrence of leukemia.

Of course, continual bombardment with poison chemicals is not viable long-term, the most obvious reason being that, given often enough and at a high enough intensity, chemotherapy will kill not only cancer cells but the patient as well. For that reason, and because of advances in medical science, doctors have developed alternative treatments, such as using stem cells, to fight leukemia.

There is a scientific basis for stem cell use, though to me it is an even darker form of black magic than chemotherapy. I prefer a philosophical explanation to help me understand this process as well. To wit: Stem cells' power is akin to that of the *tabula rasa*, or blank slate, popularized by John Locke. (For the record, Locke, a social critic from the 17th century, never envisioned anything like a stem cell.)

As generic proto-cells, stem cells have the ability to morph into specialized adult-age cells. The body continually produces new stem cells to replenish dying adult-age cell populations. Doctors theorize that these early-stage cells may still be healthy, even if they later morph into cancerous ones. To treat leukemia, doctors capture these stem cells from the blood stream and later re-introduce them into leukemia patients. Somehow these cells find their way to a person's bone marrow, where they nest and grow into healthy adult-age cells.

Stem cell therapies of this type are not controversial, unlike proposals to use embryonic stem cells, an issue in the 2004 Presidential election. Doctors are enthusiastic about the possibilities of embryonic stem cells because these cells have an even greater ability to transform into different types of adult cells. These cells also have had no exposure to environmental carcinogens, which are the root cause of many cancers, including leukemia. The malleable nature of embryonic stem cells could even lead to treatments for diseases where doctors are unsure of the root causes, such as Alzheimer's.

That's the *tabula rasa* theory: start with a clean slate and you can create anything. For all the science, the actual results are far from certain. A leukemia patient who undergoes consolidation—consisting of either multiple rounds of chemo, or a round of chemo followed by a stem cell transplant—is likely to relapse in almost half of all cases. Leukemia patients who refuse a consolidation round of treatment— perhaps because they are unwilling to undergo multiple chemotherapy rounds—experience a relapse of the disease within a few months ninety percent of the time.

I was unaware of these grim statistics as I underwent my treatment, since I didn't ask and purposely avoided doing research on the Internet, where such information is readily available. I already suspected my chances for survival were not high. Instead, I clung to a memory from the night I was diagnosed, when Dr. Roboz told me that remission was possible seventy percent of the time. Only later did I learn the difference between being in remission and being cured. Dr. Roboz discouraged me from inquiring about discomforting statistics like "cure rate five years after diagnosis," a standard measure of cancer survival.

"We could all be vaporized by a suitcase bomb before then."

By not associating my own situation with statistical averages, I sidestepped vexing and depressing issues, like possibly dying or even wondering why I got leukemia in the first place. One nurse suggested that lots of Jews seem to contract leukemia.

"Or maybe you just see lots of Jews because they tend to have good health care coverage," I replied.

Others wondered whether my proximity to the ruins of the Twin Towers had an effect. Perhaps.

Those who ask, "What are the odds?" would find that leukemia patients are especially unlucky. Though well-known as a disease, leukemia is extremely rare. Worldwide, doctors diagnose only 10,000 cases each year. NewYork-Presbyterian Hospital, the largest leukemia treatment center in the New York area, comprised of more than 17 million people, sees just 30 new cases a year.

For me, it helps to think that someone has to get leukemia, so why not me? I rationalize my bad fortune by remembering other low-probability situations where I was the chosen one among many: like at the sixth-grade fair, where I won a new ten-speed bike, or at the annual Little League dinner, where I took home the grand prize, a baseball glove signed by Mookie Wilson. (In truth, I didn't get a *signed* glove, because I was a lefty, and Mookie had signed a righty model.) What were the chances of winning those prizes? And, more generally, what were the chances that I would be born white and upwardly mobile in the United States? That's a lottery ticket in itself, in many people's estimation.

However, those were not my foremost thoughts as I began my consolidation round. I thought about such things at other points during my treatment, when I didn't have more immediate health concerns. I had that kind of time more often during consolidation, because the chemotherapy part went relatively smoothly. Side effects were mild. Sure, my stomach bloated, I had diarrhea and mild fevers, but nothing spiraled precipitously, like during my first round.

My stay in the hospital was shorter than for my first round as well, lasting a little more than two weeks. The doctors artificially boosted my marrow via an injection called Neupogen so that it would produce, and then overproduce, stem cells, the immature cells of my immune system. My white count rose quickly above the 1,000 level required to leave the sanitary confines of the hospital. I continued to take Neupogen after I went home because the doctors wanted my cell count to rise to an artificially high level, closer to 20,000—the point at which stem cells would be in such oversupply that they would be spit out of the marrow and into the blood stream, ready for collection. Before stem cell transplants were thought up, doctors had to go into the hipbone to retrieve the marrow for transplantation. Stem cell collection is far easier for the doctor and much less painful for the patient.

The nurses taught Jen how to give me the mildly stinging Neupogen injections by practicing on a clementine. Its rind is comparable in consistency to skin, providing light resistance to a needle before it glides easily beneath the top layer.

When enough stem cells circulate in the blood, a special machine is used to separate them from adult-age cells. Usually, a patient sits for three or four sessions of aphaeresis to collect sufficient stem cells for a re-transplant later on. Each session lasts about three to four hours.

My brief stint of having a port in my arm, rather than in my chest, ended that week. The doctors said they needed a higher volume line for my stem cell harvest. They booked a time for surgery with Interventional Radiology, whose doctors inserted a two-port Broviac into my right pectoral just above the scar left behind from my first "double lumen" (two-tube) port.

Inevitably, after a few days at home, I developed a fever, which forced Jen and me to return to the Emergency Room. I wasn't totally disappointed to have to go back to the hospital, because I knew I would likely be readmitted anyway when the time came for my stem cell harvest. I was happy to have had at least a short respite. The doctors had debated whether they could do the harvest with me sleeping at home at night, and attending the clinic during the day. Now that I had a fever, I was sure the doctors would decide to keep me in the hospital while they collected my stem cells.

It was nighttime when Jen and I arrived at the ER. There was plenty of action, much more so than during our visit over Christmas break. No beds were available in the hospital upstairs, we were told; it would be a long wait in the ER before they could locate a bed, and we could be admitted.

Fortunately, Adam, our usual savior, lived nearby and was able to come to the ER. Adam knew from his days as a resident at the hospital that there were always open beds somewhere; one simply had to troll the halls of various units. Open beds were not always reported to the admitting office. As for why this was so, one can offer charitable explanations and not-so-charitable ones. Suffice it to say, Adam found an open bed on the second floor in the renal unit, probably by smooth-talking the nurse who assigned beds to incoming patients. Even with Adam's assistance, it took Jen and me eight hours to leave the ER and move to the room upstairs.

I entered the hospital because of a high fever, but as I lay in the ER, I felt increasing pain in my lower back. I assumed this was because I was lying on a thin gurney in the ER. But the pain increased even when I moved to a real bed on the second floor. The nurse gave me some Tylenol and recommended some breathing and stretching exercises. I moved from the bed to a chair, hoping a change in posture would alleviate the pain. It did not. I began to feel waves of pain that literally shook me. I barely slept that night. The renal unit doctors were little help and those from the leukemia unit, who might have had an explanation, didn't come down to the second floor until late in the morning after they saw their patients on 5 North.

When a doctor did come by, he told me my white blood cell count was 22,000. This boded well for my stem cell harvest. Perhaps tomorrow they would be able to hook me up to the aphaeresis machine, he said. Meantime, the 5 North team would work on finding me a room on their floor. As for my back pain, the doctor had no explanation, but he would write a standing prescription for morphine, if I thought I needed some.

"Yes. Please. Anything. As soon as possible."

It would take at least an hour to get the morphine, I knew, because of hospital procedure. But I welcomed any relief at that point. The nurses secured me a small private room on 5 North. I moved in around dinnertime. At night, I felt another wave of pain—bad enough that I slept on the floor of my room, because the hard surface made my back feel better. A nurse passing by saw me lying on the floor and tapped me with her foot. I awoke and told her I preferred this to the bed. She seemed relieved that I had not fainted or fallen.

"That's a new one, sleeping on the floor."

From a sanitary point of view, it wasn't a bright move, though I suffered no ill effects.

The following morning the doctors had an almost ecstatic look on their faces. My white blood cell count had shot to 35,000.

"You must get to aphaeresis as soon as possible."

Within a couple hours, I was at the third floor clinic where they conducted stem cell harvests. Sharon, the nurse, whom I would come to know well during subsequent weekly visits to the clinic, attached one of my chest ports to the aphaeresis machine, which had the bulky shape of a 50s-era Univac computer. My blood flowed out through a tube and was cycled through a series of circles resembling the wheels on a reel-to-reel tape recorder. A small amount of yellowish-pink liquid—my stem cells—settled in a plastic receptacle bag, while the rest found its way back into my body via the other port in my chest. The process itself was painless, though I still requested morphine to dull cramps in my back and legs, which were exacerbated by sitting still in a plastic lazy-boy for hours on end.

I fully expected to endure a few rounds of aphaeresis in the coming days; however, that night I received a phone call from a resident who said I had provided enough stem cells for my upcoming transplant, many more cells than I needed in fact. While it was uncommon to see a patient produce enough stem cells for a transplant in a single session, it was not unheard of, according to the doctor.

"Congratulations. Someone will come by tomorrow to discuss the results with you."

Woo-hoo! Better-than-expected news. Finally. Jen and I called family and friends to tell them we were set for the final stage of our leukemia battle.

In the morning, a doctor whom I did not recognize came into the room. Dr. Schuster was tall, with a dark, bushy mustache, and was clearly the most vibrant person I had met in the hospital to date.

"Is this Tiger's room?"

I looked puzzled. He pressed on.

"I had to meet the man myself."

"You mean me?"

"Yes, you, Tiger. You know how Tiger Woods dominates the PGA tour? How no other player comes close to challenging him?"

I nodded. "Sure."

"Well, my friend, you are the Tiger Woods of stem cell harvests."

It wasn't "World's Best Golfer," but at least it was a title.

"Wow. I've never excelled as an athlete. How did I do this?"

"I've collected stem cells from patients and donors for a long time now, and I've never seen anyone produce as many stem cells as you did. In one session, no less. Guess how many stem cell transplants we could do based on your single harvest?"

"I don't know. Two or three maybe."

"Try 12."

"12?"

"You have more than doubled the highest stem cell count we have ever seen."

"That's amazing. Are you sure?"

"I called the technician to double-check. I didn't believe the results myself."

"And?"

"They're real. I'll even predict your record will never be matched. Way to go, Tiger."

"Can we put a plaque on the phoresis machine, saying that on this date, so and so number of stem cells were collected from Roger Madoff, a.k.a. 'the Tiger Woods of stem cell harvests'?"

"That's a good one."

Dr. Schuster headed the bone marrow transplant unit, which was distinct from the leukemia unit, though many bone marrow transplant patients came from the leukemia unit. Going forward, the doctors from the bone marrow team would be primarily responsible for my care.

As a statistic, my record stem cell harvest was interesting. I told anyone who asked about my latest round of treatment that I was "the Tiger Woods of stem cell harvesting." That factoid put a cheery spin on an otherwise unpleasant topic.

As for its usefulness in medicine, my stem cell harvest was less monumental. It did explain why I felt waves of pain in my back in the days leading up to the harvest. That feeling was the marrow in my bones in hyper-drive, spitting out massive quantities of stem cells. But my record stem cell harvest did not augur that my transplant was more likely to be successful than those of other patients with lower stem cell counts.

One riddle of stem cell transplants is that doctors cannot be sure whether the stem cells they insert into their patients are healthy stem cells or if there are leukemic cells hiding amongst them. The science is not there yet, as the doctors say. Overall, research suggests that transplanted stem cells are benign in more cases than not, though not overwhelmingly so.

That made me comfortable enough to go through with the transplant, which has a mortality rate of about 10 percent (again, a hard statistic with which I was only vaguely familiar while undergoing treatment). A person can never know whether his or her specific case will be among the success stories based on statistics alone. For that kind of assurance, one must rely on hope and/or faith.

12

A Better Mouse Trap

After completing my stem cell harvest, I earned a three-week respite from hospital life before I was scheduled to return for my transplant. This third and final phase of my treatment would perhaps be the most difficult to bear, I was warned by the doctors. First, new chemotherapy drugs would be employed to kill my bone marrow cells, not just stun them, as had occurred in two previous rounds of treatment. Once my bone marrow was ablated, the scientific term for killed, the stem cells collected during my harvest would be given back to me via IV. These cells would take root at the sites of my now-dead bone marrow and spawn a fresh new immune system. Such is the miracle of stem cells: they go where they're needed and morph into cells that resolve the problem. After my new bone marrow produced new blood cells, and the doctors deemed my immune system self-supporting, I would be released from the hospital.

All this could take as long as five weeks, I was told, longer than the thirty-one days I endured in the hospital during my initial phase of treatment. The risks inherent in the transplant procedure were plain. For weeks, when my old bone marrow was dead and my new immune system had yet to establish itself, I would be vulnerable to all sorts of infections. The doctors would give me drugs to kill these infections, but these drugs might not be effective. The second major risk was that my stem cells might not take root, or graft, as the doctors term the process by which the cells magically find their old home and nest again. If no graft occurred, I would remain immune-compromised and vulnerable to infection indefinitely.

Neither of these complications was likely to happen, though each was a possibility. Another risk I faced was that even if my transplant was deemed a success, I might still experience a relapse of leukemia. It happened in about 40 percent of all cases. A relapse might occur if there was leukemia in my stem cells, or if my supposedly dead old bone marrow was not completely destroyed and its remains continued to produce leukemia cells.

Overall, the doctors said there were fewer risks to undergoing a re-transplant of my own stem cells, known as an autologous transplant, than to not doing a transplant. The risks were also fewer than if I underwent an allogeneic, or donor stem cell, transplant, where stem cells from another person are infused into a leukemia patient. Donor transplants are riskier because a donor's cells are less likely to graft in the host. Even if a donor's stem cells do graft, the new immune system from the donor may fight the host's body, causing all sorts of complications, anything from skin chafing to liver failure. Patients die from donor transplant complications in about twenty percent of cases, almost twice as often as when they undergo autologous transplants.

One argument in favor of donor transplants, as opposed to autologous ones, is that those who receive donor transplants experience fewer relapses. Even so, many doctors believe that this benefit is outweighed by the greater risk involved. They often advocate performing an autologous transplant first. If that transplant fails, a donor transplant can usually be performed after that. As for the suffering that two transplants can exact on a patient, both physically and mentally, well, you cross that bridge when you get to it.

To get approval to undergo a stem cell transplant, private health insurance companies require a series of diagnostic tests that demonstrate a leukemia patient is strong enough to survive and truly needs a transplant as a last resort. This is mostly due to the six-figure cost of the procedure and treatments that accompany it. The tests include measures of lung functions, dental X-rays, and other procedures that seem unrelated to receiving a transplant. Though my health insurance approved my stem cell transplant without undue fuss,

my doctors said they had fought many times in the past with insurers
to pay for the procedure.

During my break between the second and third round of
treatment, I felt reasonably confident of my prospects, as did my
family, though perhaps we were being premature. My parents began
thinking beyond my own care needs, about the larger issue of leukemia
treatment. They came upon the idea of making a gift to the hospital.
Though they could have given money to The Leukemia & Lymphoma
Society, the principal fund-raising organization for the disease in the
U.S., they thought there was a way in which they could more directly
aid the efforts of the doctors and nurses who looked after patients on a
daily basis. From their vantage point as frequent visitors to the
hospital, they saw how even this well-funded institution lacked money
for many services and projects that might seem peripheral to patient
care, but were essential to running a solid leukemia program. When
we asked the team for proposals in need of funding, the amount of the
gift quickly rose into the millions, though the final total and the focus
of the donation remained undecided for a few months more.

Also, in the break between hospital stays, Jen and I took a brief
vacation. This time we traveled south to my parents' vacation home in
Palm Beach, Florida. It was late February 2003. Jen and I spent most
of our time there lying in the shade. Because my leg muscles were
atrophied, I did not have the strength to play golf or go for a jog. I
couldn't swim, because I couldn't risk wetting the tubes protruding
from my chest. I did take my dad's Ferrari for a spin once, though I had
trouble feathering the clutch. Being ill can make an extravagance like a
Ferrari seem totally ridiculous. Still, I felt good smelling oil waft
forward into the cockpit from the engine in the rear.

I read *The New York Times* cover-to-cover every day. The major
stories at the time described the looming war in Iraq and the
coincident capture of a top Al Qaeda leader. Lots of articles speculated
that future terrorist plots might be stored on the terrorist's laptop
computer, which captors found in his Lahore hideaway. For the first
time in months I let my thoughts run far beyond my private terror of
having cancer to the many terrors faced by the world at large, though
that reality had never been far from my mind. Sometimes I found
myself trying to not read to an article's end, where I knew I would find

the most frightening description of a hypothetical attack, only to find that I could not divert my eyes.

Could I rightfully blot out others' suffering simply because I had worries of my own? As I sat beside the pool, I read an article describing the inequities of life in Iraq. One anecdote told of a young Iraqi with leukemia, who would likely die. The Iraqi government had medicine to treat the boy, but only hospitals that served a privileged elite provided treatment, the article said. This hit me harder than imagined terrorist strikes. My plight seemed near impossible, with access to the best medicine had to offer. The Iraqi boy didn't even have a chance to fight.

Other than reading, I spent most of my days eating and trying to gain weight. I needed to gain at least ten pounds before I returned to the hospital, because I knew I would lose that much while there. I ate stone crabs almost daily, only to have my aunt tell me that the tasty crustaceans were a favorite of dieters, because they contained virtually no calories. Unable to pass them up, I added snacks of nuts and ice cream to my diet.

We returned to New York in the first few days of March. The night before I entered the hospital, Jen and I went to dinner with my parents, my sister Shana and her daughter. During the meal, Shana said offhandedly that our cousin Andy had found a lump near his neck that had been biopsied the prior week. In fact, Andy had not found the lump: a masseuse who was giving him a chair massage at work had found it.

The initial pathology report on Andy's lump stated that the cells from a biopsy appeared cancerous, but there was now a debate among the doctors as to whether this was the case, my sister said. They needed to do more tests on the mass.

Me: "That's awful. Andy must be freaking out."

Shana: "Not yet."

Many people get biopsies of lumps, and the lumps often turn out benign. But my family's luck of late made me wary, given that I was the second person in our family to get leukemia since September, following my nine-year-old cousin, Ariel. Still, I admit I did not think often about Andy's plight during the first half of my transplant procedure, in part because I didn't hear much more about it from my family during those weeks.

For my third round of chemotherapy, the doctors added the drugs busulfan and cyclophosphamide to my usual battery of toxins. I reacted to this new mixture of chemo much in the way I reacted to my other treatments; that is, grudgingly. One peculiarity of this round was that busulfan was known to cause mucousitis, defined as swelling of the mucous glands.

This swelling would cause sores in my mouth and throat. I would find it difficult, then impossible, to eat and drink for a few days, the doctors said. To lessen the pain, they would provide me with a continuous drip of morphine, coupled with a button I could press to boost the dosage when I felt more acute soreness. I didn't develop mouth sores for a couple of weeks, not until after I received my stem cell transplant.

In the meantime, Jen and I tried to make some alterations to the usual hospital room routine. First, we limited the amount of time anyone could watch CNN (or any other news channel). I recognized war with Iraq was imminent, though it was hard to believe at the time. I knew nothing we would hear or see on television would make the war come any sooner or later. Besides, I had a history of freaking out at simply the idea of war. I didn't need nonstop conflict coverage to add to my already wrecked nerves. Jen and I decided we would get our daily dose of misery from the newspaper.

The transplant ward was located on 10 West, a separate floor from the leukemia ward. My room had south and west-facing views of Manhattan. Each room on 10 West was designed for a single patient, because each patient was extremely vulnerable to infection during transplant. The doctors discouraged patients even from going into the hallway until their counts returned to near normal levels. Rooms were equipped with standard-issue 19-inch TVs. They also each contained a DVD-VCR player and a laptop computer linked to the Internet. Upon request, the hospital provided exercise bikes and sleeper couches for visitors. As long as patients were going to be in the hospital for the long haul, the doctors figured they might as well offer some of the comforts of home. The stem cell transplant unit also gave out a daily parking pass worth $25 for each day a patient was in the hospital.

These small luxuries were not major expenses, considering the cost of a transplant, but were appreciated by those of us who had had extended stays on the "regular" floors before.

Jen and I used the laptop to e-mail our friends about my progress in the transplant unit, since we had to restrict visits due to my compromised immune system. My mom discovered an Internet Bridge league, where a worldwide community met to play cards and chat with each other, as often in Polish as in English. Though she would sit just a few feet from my bed, my mom could get lost for hours in a bridge tournament, rising from her seat only for runs to the bathroom. Sometimes I tried to follow along with her games, but the concentration required was beyond me at that point.

I had my own distraction: March Madness, the annual college basketball playoff that begins with regional conference tournaments and is followed by the 65-team race for the national championship. I often maintain a rooting interest throughout March, because my alma mater, Duke, usually is among the finalists for the championship, making it to the "elite eight" or "final four" most years. In 2003, Duke provided me almost a full month of viewing entertainment before they lost to Kansas in the round of eight.

Before Duke's loss, I passed a few significant milestones in my treatment. My stem cell transplant was performed on March 18. It was an anti-climax if there ever was one. The nurses brought my stem cells into my hospital room in a plastic bag no different from one that would contain generic antibiotics or platelet transfusion. The bag's contents looked like papaya juice, that same yellowish-pink color I remembered seeing during the collection. A nurse hung my stem cells from a metal pole and connected the bag via a tube to one of the ports in my chest. The sole notation indicating that this bag indeed contained my stem cells was written on a white sticker. In black Sharpie ink, it stated, "Madoff. Auto Transplant."

That was it. I'd seen saline bags with IDs that looked more sophisticated.

"My stem cells have been sitting in a freezer for a month, and that's the bookkeeping method the hospital uses to keep things straight?"

"Yep."

"And you're sure those are my cells."

"Yep."

"How much of my 'record haul' of stem cells is in that bag?" I was referring to the 125 million or so stem cells per unit of measure that the phoresis machine had extracted from my blood.

"About 60 million."

"So, half, then."

"More or less."

At which point the nurse began the drip of stem cells that would enter my blood stream and somehow find their way to their home in my bone marrow sites, eventually creating my new immune system. Soon after the stem cells began dripping, I got that "shnoggy" feeling, the colorful term used by nurses to describe the sleepy-time effect produced when a patient receives 50 milligrams of Benadryl, as is often prescribed for transfusions to limit an allergic reaction. In less than an hour, the transplant was complete.

It would be another ten days before the doctors would see evidence of white blood cells in my daily lab reports. This would prove that my stem cells indeed had grafted, and I could be certain that the Sharpie-marked plastic bag with yellowish-pink fluid inside had been mine.

On March 20, two days after my transplant, the U.S. invaded Iraq. I learned this almost at the moment of the first strike, as my father called at about the same time that evening to tell me that the U.S. was dropping bombs. I was not happy to hear this for a few reasons: War is painful, I was worried about reprisals in New York, and my ban on watching CNN in the hospital room hadn't enabled me to pass this moment in peace.

My dad didn't revel in the fact there was a war going on. At the time, he was even more of a pacifist than I was. Still, there was an excitement in his voice from which I recoiled, as I considered my own vulnerability at that moment. I probably couldn't survive even for a few days outside my quarantined existence. Without a functioning bone marrow, I had no ability to prevent infection. Because I could not produce platelets, my body wouldn't heal if I received any kind of cut or wound.

Sometime between the invasion of Iraq and Duke's loss to Kansas, I developed mucousitis, just as the doctors predicted I would. As the soreness in my throat increased, I shunned crunchy things like pretzels and chips. Soon even mushy food such as noodles became hard to swallow. Eventually I couldn't put anything down my throat without feeling pain. The doctors switched my medications to IV so that I no longer had to take them orally. They also started the morphine drip around then. Because it hurt to swallow even my own saliva, I slept with my mouth open so that I could drool onto the pillow. I slept for no more than fifteen or twenty minutes at a time, because I needed to spit what still remained in my mouth into a cup. Drug-addled and sleep-deprived, I had one of those clarifying moments. It was 3 a.m. I developed a theme for a story I would write about my experience battling leukemia.

It was about overcoming fear, I realized. For most of my life I had shied away from conflict, was a "chicken," so to speak—though the battles I had run from up to that point were hardly monumental. Now I faced a real fear: that my life might be cut short by cancer. And I looked that fear in the face. Why? Maybe it was because I had nowhere to run; there was no one or nothing to bail me out. That made me strong. That made me appreciate what life I had. That was reason enough to feel lucky and to battle on.

Writing down these thoughts on a four-inch-by-six-inch pad, I began with an anecdote about my greatest fear as a seven-year-old: that I had left the toaster on overnight...

13

Bad News Comes in Threes

I had been waiting to hear an update about my cousin Andy's biopsy since he'd had a lump removed from his neck a few weeks earlier. The occasional word I received was that things were okay, in spite of the initial pathology suggesting he had cancer. As I became less vulnerable to infections, I invited more guests to come visit. Andy told Jen and me that he would come by. We would get the full story from him then.

The day of his visit, we talked to Adam. We knew he would know what was going on—he was Andy's brother's best friend and had helped Andy contact a handful of experts at NewYork-Presbyterian Hospital and across the country to help diagnose the problem. When we told Adam that we'd heard things were okay, he dodged making a direct reply.

"I think you should talk with Andy."

When Andy arrived, Jen and I avoided asking him about the issue we both wanted to know about, but Andy quickly got to the point.

"I have lymphoma."

Silence, as I tried to comprehend what he had said. Andy and I were never extremely close; he was nearly eight years older than I and I was still the baby of the family when he was leaving for college. Even when I was working for the firm, we were in completely separate divisions on different floors and didn't have much contact. He and his wife, Debbie, were both smart, interesting people. They always seemed a very down-to-earth couple, for a stock trader and an Upper East Side preppie. They lived in the city with their two young daughters, but we rarely saw them outside of the office and family functions. Still, I always thought that had we been closer in age, we would have been friends. He was also obsessed with gadgets and technology, so I enjoyed checking out his latest acquisitions. Debbie went to Duke and loved the Adirondacks from the time she went to camp there as a young girl, so she and I had a few important things in common as well. Now, given our newest commonality, our age difference seemed negligible.

"My dad told us that you were okay."

"No. The initial pathology showed cancer. Everyone agreed on that. The question was, 'What kind?' Your dad probably didn't want to get into it while you were in the hospital."

Andy said the initial pathology of the lump in his neck suggested he had Mantle Cell lymphoma, a very rare and often fatal form of the disease. There weren't more than a few reported cases of people under fifty-years old who had Mantle Cell lymphoma. Because the condition was so rare, his doctors questioned the report. Lymphoma diagnoses are tricky, given that there are so many different kinds. He and Debbie had spent the past few weeks talking with experts around the country. The advice they had received was all over the map: everything from "do nothing, and wait until you get sick," to "get a donor stem cell transplant immediately." None of the experts agreed, probably because no one seemed to have much expertise with Mantle Cell lymphoma.

All this was unbelievable to hear, as Andy showed no signs of even being sick.

"We still don't know for sure if it is Mantle Cell," Andy said.

Jen and I tried to absorb what we were being told. We offered our sympathy, even though we knew from experience how difficult it is to put oneself in another's shoes, especially when the news is bad. Andy and I faced similar circumstances, to a degree. Leukemia and lymphoma are both diseases that affect the immune system. To be cured of either, a patient undergoes an arduous regimen involving chemotherapy and sometimes radiation. Stem cell transplants are often prescribed as a final way to keep the disease from returning.

Yet Andy faced a host of issues that I was lucky enough not to have to consider. I was diagnosed with leukemia the first day I was admitted to the hospital, and I began chemotherapy within twenty-four hours of that. Andy's diagnosis remained uncertain weeks after he had been told he had lymphoma. It still wasn't clear what treatment path Andy should take. He had every option available to him and seemed to have time to figure it out, as he was asymptomatic. In contrast, I had only one path to follow. By chance, I was admitted from the Emergency Room directly to the largest leukemia program in New York, but from what I was told, my treatment was the same standard of care that had been followed for almost thirty years. The only question I had faced was whether to enter a clinical trial. When I did have time to look into other programs before my transplant, we didn't consider them for long because we were comfortable where we were at that point.

Andy had far more than himself and his wife to be concerned about. He was a father and head of the trading desk at our family firm. Both his family and the company would sorely miss him if he chose to undergo the most extreme treatment regimen, a donor stem cell transplant, which would quarantine him for at least half a year.

Andy had time to consider his options. There was no obvious moment when it would become clear he had to do something about his cancer. Some very smart people were telling him to do nothing at all. I saw this last aspect of his situation as perhaps the most difficult to bear. It must have been an enormous strain for him to act as if things were relatively normal. He hadn't told anyone outside his immediate family about his condition. He hadn't even told his daughters yet.

Andy and Debbie were still planning to go on an upcoming vacation to Belize with their kids. He would find out more about whether he had the dreaded Mantle Cell form of lymphoma when he returned. He promised to let us know the verdict when he got back.

The one thing we could all agree on is that we should curse the Madoff bloodline. We were each told repeatedly that neither leukemia nor lymphoma is transmitted genetically. But the facts seemed to contradict this theory: now three relatives had come down with closely related, rare blood cancers within six months. Our pain was probably shared, although surely to a lesser degree, by the actuaries at

Guardian, the health care insurance provider that was responsible for paying the cost of all three treatment protocols.

Andy's news dampened the enthusiasm I had for my own recovery, which was proceeding apace. There was one scary moment, when the doctors said my white blood cell count was taking too long to rise over the 1,000 threshhold, the signal that I was moving along the recovery path. The doctors warned that to treat a lingering fever I would have to start nightly doses of Abelcet, the powerful, rigor-inducing, anti-fungal drug I had taken during my first round of treatment. My body must have heard the fearsome warning, because the next morning's lab test showed a white blood cell count of 1,600, well beyond the required threshold to ward off Abelcet and give my body a chance to fight the fevers on its own.

As my white cell count rose, the sores in my mouth that had made it so hard to eat faded. But as those sores improved, for some reason I developed chafing in the "folds" of my body, like my armpits and between my legs. The doctors said these side effects, though uncomfortable, were not unusual for someone undergoing a transplant. My raw skin would grow back normally, as my renewed immune system adjusted to its environs.

With things generally improving, the doctors began estimating how long it might be before I could be released from the hospital. Perhaps I could leave in early April, about a week away, they speculated. First, though, they wanted to see my platelets and white blood cell counts stabilize at close to normal levels, which appeared to be sometime away.

Then, at a moment when Jen and I expected nothing to go wrong, the nurses noticed something odd, almost unbelievable, during a routine "vitals check." My pulse rate showed that my heart was beating at 250 beats per minute. It may have been going faster, in fact, but 250 represented the upper limit for the electronic heart monitor attached to my finger. The monitor blinked "250, 250" and emitted a shriek, in case anyone missed the readout.

"Maybe the monitor's wrong."

My heart rate had been running above average for six months, but never that high. This didn't feel that out of the ordinary.

Nurse: "I don't think it's wrong. I'm going to get a doctor."

The doctor measured my pulse the old-fashioned way, by putting his fingers against my wrist, but said he couldn't get a read. He did note that my hospital gown was rising and falling rapidly against my chest.

Jen and I watched the team of doctors and nurses move quickly in and out of the room, though not with any outward sense of alarm. A technician rolled in an electrocardiogram machine. He affixed stickers to my chest, arms and legs, and then attached metal clips to the stickers. A computer screen on the machine produced a multi-graph chart of my heart's function.

"It says your heart rate is 263. Do you feel dizzy?"

"Not particularly. Maybe a little short of breath."

"I'm amazed you haven't passed out."

The team decided that I needed a drug called Adenosine. This medicine would return my heart rate to a normal range, after actually stopping it, momentarily. They told me I would feel my heart stop for a few seconds, but I shouldn't be alarmed.

Yeesh. The drug actually gave me a sensation that I'd only imagined while watching science fiction movies. I felt as if my body "de-materialized" and funneled into a cone, as if I were being sucked into a black hole. I moaned in a drawn-out way, or at least I think I did. My vision faded. The feeling lasted no more than ten seconds, and then I felt normal again. The heart monitor agreed, now beeping at a more familiar, slower pace. Strange.

The doctors seemed pleased, and we didn't hear much more about my super-fast heart rate that day. Jen and I thought it was just another episode like the one I'd had after I was first released from the hospital in late December when we had to go to the Emergency Room because my heart kept racing. The next morning, a Saturday, the doctors joked that I just couldn't let my final week pass uneventfully. They did not suggest that anything particularly unusual had happened.

That Monday, though, a doctor from the cardiology team came into the room as Jen and I were eating dinner. The doctor told us that I was going to be transferred out of the stem cell transplant unit to the cardiology unit on the fourth floor so my heart could be monitored constantly.

"Wait a minute. I'm immune-suppressed. I don't think I'm allowed to leave 10 West right now."

She said that the cardiology team had talked to my doctors in the stem cell transplant unit, and they were comfortable releasing me to the care of the cardiology team, given that my blood counts and other measures were improving.

"Well, why didn't anyone from the stem cell unit tell me this?"

"We just made the decision together."

The cardiology staff had gone over the record of what I had experienced on Friday and decided that I would be better off on their floor, where their staff was more prepared to handle situations similar to what I had experienced. She continued, saying that I had an arrhythmia, or abnormal heart rate. Someone from the cardiology team would give me the full details the next day. For the moment, the doctor asked that I not exert myself and suggested that Jen could pack up whatever things I would need in my new room.

"I don't understand. I thought this was no big deal. This has happened a few times before, and nobody seemed particularly concerned then."

I had felt my heart beating unusually fast on a few occasions in recent months. When I reported these symptoms to my doctors, they assumed I was probably fatigued or dehydrated and suggested that I down Gatorade. After following the advice, my heart rate usually settled back to normal in fifteen minutes or so. Occasionally, I would also take an anti-anxiety drug, Ativan, to help me calm down. Once I thought that just chewing a Tums had managed to do the trick. It was only that first time, when I felt the palpitations in December, that I felt I had to go to the Emergency Room.

A member of the transplant unit did come by later to confirm that the team had given the okay for me to switch units. So I left my relative palace of a hospital room on 10 West with my river view, and passed through the exit doors of the transplant unit for the first time in about a month. My new room on the fourth floor was a cramped, badly lit square.

At least I had another private room, an accommodation to my still weak immune system. And it didn't matter much that my total space had shrunk, since the heart monitor I was attached to limited my movement to a small circle around my bed and the bathroom.

Once I settled in, a cardiology nurse wheeled in a bright yellow defibrillator on a movable stand, placing it beside my bed.

"Is that really necessary?"

"Just a precaution."

The atmosphere in the cardiology unit seemed the opposite of that in the transplant ward. Nurses did not expect to see their patients more than a few times, just before and just after surgery. That these relationships were transient was obvious from the get-go. In the morning, Dr. Mittal, an electrocardiologist, came by. As an expert on the electrical currents that regulate the heart, he explained that my recent electrocardiograms showed a pattern called Wolf-Parkinson-White syndrome, or WPW, as everyone in the medical profession referred to it. On an EKG, the syndrome revealed itself as a small blip occurring just before the regular jump one sees in the trend line. That extra blip of mine was called "pre-excitation," and its presence suggested there was an additional electrical pathway in my heart. Dr. Mittal said WPW was a congenital defect, which had probably surfaced as a result of the strain on my body from multiple rounds of chemotherapy and the transplant. When the extra pathway was triggered, it had the potential to literally short-circuit my heart, sending my heart rate into an abnormally fast rhythm. Unless it returned to its natural rhythm, it would eventually tire, causing a heart attack. That was the theory of what was wrong. The only way to test it would be to insert a probe into my heart, identify the pathways and "burn off" the abnormal node that was sparking the extra pathway, in a procedure called catheter ablation.

Performing catheter ablations was the specialty of the electro-cardiologists at NewYork-Presbyterian Hospital. The catch to my surgery was that the doctors would have to pierce the wall that separated the left and right chambers of my heart so that the probe could reach the trigger point of the extra pathway, which was located in the right chamber. Accuracy was important, because my heart would be beating during the surgery. If the doctors made a hole that didn't seal properly, they would have to crack open my rib cage to stanch the bleeding. Minimally invasive surgery would suddenly become massively invasive. This complication happened rarely, Dr. Mittal said, though surgeons had to inform their patients of all possible outcomes.

Without the complication, the abnormal node would be burned off with an electrical charge sent through the catheter and then Adenosine would be administered once again, to stop and restart my heart. The catheter wouldn't be pulled out until a monitor showed that the extra blip was gone.

Surely this was twenty-first century medicine. To me, Dr. Mittal and his ilk were master solderers on a microscopic-level—the successors to the daredevil ironworkers who erected the last century's skyscrapers by melding I-Beams while suspended hundreds of feet above the ground, in nano-sized form.

If only I could continue to marvel at the wonders of science instead of having to dwell on the newly revealed fact that on top of everything else that was wrong with my body, I was also prone to a heart attack. Dr. Mittal's straightforward analysis didn't do anything to ease my concerns. There wasn't much in the way of good cheer in what he had told me with which I could make myself feel better.

Dr. Mittal recommended that I start taking a medication designed to prevent a WPW short circuit in my heart. The problem with the drug that he recommended was that we couldn't be sure whether it worked. If I didn't experience a recurrence of my arrhythmia, it would be as good a sign as any we would have that things were going well. Meantime, Dr. Mittal said he would like to watch me in the hospital for a few days, while I started taking the drug. Only then could I be released, until I wished to return for the catheter procedure, perhaps in a few weeks time. Dr. Mittal, too, recommended that, as a precaution, I not exert myself in the next few weeks.

Dr. Mittal had explained all this as my father and mother were sitting in the room. Just as he was finishing, Jen arrived from our apartment. My mom and dad correctly assumed I wanted to talk with Jen alone about this latest challenge, and left the room. As they walked out, I cried, much as I had when I left the hospital for the first time in December. Jen was overwhelmed, too, but tried to comfort me as we held each other and tried to process what was happening.

Apparently, I was nowhere near the end of my treatment, as it had been laid out to me at the start.

Dr. Roboz came from the leukemia unit upstairs to visit me in the cardiac ward. She tried to put my newly discovered heart condition in as cheerful a context as possible. At least this problem was clear and there was a ready fix, she pointed out. This was true, if cold comfort, I thought.

I had obviously willfully deluded myself that the completion of my stem cell transplant would signal an end to my woes. Only now did I begin to consider the after-effects, small and large. I was still bothered by chafing. A dermatologist came by and prescribed a liquid form of lidocane, which she said I could apply directly to my testicles, which currently resembled ripe strawberries. The soreness between my legs made for a light-hearted moment as I took a shower one morning. As water dripped into the area, my pain pushed my heart rate up to 160, triggering an alarm at the nurse's station. I heard a frantic knock on my bathroom door, but warded them off trying to explain what was going on and that I thought I was probably okay. My cousin Mark subsequently dubbed my mid-section woes "Roger's Great Balls of Fire."

Dr. Roboz also had some news of her own to relay to me. The clinical trial I had agreed to participate in during the first phase of my treatment had an additional, post-transplant phase, in which I could also participate. This additional "maintenance" protocol called for daily injections of Interluken-2, a drug that previously had been shown to be effective fighting melanomas and that some researchers thought had potential in keeping leukemia relapse at bay. The maintenance phase of the trial would last three months. For the first ten days I would get low-dose injections, while during the following three days I would get high-dose treatment. Then I would get one day of rest and the cycle would start again. For the high-dose periods, I might want to stay in the hospital, Dr. Roboz said, in case I experienced side effects that required immediate attention.

That certainly sounded like a roundabout way of saying, "It won't be pretty."

Me: "You're joking."

"No. This is good news. This may help reduce your chances of experiencing a relapse."

"I thought that was why I did the stem cell transplant. So that I wouldn't relapse."

"The transplant helps your odds, but it's not a cure-all."

"But ninety days. That's what, half again as long we planned on when this began?"

"Hey, look at the bright side. Your counts are up. You look great. You'll be going home very soon."

All true, I conceded. But in the back of my mind I was still trying to come to grips with yet another indication that my battle with leukemia was far from over.

Jen and Roger, October 2000

Clockwise from left: Marty, Peter, Grandpa Lee, Roger
and Evan, August 2001

Roger at sunset in the Seychelles, September 2001

Jen and Roger on their honeymoon, September 2001

Roger and Milo, March 2002

Roger before the shave, November 30, 2002

Roger post-induction in Lake Placid, January 2003

Jen and Roger, January 2003

Roger's 30th birthday with Jorge, Noah, Ben and Rich,
April 2003

Roger, Milo, Jen and Evan, May 2003

Rebecca, Shana and Roger, July 2003

Jen and Roger in Lake Placid before his second transplant,
September 2003

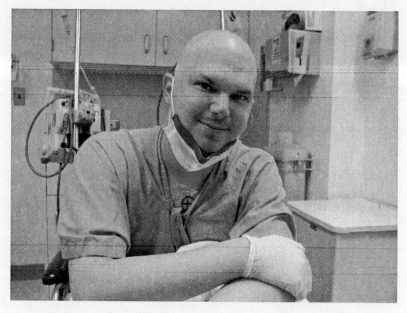

Roger waiting for his first session of total body radiation,
October 2003

Adam visiting in the hospital, October 2003

LEUKEMIA FOR CHICKENS

Part II: Allo

LEUKEMIA FOR CHICKENS

14

End of Military Operations

April 2003

This was to be my moment of triumph. After enduring six months of treatment for leukemia that began just before Thanksgiving, I neared the end of the line in early April. The treatment protocol had required three rounds of chemotherapy, followed by a stem cell transplant to build me a new immune system, which would all add up to my being better equipped to fight off the disease. Each round of chemotherapy had sapped me, draining me of what I came to call my "life force." Each time, my body had managed to rebound from that almost will-less state. With the transplant now mostly behind me, the doctors said I could leave the hospital any day.

Now that I was reaching the end of it, I was able to reflect back on the harsh treatment regimen that the doctors had prescribed for me. Even in my weakest moments, the doctors stressed the importance of sticking to the protocol. At those times my family and I were torn between easing my pain at the moment and trying to keep in mind the bigger picture of ridding me of the disease. Now that I was stronger (my blood counts, the broadest measure of my health, were nearing healthy levels), the doctors felt vindicated and confident for my future. A bone-marrow biopsy showed no detectable sign of leukemia in my body. It was fair to say that the rigorous protocol had at least prevented a catastrophe for the moment.

Though it was purely a coincidence, my doctors' obvious satisfaction with their work mirrored the newfound confidence shown by our leaders in Washington, who were increasingly certain of victory in Iraq. The press had pilloried the White House and the Pentagon in the early weeks of the invasion, begun in March. The U.S. battle plan sought to undermine support for Hussein's regime by attacking any Iraqi who was brave enough to back it. They callously described their plan as "shock and awe," though later it probably could have been better characterized as "horror and death." Regardless, the bombardment stunned the Baath regime and led to the quick demise of Saddam Hussein's rule. We in the U.S., even those of us who had our doubts, breathed a sigh of relief as the battle ended quickly and no weapons of mass destruction were released in Iraq or in the U.S. We didn't know at the time that they didn't exist.

In any event, the defunct Iraqi nation now faced an uncertain period where it was expected to heal its wounds and rebuild itself. I kept seeing all kinds of parallels to my struggle. The political pundits were optimistic. There were few signs of the rebel insurgency that would soon cripple Iraq's redevelopment—just as the rebellious remnants of my leukemia lay momentarily dormant within me. Though the doctors were optimistic for my future, they knew from prior experience that many seeming successes still could result in failure. This knowledge tempered their enthusiasm somewhat, and made their forecasts less grand. The politicians in Washington were not nearly as humble.

In the days before I left the hospital, the doctors had dropped daily hints that I faced a longer recovery process than I probably had anticipated up to that point. At the time of my diagnosis in November, the doctors had told me only about the six-month attack plan. Now as that plan neared its end, they filled me with details about the next phase. It seems naïve now, but I had assumed that recovery would not be a full-time occupation, but rather, something I could deal with part-time, as I returned to my "normal" life. By the summer, I expected I would be able to do most of the things that I had done before I was diagnosed. I did allow that maybe it would take a little longer to get there, depending on how I dealt with some of the post-treatment medical issues that I faced, like my arrhythmia and that maintenance protocol into which I had been randomized.

I was glad to learn about these ongoing issues only as I was finishing up the protocol. Prior to that, I hadn't thought much about life after treatment, except to assume my routine would be similar to what it was before. As if fighting leukemia was akin to taking an exit on the highway, then, after that brief detour, once again heading towards my destination. I would be able then to pursue openly the new career I wanted. But after six months of treatment, normalcy seemed like a refuge and my loftier dreams seemed beyond reach. Could I be blamed for craving drudgery?

Jen pushed me not to give up. Hadn't I learned from all this that time is the ultimate luxury?

"Yes," I replied, "but give me a minute to rally."

Fortunately, I did have some time before I needed to choose my route forward. To begin with, day-to-day life outside the hospital demonstrated that my plan for returning to normal in a few months' time had been overly optimistic. The doctors had warned me in the hospital that I would feel exhausted when I got home, because my body was expending enormous energy rebuilding itself. They also said I wouldn't realize how confined I'd been in my isolation room in the transplant unit until I left it. Moving even a short distance out into the real world would feel like a major expedition. They weren't exaggerating. For weeks, I would sleep ten to twelve hours a night, plus naps.

Even if I had wanted to exert myself more, I had my heart condition to think about. Once the cardiologists discovered my arrhythmia, they put me on a drug called Flecainide. While the drug suppressed my heart's propensity to kick into an unnaturally fast rhythm, the doctors said they could only know the drug was working if my heart rate remained stable. In other words, I shouldn't do any activities that might agitate me until I had surgery to fix the problem permanently. It was up to me to tell the doctors when I felt well enough to undergo the catheterization procedure, sealing off the stray electrical node in my heart that was the culprit. That was still a few weeks away.

In the meantime, I would be reminded of my fragile state by my chest port, which Dr. Roboz decided to leave in after I left the hospital. She didn't like to pull out the tube too soon, because patients often needed transfusions to boost their blood cell counts and platelets until the stem cell transplant took complete root in the marrow. Though my counts were strong, I understood Dr. Roboz's reasons, even if I knew they were part superstition. I didn't fight to have my port removed sooner.

Even more than being a physical reminder, my chest tubes required a significant amount of care. Any time I showered, I had to cover the ports with saran wrap and adhesive tape. The porthole had its own dressing, a see-through bandage, that was changed three times a week by a nurse at the clinic, or by Jen.

When Jen changed the dressing, it would usually be just before we went to bed. I would lie back on my pillow while Jen sat cross-legged on the bed next to me and set up the materials needed to change the dressing. The task was highly ritualized. Donning rubber gloves, Jen would remove a paper towel from the dressing kit and place it under my tubes. Next, she would peel away the old sheer bandage covering the hole, discarding it with her first pair of rubber gloves. A new set of sterile rubber gloves was provided in the kit for the next step: cleaning around the port. She tore open packets of iodine and betadine that were about the size and shape of ketchup sleeves at McDonalds. Each packet contained applicator swabs, which she used to spread out the iodine, then the betadine, slowly drawing concentric circles of increasing size around my chest port. Lastly, she placed a new clear bandage over the site. Jen leaned close over my chest as she cleaned and sealed my port. Usually Milo would watch as well, standing very still beside the bed, his head at the height of our mattress as he followed every move. I looked forward to these quiet, intimate moments that we shared as a family.

Jen and I didn't get much more intimate than that in the weeks after I left the hospital. My pride at having beaten back leukemia hadn't translated into any "manly" urges for a number of reasons. First, there was the matter of my heart condition. Getting aroused was potentially perilous.

I was constrained by psychological issues as well. Since being diagnosed, I had given up much of the control for my life to others. The onus of survival was on me, but many others' hands were outstretched to help me in large and small ways. While in the hospital, I almost had to make excuses to get out of bed. Even going to the bathroom stall was an option, not a necessity, because there were empty Thermos-like "urinals" hanging from the side of my bed into which I could urinate. When I chose to walk to the bathroom, I still used these plastic tubes, because the doctors liked to measure how much fluid flowed out of my body. So standing at a toilet to urinate was pointless, other than for the minimal exercise it provided.

My food was brought to my bedside. I sent family and friends to buy reading material or rent DVDs. It made sense to leave heavy lifting to others, as I was physically weak, but my friends' and family's desire to help in every way left me few things for which to be responsible. Aside from the brief moments in the hospital before I went to sleep, I hadn't been left alone at all. I was a ward of the medical establishment and my family unit; at least one member from either group was posted at my bedside most hours of the day.

It is said that one needs to love oneself before he or she can love another. I'll add to that: people need to have a sense of who they are and what their role in life is, as well.

Add to my lost sense of self my weight loss, muscle loss, and hair loss. Looking in the mirror, I wasn't who I had been a few months before and I wasn't particularly attractive. Although I had come to like my head with a short-shave look after my hair had started growing back from baldness. How had I lived with a bouffant all those years?

From a sexual perspective, I worried that leukemia might have emasculated me entirely. After each round of my chemotherapy treatment, I had gone to the sperm bank to give a "sample" to the lab. In each case, the lab had found no motile sperm. This wasn't unusual, the doctors said. It took time for the testes to heal, like everything else. I put faith in their patience, but I knew from the beginning that it was possible that I might now be sterile.

Before my leukemia, Jen and I hadn't much discussed trying to have a child. We both knew we would want one soon. Following my treatment, we realized we were nowhere near ready to have a baby.

The forced delay we faced contrasted starkly with what many of our friends were experiencing. Three couples with whom we were close were just weeks away from welcoming babies to the world. As much as our friends' good fortune was a reminder of our own bad luck, their excitement was also a pleasant distraction. When Lauren and Tom had a baby at NewYork-Presbyterian Hospital a week or so after I was released from the same hospital's transplant unit, I felt good returning to visit someone else there, especially on a happy occasion. The maternity ward was one floor of the hospital I had not yet seen, though it looked the same as the others. A few weeks after Lauren gave birth, Noah and Nancy's son Isaac was born. They asked Jen and me to be Isaac's godparents. Noah and Nancy said they saw strength in my relationship with Jen and in my resolve. They also knew what we were up against in having children of our own and said simply they wanted to share him with us. We felt good about that.

Getting leukemia is distressing and confounding at any age, though there may be worse times in a life to be afflicted than at 29, my age at the time. It would have been more difficult for me to deal with leukemia if I were younger, I believe. Especially if I were the same age as Mike, the leukemia patient I met on the day I was first admitted to the hospital. He was twenty years old when diagnosed with the childhood form of leukemia. (Technically, I had the adult form). Mike's treatment regimen was less intense per admission, though his protocol lasted longer—a total of two years. In between stays at the hospital, Mike tried to live his life as his friends did: working in a bar, smoking, hanging out, and on one occasion wrapping his Audi around a tree. I'm sure he would have preferred to feel as indestructible as many people do at that age, rather than have the very adult knowledge of his own vulnerability.

Mike had a tough time fighting the disease, getting ill sometimes between treatments. His upbeat attitude was laced with cynicism. Once, when he wasn't trying to maintain his cool exterior, he left a ceramic angel figurine in my hospital room for me to keep at my bedside. Mike relapsed six months after he completed his two-year treatment protocol. The doctors weren't able to keep his leukemia from spreading before they could perform a stem cell transplant that might put him back in remission. Mike didn't make it.

There are a million reasons why people don't survive. I don't pretend to know any of them. In my experience, which is all I can offer, a person needs to let leukemia rule him or her for a little while at least. By giving up control, you maintain some strength to fight the disease and, eventually, at a later date, you can try to regain control of your life. I knew after finishing the "attack" stage of my treatment that I'd lost a lot of myself in the process. I would have liked to return immediately to being my prior self, but that would have been like trying to become a totally different person.

My recovery included more than just being restored to good health. I needed to reassert control over parts of my life—little things, like cleaning up after myself, and bigger things, like restoring the fullness of my relationships. Likewise, my family and friends—especially Jen, who had assumed many of my responsibilities—now needed to loose the reins and trust that I could fend for myself. Not immediately, though. My weakened state precluded that. But this transition was a necessary element of my recovery. Otherwise the people who had been so helpful to date risked becoming obstacles to my future progress. We were all weary at this point from focusing laser-like for six months on my illness. The acute threat to my health was past. But now we lacked a strong impetus to move forward quickly.

This was the grinding nature of recovery—building a new self out of the old one and the one that had been through leukemia. Once again I turned to political metaphor as a way to understand my situation. I imagined myself as a microcosm of the Iraqi people, liberated after having surrendered to dictatorship decades earlier. For us, the most difficult task lay ahead: Becoming a self-governing nation again.

LEUKEMIA FOR CHICKENS

15

Take Charge, Remove Charge

While I recovered at home following my stem cell transplant, my cousin Andy prepared to be treated for lymphoma. When he was diagnosed in March 2003, doctors had removed a lump from the crook of his neck and the pathology of the lump had shown cancerous cells. For weeks, doctors debated what type of lymphoma had been found, until finally agreeing on Mantle Cell lymphoma. Almost everyone diagnosed with Mantle Cell lymphoma is over 50. To be diagnosed at the age of 37, Andy's age at the time, was practically unheard of.

Because there is no standard treatment for Mantle Cell lymphoma, since it is an extremely rare variant of the disease for which there is no known cure, the options run the gamut. Doctors typically remove any known tumors from the patient. Then the patient undergoes radiation and/or chemotherapy to eliminate all remnants of the disease. The treatment is not intended to cure the patient, only to delay the onset of a relapse, perhaps for as long as five years. Because Mantle Cell lymphoma typically attacks older people, patients are usually ineligible to receive a donor stem cell transplant, which might cure them of the disease but would be extremely difficult to endure without the strength of youth. At 38, Andy was young enough to have as good a chance of tolerating a stem cell transplant as anyone, but he displayed no symptoms of lymphoma besides the lump the doctors had removed. Because allogeneic stem cell transplants are fatal 20 percent of the time, some doctors still considered doing one too risky under the circumstances. Other doctors had recommended that Andy simply wait and do nothing until symptoms developed.

Andy finally chose a middle-of-the-road option: a moderate dose of radiation and chemotherapy. The doctors expected Andy to tolerate the treatment well enough so that he could remain an outpatient. Andy planned to continue working at our family firm, albeit with a lighter schedule, while receiving treatment. For medical supervision, Andy chose a lymphoma specialist from Memorial-Sloan Kettering Cancer Center, located across the street from NewYork-Presbyterian Hospital. This middle-ground approach seemed reasonable to all of the lay people Andy discussed it with. If Andy could put off intensive treatment for lymphoma for even a few years, there was a good chance he could benefit from medical advances that would occur in that time. Stem cell transplants have only been conducted regularly for the past fifteen years. The science is evolving quickly enough that each year they become safer and more tolerable.

Before deciding on his treatment, Andy devoured medical reports on stem cell research and talked to specialists in the field from around the country. In his case, doctors' advice varied widely. The onus was on him to choose a path and then trust a single practitioner's approach to his treatment. That role suited Andy better than it suited me. For all the classes I took as an undergraduate on decision analysis, I thought the whole concept of analyzing probabilities and percentages was somewhat bogus. Maybe I just didn't want to think so hard, but I found it easier to go with my gut. Andy, on the other hand, acted as if he could truly improve his chances for survival not only by learning more but also by actively supporting scientific research related to his disease.

Towards that end, in the spring of 2003, the Madoff family put the final touches on a foundation that would fund leukemia and lymphoma research and treatment, something they had begun thinking about a few months earlier. Using resources from the family's trading and investment businesses, the fund ballooned in size to well over eight figures. To me, the sum was enormous. Not being closely involved in the trading operations, I hadn't realized the extent of the wealth that existed there. The sum further showed a boldness and scope on the part of other members of my family that I lacked. My dream to create a bottled water company seemed, by comparison, like a mere drop in the bucket, so to speak.

Among the projects the foundation would fund was an endowed chair at NewYork-Presbyterian Hospital for "translational research," that is converting studies conducted in the lab more quickly into clinical trials for patients. NewYork-Presbyterian Hospital awarded the chair position to Dr. Roboz. She was the most qualified candidate, because the head of the leukemia unit, Dr. Eric Feldman, was already in a senior position. The foundation also gave money to the Fred Hutchinson Cancer Research Center in Seattle, the largest stem cell program in the U.S., to study ways of making stem cell transplants more tolerable to patients. The Leukemia & Lymphoma Society received funds that it could use to support its own research grant programs, and a group called Gift of Life was given money to expand its efforts to identify matching donors for Jewish patients in need of stem cell transplants. (About one-third of potential stem cell transplant recipients lack a qualified matching donor.)

In less than a year, the Madoff family became the largest private benefactor for leukemia and lymphoma research in the U.S., and probably the world. We didn't make public pronouncements about our charity. Different members of the family had different reasons for keeping quiet, I'm sure. For me, the fact that three family members were suffering acutely from blood cancers seemed reason enough not to crow about research funding. We all felt good that we could contribute to the broader effort, and we knew that whatever researchers discovered had the potential to help us, too. I admired Andy's ability to look ahead and see the possibility of more treatment options for him and others. My concern was to get better now. In my current condition, I couldn't wait for medical advances.

With all this going on, there were still very few people, other than close members of the family and the doctors with whom we consulted, who knew that Andy had contracted cancer. That changed when Andy sent an email to his friends and co-workers describing the nature of his disease and the treatment he would undergo. He didn't say specifically that the doctors had found Mantle Cell lymphoma. His straightforward prose, sensible and tough-minded, asked that people not treat him differently and that they not ask him how things were going, cancer-wise. He would give them an update when there was something to report. He added that he would be taking more vacation time in coming months, including a trip to Alaska to fish for salmon. The letter ended positively, promising he would fight hard, and encouraging everyone to enjoy their time now, because life was short. The clarity with which he described his strategy was a stark contrast to the mayhem I experienced in the hospital the day after I was diagnosed. Andy successfully completed his treatment six weeks later. He suffered no complications, but came out of the experience with a shaved head, a newfound interest in yoga, and an outward soulfulness I hadn't seen before.

Meantime, I prepped for my catheterization procedure, which was intended to fix my WPW. It had been about three weeks since I had left the hospital. I was tired, but my condition was stable. My transplant doctors wanted me to complete the catheterization before I began my maintenance treatment, the experimental three-month program of daily shots intended to keep my leukemia from reemerging. Better to undergo the heart procedure while I was in my strongest state, without potential complications from the maintenance protocol, they reasoned.

I scheduled surgery with the electro-cardiologists for a Friday morning in April. At first the cardiologists told me it wouldn't be a problem scheduling an appointment, but it turned out an open slot wasn't so easy to find. Eventually one was found for a Friday, not my favorite day to enter the hospital, with my mistrust of weekend staff. As is routine for surgeries, I was told to report to the hospital admitting nurse at 6:30 a.m. Surgery would probably begin about 9 a.m. Dr. Mittal would perform the surgery as his first appointment for the day.

The doctors were expected to take about two hours to perform the procedure, officially known as a catheter ablation. They planned to insert two catheters into veins, one on each side of my groin. One catheter contained a small camera attached to a fiber-optic cord. The catheter with the camera would examine the electric pathways embedded in the muscles of my heart and would be used to guide the second catheter, which was capable of sending out an electrical charge.

Just before the procedure, a nurse came by with an industrial-grade Bic razor, planning to trim the hair near my groin.

Me: "No need for that."

Nurse: "Why not?"

"One of the few benefits of chemotherapy, I guess. No hair."

"Ahhh. Okay."

I received Versed, the "twilight" drug. As usual, this blocked much of my recall beyond the sudden relaxation I felt after receiving the drug. During the procedure, I remember feeling a lot of pressure in my chest at one point. Later, at another point, I remember feeling the characteristic groaning sensation that comes from Adenosine. The last thing I remember was the doctors pressing intently on my groin to stanch the blood flow after the catheters were removed at the end of the procedure.

The doctors took off the breathing mask and I rose into consciousness.

Me: "That's it?"

Dr. Mittal: "Yep."

"How long was that?"

"About an hour and forty-five minutes"

"You're sure you fixed everything?"

"Yes. We found exactly what we expected."

"And I don't have to worry about this any more?"

"No."

"That's really it?"

"Yes."

After a few hours in the post-op room, I moved to a shared room on the cardiac unit floor. My neighbor, according to the sign on the door, was a Mr. Lattanzi. He was older, and spoke Italian or English, depending on the person to whom he was speaking. Generally, the older a person, the more likely it was that Mr. Lattanzi spoke to him or her in Italian. We kept overhearing references to a restaurant, and wondered if he was the owner of a restaurant with his name where my family used to eat. Finally, my dad walked over to his side of the room (our beds were separated by a sheet), and asked him the name of his restaurant. Turned out he was not the owner of the restaurant of which we were thinking, but of Paper Moon, a modern Italian bistro across the street from the Four Seasons Hotel. The original Paper Moon is located in Milan, and I ate there frequently during my year in

Italy. After visiting hours ended and our guests had departed for the night, I spoke through the curtain to Mr. Lattanzi. I debated speaking in Italian, but decided I'd be more comfortable telling a story in English.

"I had an Italian friend who used to go to Paper Moon in Milan for dinner by himself. He would pay the maitre d' 50,000 lire ($30) to be seated next to any woman who was eating alone."

(There were always lots of American women on business in Milan, usually working as buyers for the department stores.)

"My friend would strike up a conversation with her and then invite her back to the hotel bar at the Four Seasons, where they usually were staying. I never asked him for details about what happened afterwards."

Mr. Lattanzi gave a gruff laugh. Though I couldn't see him on the other side of the curtain, I imagined him making a typically inscrutable Italian gesture indicating his lack of surprise at the behavior of Italian men.

He left the following morning, inviting Jen and me to come and eat at his restaurant. I stayed in the hospital for another forty-eight hours for observation. The doctors wanted to make sure I suffered no complications from the surgery and that the wounds in my groin healed properly. The wounds were covered by sheer, plastic bandages similar to the dressing I had over my chest port. I was happy to be hairless again, with no need to worry about how painful the bandages might be to remove.

The doctors told me not to exert myself for another two weeks after I returned home, because they didn't want me to injure my groin, which would remain sensitive for a little while longer. That was okay; two weeks was nothing. It felt good to know that some of my medical issues could be addressed, and then I no longer had to worry about them. And in this case, I really didn't.

16

Fix it again, Tony

You call this maintenance? Warding off leukemia is more than just an oil change every three thousand miles and the occasional tire-pressure check. Let's get this straight. To boost my chances of preventing a relapse I will maintain the following two-week schedule, repeated six times, for a total of three months: Spend three days in the hospital on a high dose of Interleukin-2, followed by a day of rest, and then spend the next ten days out of the hospital while receiving a lower dose of the medication. Other than being in the hospital three out of every fourteen days, it sounds reasonable, no?

Let's dig a little deeper: On those days when I am in the hospital, say Monday through Wednesday, to receive a high-dose injection of IL-2, its common name, I will be watched closely by the nurses. They will check my blood pressure and temperature every half hour. This is because my body does not tolerate the drug well. After I receive the shot, usually late in the morning, my blood pressure jumps, I get sweats, and, more often than not, I throw up whatever meal I ate following the injection. No matter how long I delay eating my next meal, my body seems to want to eject what I swallow. Nor does my body get used to the injection on subsequent days in the hospital or on subsequent visits. This makes the anticipation of returning to the hospital for treatments almost as hard to endure as being in the hospital.

On the fourth day of a typical two-week cycle, a Thursday generally, when I get a respite from injections, I return home and go to sleep, exhausted from my previous days of sweating and vomiting. On days five through fourteen, I receive low dose injections of IL-2. Jen gives me this injection before bedtime. Some days it is part of the ritual of cleaning my chest port. Some days it is her sole task. To prep for the injection, Jen ices an area of my leg or hip before she inserts the inch-long needle. Because the injection stings, Jen varies the speed at which she courses the fluid: sometimes it trickles in slowly; other times, she pushes it in a quick burst. Jen must pick a new site for each injection. This is easier than it might seem, because previous injections leave almond-sized, pink-hued marks that the doctors call "nodules" because of the raised, hard surface they form on my skin. The site wounds take a week or two to heal. A few weeks into the protocol, I can identify dozens of prior injection sites on my body. After ten days of this low-dose therapy, I return to the hospital for high-dose injections.

I am taking IL-2, a reproduction of a chemical compound found naturally in the body, to stimulate my body's production of T-cells, specialized white blood cells that fight cancer. Doctors have found that raising IL-2 levels in the body helps patients fight skin melanomas and other cancers. The maintenance protocol in which I am enrolled is a clinical trial to test the theory that IL-2 treatment is effective also in fighting leukemia.

As far as suggested maintenance goes, staving off leukemia with IL-2 is something like keeping an old Fiat in working order. Fiat didn't earn the nickname "Fix It Again, Tony" for nothing. The name "Fiat" actually stands for Fabbrica Italiana Automobili Torino. (That's just the former Italian transportation reporter for Bloomberg in me talking). As it happens, Tony was the name of the person at NewYork-Presbyterian Hospital who oversaw clinical trials for the leukemia unit. Whenever I had an issue with my IL-2 treatment, whether about scheduling a private room for my high-dose regimens or talking about the size of my injection-site nodules, I would call Tony.

The doctors made lots of changes to my maintenance regimen, unlike my leukemia treatment protocol, which was never amended. For example, they tried to reduce the size of the nodules on my hips and legs by lowering the dose of IL-2 that I received, and they cut short my third visit to the hospital for high-dosage treatment, because the side effects (a combination of high blood pressure and high fever) were deemed too severe. The doctors also gave me extended breaks between high-dose and low-dose regimens.

The discomfort that was caused by the maintenance protocol might have been more tolerable had I had some confidence that taking IL-2 would be beneficial. But as Dr. Feldman, the head of the leukemia unit, told me when I was being released early during my third high-dose session:

"You know, the initial results from previous IL-2 trials have not shown it to be effective fighting leukemia."

"Do you think it works?"

"I don't know. Of all the trials we're conducting, this has been the most disappointing."

"But they've been studying this for a while, haven't they? They wouldn't be conducting this test it if they weren't at least somewhat optimistic it would work this time, would they?"

"They say they think this regimen will be effective. But they said that about other regimens that failed as well. This time could be different, but you have to weigh that against how you feel now. You could be feeling better."

Add to Dr. Feldman's lack of enthusiasm the fact that I was taking continually lower doses than were recommended by the protocol. Lower dosages made it easier to tolerate, but also no doubt made the treatment less effective.

I had a choice. I could quit the trial, deeming it not worth my time and effort. Under the circumstances, it was a reasonable choice, though few of my friends and family thought it was the right one.

As Noah and Nancy put it to me at dinner one night: "You're in remission, but you're still fighting cancer. If you give up, and you relapse, you'll regret not having done everything that you could have."

There was an argument contrary to this. If I completed the protocol and still relapsed, then having stuck to the maintenance regimen would have needlessly kept me from enjoying the healthy time that I had available. This argument was harder to defend, as it was pessimistic at its heart, assuming I would relapse regardless of my attempts to fight leukemia. In reality, that wasn't my assumption. I was young, strong, and had withstood the full treatment protocol. Even if the odds of relapsing were fifty-fifty, wasn't it likely that most of those who did relapse were weaker and older than average? I had also heard some anecdotes that made me optimistic for my health. A father who lost a daughter to leukemia told me that his daughter had not had difficulty tolerating chemotherapy. Later he surmised from her "easy" experience that the leukemia had been stronger than the chemo. People who had a rougher experience during treatment probably were able to fight harder, he said; my difficulty during treatment boded well for my ultimate survival.

I chose to stick it out with the maintenance protocol and continue taking IL-2, though I found a way to make it easier on myself. After talking with my therapist, Dr. Curcio, my internist, Adam, and finally Dr. Roboz, we decided together that I should begin taking Lexapro, an anti-depressant. For all the attention I received from doctors while in the hospital, very few times did any of them ask, "How are you feeling, mentally?" This was partly because I usually put on a cheery face for them, but the issue of patients' mental health runs deeper. The few times I told the doctors I was miserable, they were not surprised. After all, I was going through something miserable. I doubt the doctors thought there was much they could do to make things better. Though psychologists work at the hospital, they do not work closely with oncologists or their patients. Therapists don't make regular rounds; doctors only call them in for an emergency—based on my experience, at least. It doesn't make much sense.

When I told Dr. Roboz that I was thinking about taking Lexapro, she encouraged me to do so. She also said that other patients of hers were taking the drug. Beyond that, she did not offer much insight.

The Lexapro worked as advertised. It gave me an energy boost that helped me to better endure the maintenance protocol. Perhaps the drug helped me to brush aside, at least temporarily, the fact that my weekly blood tests were faltering. Specifically, the tests showed continued drops in my number of platelets, the clotting agent in my blood. Where once they had measured more than 200,000, near normal, they had since fallen to 100,000. Dr. Roboz said that IL-2 sometimes reduced platelet levels and that I should not stress about weekly fluctuations, but the declines were hard for me to ignore.

When I was on the low-dose part of my schedule, I tried to return to normal as much as possible. We visited some of our friends and their newborns and planned a last-minute trip to Lake Placid. A few times I weighed in on some tasks at the office. One of my duties had been keeping the website up-to-date. My boss asked me to look over the site and update any information that seemed stale. Also, I proofed a press release that my colleagues had prepared. I focused on these tasks for a couple of hours before I became tired and petered out. Though just being able to do some of my old work felt good, I was conflicted about doing these tasks, because I was unsure if my job of getting better should include doing office work. Jen didn't think so.

I avoided making an appearance at the office, which was housed in the same building as the family's trading firm. I told my father I didn't want to see so many people whom I had known since childhood when I was so skinny and weak. I thought that I would be put on parade and have to be extra chatty to avoid discussing the "elephant in the room," my illness. Nor was I ready to answer repeated questions about how I was doing with an exaggerated "Grrrreat!"

For my thirtieth birthday, I bought myself an Apple laptop, with the intention of starting to write that book I dreamed up in my epiphany during my stem cell transplant. I didn't get very far with the writing, but I felt some sense of subversive independence in just owning an Apple, the anti-corporate PC. I marked that watershed birthday, an event many of my peers celebrated loudly, in a subdued fashion with just a few of my close friends at our apartment for dinner.

I completed the fourth and fifth high-dose sessions of the maintenance regimen, leaving one final session, scheduled for Monday, July 21. Before being admitted to the hospital, Jen and I waited in the outpatient clinic for the results of my weekly blood test. The wait was long, but not unusually so. We asked Monique, the office manager, if we should go straight to 10 Central, the new leukemia unit, or if we should wait in the clinic. She called Dr. Roboz's office. We were instructed to wait.

Soon after, we went back to Dr. Roboz's office. Sometimes she came in smiling and radiant, though not always. Her mood often depended on how far behind she was in her patient schedule. Dr. Roboz was always behind schedule, in equal measure because she was always overbooked and because she couldn't cut herself short when talking to her patients. That day Dr. Roboz offered no small talk when she entered the room.

"I'm going to tell this to you straight. We saw some bad cells in your peripheral blood that we didn't like."

Dr. Roboz was referring to "blasts," or immature blood cells. She paused to let either Jen or me respond, but we said nothing.

"The technicians saw some in the blood test you gave Thursday, and the computer scan of your blood today raised red flags as well."

There are few explanations for blasts in the blood stream other than a relapse of leukemia.

Me: "Are we talking about a relapse?"

"We won't know for sure unless we conduct a bone marrow." Dr. Roboz left the word "biopsy" unspoken. "I want to do that now."

Jen and I looked at each other but found little to say in front of Dr. Roboz. Jen grabbed my hand. I turned back to Dr. Roboz.

"What are the chances that this isn't a relapse?"

"Not good."

17

Another 48 Hours,
Or Chaos Has Its Merits

As soon as Dr. Roboz told me that she wanted to perform a bone marrow biopsy, my mind switched gears. I momentarily put aside the possibility that my leukemia may have returned. That grim news could only be confirmed after Dr. Roboz analyzed the biopsy results, something that would take a couple of hours at least. It was premature to dwell on the ramifications of a relapse. There were minute details to attend to, such as canceling a vacation to Italy planned for August, and enormous issues to consider, like undergoing a donor stem cell transplant, the provider of which would be my sister, since Shana already had been identified as a "perfect" match.

Rather, for the moment, I focused on minimizing the pain inherent in a bone marrow biopsy. Jen and I had tried a number of ways to make the brief, though agonizing, procedure more tolerable each of the half dozen times I had gone through it. Taking anti-anxiety drugs and creating distractions were the most effective. Before the procedure, I asked Dr. Roboz to order two milligrams of Ativan from the hospital pharmacy. Ativan takes the edge off and lessens the physical pain by keeping the mind from concentrating too much on any single topic.

As Dr. Roboz left to fill my prescription, Jen and I had our first moments alone since Dr. Roboz had dropped the bombshell that I had probably relapsed, just three months after I had completed a supposedly curative stem cell transplant. We found little to say, other than "I can't believe we might have to go through all this again." Embracing each other, we still held back our emotions on the slim hope that the biopsy would contradict the blood test results from earlier in the day.

Dr. Roboz returned with the Ativan and a foam cup filled with water. It would take about twenty minutes for me to feel the drug's calming effect. She left again to prepare for the biopsy. I don't know if she would have given Jen some Ativan as well, but Jen didn't ask. How my wife managed to handle the stress of all this while remaining mostly drug-free—not only on this occasion, but many others as well—remains a mystery to me.

Dr. Roboz returned once again with a nurse. The nurse wheeled in a cart that held a box covered in blue tissue paper, like a gift that had been wrapped at home. Inside the box were the tools needed to perform the biopsy. I didn't watch Dr. Roboz unwrap the "present." Instead, I flipped to my stomach and tuned into my iPod, listening to songs selected randomly. Dr. Roboz numbed the area around my hip with an injection of lidocane, which stung momentarily before the pain subsided. My iPod jumped from rhythm and blues (Erykah Badu's "Next Lifetime") to classic rock (Led Zeppelin's "Dazed and Confused").

Dr. Roboz then inserted the long needle into my hip to extract the telltale marrow. With each sample Dr. Roboz drew through the needle, Led Zeppelin's guitars whined, and I wailed a long, flat note. It was all strangely concordant.

Dr. Roboz: "Whatcha listening to there?"

Me: "Dazed and Confused."

"Um, that works, I guess. I prefer opera."

Dr. Roboz chiseled off a few bone fragments from my hip, signaling the end of the procedure. I had a brief recovery period, lying on my backside, which was sore, but nothing worse than I'd experienced before. Then a nurse told Jen and me that we were free to go. Dr. Roboz would look at the samples under the microscope and call us at home later that afternoon.

Jen and I searched for a way to kill time and distract ourselves. Going to a stupid, funny movie seemed like the best option. We looked through my Palm organizer, which had a downloaded list of movie times, and settled on a 3 o'clock showing of *Johnny English* at Union Square. The James Bond spoof starred Rowan Atkinson, who had made a name for himself as "Mr. Bean," and definitely represented the silliest entertainment option on offer. It held my attention just well enough to keep me from constantly thinking about the prospect of a relapse.

We returned to our apartment and listened to the messages on the answering machine. There was a message from Dr. Roboz, who said only that we should call her back at her office. We didn't read much into the fact that Dr. Roboz had left no details in her message. It wouldn't have been appropriate (or legal) to leave medical information, whether good or bad, in a phone message. But when I called her back, she told me what we suspected and feared: The biopsy confirmed the blood test results from earlier in the day. Indeed, there were leukemic cells in my marrow. I had relapsed. As Dr. Roboz gave me the news, I nodded to Jen, who was sitting next to me on the bed. Jen leaned her head into my shoulder while I quickly wrapped up the call.

Dr. Roboz: "I'm so sorry about this, but I want you to know that we're still thinking in terms of curing you. This is a terrible setback, but we are not out of options. We want to start you again on chemotherapy tomorrow in preparation for you to receive an 'allo' transplant." (Again, "allo transplant" was doctor-speak for an allogeneic stem cell transplant).

Me: "Isn't this fast to have a relapse? I thought I read somewhere that the average time spent in remission was something like seventeen months."

"Sometimes an autologous transplant does last longer. Sometimes not so long."

"So when should we come to the hospital?"

"I'll have admitting set up a room for you. You should be here by noon. Tell your family they can meet you in your hospital room. Eric [Feldman] and I will debrief everyone when they arrive."

"Okay. Thanks. Let me go talk to Jen now."

"Not a problem. See you tomorrow."

Jen and I held each other and cried for the second time that day. We could no longer avoid thinking about the agony that lay ahead. I didn't need to know details about future rounds of chemotherapy and an eventual donor stem cell transplant to know what we were up against. Never mind that my relapse now made me question everything that I had done up to this point. How did it go wrong?

From the outset, I trusted that my doctors would make me better, even though I had been warned that it could all be for naught. If Jen and I hadn't had so many little details to take care of in the eighteen hours before I checked into the hospital, I don't know how I would have dealt with the doubts and insecurity. Which is to say, having a hectic schedule of tasks to complete helped me to put aside those larger issues for the moment.

First on our list of things to do was call our parents and my sister, Shana, to tell them what had happened that day. Jen called my dad's cell phone and pulled him out of a movie they were seeing with my Aunt Ruth and Uncle Bernie. The news hit like a brick, but the conversations were kept short, punctuated by deep sighs and resolutions to fight on. All of us were too shocked to come up with anything poignant or comforting to say.

I broke down again as I spoke to my sister: "I'm really going to need you this time. I'm sorry. I have to go. Love you. Bye."

Our parents agreed to come by our apartment later that evening, after Jen and I went to dinner. Shana stayed home with her daughter, Rebecca. The last person we called before going to dinner was Adam. He said he would meet us at the hospital the next day to listen to Dr. Roboz and Dr. Feldman.

For dinner, Jen and I decided to go Da Andrea, one of the local restaurants where we'd come to know the waiters, as well as the restaurant's chef and owner. Our neighborhood, the West Village, still had a small-town feel. If you cared to, you could befriend the local shop owners—all in the midst of the bustling city. From our apartment on Greenwich Street we walked slowly to the restaurant, taking in a warm breeze coming off the Hudson River. As we straggled along, a taxi driver veered around us and bellowed:

"Move it. You look like you have AIDS."

New York City, apparently, was still living up to its reputation for brusqueness. Long after the driver had moved on, I made my retort.

"Not AIDS, leukemia," I murmured to myself. "You were close."

The Da Andrea staff were sympathetic when I told them that the meal they were cooking would be the last freshly prepared dinner I'd eat for a while. Their basic but delicious homemade pasta was what we needed, although Jen had a hard time getting much down. Our waiter brought us a an additional, special dessert of homemade biscotti and zabaglione cream:

"Fatta dalla nonna, che abita sopra," he said. "Made by Grandma, who lives upstairs."

We met our parents back at our apartment. Jen's parents had brought Milo with them. He had been taken to his country home the day before, since I was scheduled to be in the hospital for my high-dose treatments. I appreciated seeing Milo for a few hours before checking into the hospital, knowing it would probably be weeks before I could see him again. He was a calming presence for both Jen and me, even more so since I became ill. Neither of us had worked for a while, so we spent most of our time outside the hospital with Milo, who returned our affection by making funny faces at us, emitting expressive moans, and rubbing his nose against our limbs and heads. He had become much more than a pet: Milo was our child.

Our parents and Milo departed, and we received a call from Adam.

"I didn't want to bother you guys. But I just spoke with a friend at the hospital who is a fertility specialist. I told him your situation, and we discussed some options. I hope you don't mind."

Me: "No. We appreciate you thinking about it for us."

"There are some sperm banking options you could consider before you begin another round of chemotherapy. This might be your last chance. Once you receive an allogeneic transplant, you will be sterile."

One of the options available was to undergo a testicular biopsy, Adam said. I cringed. He conceded the surgery would be painful, after the fact at least. (I would be under general anesthesia while the doctors performed the operation.)

"But don't give it too much thought until you talk to the doctor tomorrow and get the full details."

Jen and I took Adam's advice. We still needed to get word out to our friends that I had relapsed. Once I entered the hospital, we wouldn't have time to talk to them, nor would we immediately have access to a computer for sending emails. Jen and I composed a group email with the subject "Some bad news," which updated a small circle about my latest struggles. We said we hoped to speak with everyone in the coming days, but we were too tired to talk that night and needed to rest up for the following day. That task accomplished, Jen and I tried to get some sleep. I don't recall us having pillow talk. Whatever my thoughts, I couldn't think of anything to say to make Jen feel better.

The next morning we packed clothes, pictures, and some bath products and headed back to the hospital. The admitting process was typically slow, so slow that the office provided a dozen chairs up front and a TV perched in the corner. We watched "The View." I was now familiar enough with daytime television to know that this was the best option for the hour. Once checked in to my hospital room, I called family members to tell them where they could find us.

"10 Central, not 5 North. The whole leukemia unit moved… Yes, still Greenberg Pavilion, the same elevator bank as before."

After everyone had filed in, Dr. Roboz and Dr. Feldman came by and gave a joint speech on the treatment protocol that lay ahead.

Dr. Feldman: "Roger was in remission for almost eight months. That's a pretty good period of remission."

Dr. Feldman was counting forward from late December, when I underwent a bone marrow biopsy that showed no signs of leukemia. His tabulation, while reasonable, was longer than my count of three months since the completion of my stem cell transplant.

Dr. Roboz: "Our goal now is to put Roger back in remission so that he can undergo an allogeneic stem cell transplant from his sister, Shana."

With that, Dr. Roboz looked at Shana and smiled. Shana blushed a little and looked down. We all felt fortunate that I had a sibling match, since transplants from siblings were among the most successful donor stem cell transplants.

"Shana's stem cells will be harvested when Roger is ready for his transplant. Before that happens, Roger will have at least one round of chemotherapy and then one round of total body irradiation."

Dr. Roboz didn't say it to the assembled audience, but Jen and I knew that the radiation would be the cause of my sterilization.

Dr. Roboz: "Roger is young and strong. We expect him to pull through this difficult process and make a full recovery."

Dr. Roboz and Dr. Feldman asked if there were any questions. A few were asked and answered. Then the doctors left the room. Were there any doubters, their faith had been restored by the doctors' smooth and confident presentation. Jen and I then asked everyone to leave, not mentioning that the reason was that we had an appointment to meet with the fertility doctor. There were a few things we preferred to keep to ourselves.

When he came to the hospital room, he discussed the few options available to us to capture and store sperm for later use. The doctor confirmed that the procedure with the best prospect for success was a testicular biopsy. Should Jen and I decide to go through with this, the doctor was available to do the operation the following day. For the procedure, the doctor would extract sperm lodged within the testes. Any sperm recovered would be frozen and could be used later for in-vitro fertilization. Though it was the best available option, the biopsy had a relatively low probability of success, just thirty to fifty percent, the doctor said. Even if viable sperm were found, it might not be healthy. Leukemia wasn't considered a genetic disease, but the multiple rounds of chemotherapy that I had undergone already might have damaged my sperm. The current science couldn't tell us the state of the sperm that would be extracted. As for the pain associated with the surgery, the doctor said:

"For a couple of days at least, you'll feel like somebody kicked you between the legs."

None of this sounded good to Jen or me. Still, we mulled over the idea, because chemotherapy that I had undergone already might have damaged my sperm. The current science couldn't tell us the state of the sperm that neither of us wanted to look back and think we could have done more. We needed to decide in a couple of hours, so that the doctors could reserve space in the operating room. We sought advice from Adam and our friend Noah, whose wife had just given birth. Noah said he loved that his child had been of his own making, but there were other wonderful options for having a family. Dr. Roboz said it was important that I remain strong in the coming weeks; the testicular biopsy would surely weaken me. Jen and I reflected back on the many moments of weakness I had experienced in the past nine months. In addition, we still had the viable sperm sample that we had banked in November, before my first round of chemotherapy. It was a solitary chance, but it was a hope, a healthy hope. That settled it. With heavy hearts, Jen and I called back the fertility doctor and told him that we had decided against the surgery.

That would have been enough for any single day, but I had one more mini-drama to play out. After visiting hours ended and Jen had left for the night, I tried to get as good a sleep as I could. The following day I was scheduled to have yet another chest port inserted. (The last one had been removed just six weeks earlier.) Also, I would begin receiving chemotherapy, probably overnight in some cases. These two developments would make future nights' sleep both uncomfortable and short-lived. As I tossed in bed, I caught my right arm in the sheets. I tried to pull free and instead I pulled my shoulder out of its socket.

Imagine your shoulder is the cap that seals your car's fuel tank. You crank the cap and feel it lock into place. But you don't release at that point. You continue cranking until it clicks forward thirty degrees or so. That second crank, with its crunching sound, is what a person feels when his or her shoulder dislocates. I knew it immediately. This was the fifth time I had dislocated my right shoulder. Getting it fixed was one of those things I had planned to do for years but had postponed, for one reason or another, usually fear. The latest reason had been leukemia. I had dislocated my shoulder enough times to have learned how to put it back into its proper position myself, a la Mel Gibson in *Lethal Weapon*. This time, however, I knew the dislocation was too severe for self-service. I reached with my left arm, the good one, for the nurse call button.

"I need help. I threw out my shoulder. It's an emergency."
Nurse: "You what?"
This was not something heard every day on the leukemia ward.
"I dislocated my shoulder. Please send in a nurse. It hurts."
A nurse came in. I lifted the sleeve on my t-shirt to show her the depression in my shoulder where my arm bone would normally reside. I have been told that I turn green when my shoulder dislocates, a result of the adrenalin rush. I'm sure I was a sorry sight for the nurse.
Nurse: "We need to call an orthopedist."

"We can put it back. Have you ever reinserted a shoulder?"

"No."

The nurse got some morphine for my pain and injected me with it.

"It will take some time for the doctor to get here. They'll first want to get an X-ray.

No matter. I was floating now. The nurse and I began to chat about how I had first dislocated my shoulder: Climbing in a slippery gorge in Ithaca, trying to get a better photo of Jen and her friend Elizabeth who were standing amidst a waterfall, slipping after taking the shot, then trying to save my camera, not myself, from the fall. After twenty minutes' discussion, the nurse gave me a booster shot, loosening me further.

The orthopedist, a muscular young doctor, arrived about a half hour after my dislocation. I recounted my story to him, and he examined my shoulder, before going to look at the X-ray. He returned and said that he would round up the materials needed to reset my shoulder. I thanked him, and, without thinking, offered my right hand, the bad one, to shake his.

Pop! I felt the shoulder magically snap back to place. Relief...

Me: "You won't believe this. My shoulder just reset itself."

Doctor: "You're kidding."

"Nope. Check it out. You're an amazing doctor"

I looked past the doctor at his younger female assistant.

"You should be very impressed with him. He reset my shoulder by his presence alone."

She didn't play along with me. Then again, she wasn't high on morphine. The orthopedists departed soon after, and I fell into a deep sleep.

After that, my days quickly settled into a more normal routine. I thought that I would welcome that. I didn't. With more time to think, my troubles could fill my head.

LEUKEMIA FOR CHICKENS

18

♪ Where Were You When the Lights Went Out?

Any time I begin a new round of chemotherapy, I find myself fraught with ambition. I think of new projects to start, like watercolor painting or loading my iPod with music. I choose new books to read (never anything related to illness) and make sporadic entries into my journal. Here's one entry I wrote shortly after being admitted to the hospital in late July:

Saturday, July 26, 2003

Are these drugs pumping me up too much? It's probably not the drugs. It's 7 p.m. here. I took my two-hour nap at lunchtime. Jen's exhausted from the daily ritual, while I'm bright as a bee, to coin a term. I took two walks today and talked a lot to Rich.

It was more difficult to speak to Noah, because we couldn't leave the room. There was a lot of cross conversation [among other visitors], so it was hard to concentrate. He was great, though. He found someone who could come by and lead me in some meditation exercises. I enjoyed the meditation I did with Joe [the in-hospital physical therapist], so maybe this new woman will help me mellow out. The claustrophobia makes me antsy. You just want these days to go by, to some degree.

But they may be important, or they are important, or they are what they are, and it's my life...

We've set up the room. The people and doggie pictures have been fun-tacked to the wall. We've shown the photo album on the laptop to our visitors. We've arranged some background music playing out of the computer, and we've done a lot of Scrabble games, as always...

Day by day, it gets darker earlier. Soon it will be a full four seasons looking out these windows. Mom keeps checking in, saying she doesn't want to listen to more sympathy calls from her friends. Dad surprised us this morning with bagels. Usually he goes to temple on Saturday... Everyone wants to do something, change in some way, show acknowledgment, or respect, or empathy. It's not a burden, but it makes me feel like my situation is making other people stagnate...

The physical day-to-day doesn't feel as fresh as before. Sometimes I even feel like new nurses would add some variety. But I've got to shed this craving for variety. Eventually things will settle down and I'll adjust to this routine. This may be the ants talking for now... I feel like signing this note to myself, so I will:

Love, me.

The "ants" (as in the antsy person inside of me) stopped talking pretty soon after that entry, which turned out to be my last for a few weeks. That's because the effects of the chemotherapy kicked in about that time. I soon felt weak, sleepy, and generally lacking in energy. For this round of chemotherapy, doctors prescribed the usual medicines plus Mitoxantrone, the most distinctive side effect of which is that it turns patients' urine blue-green. The doctors also prescribed Decadron, a steroid, to limit inflammation. The steroid offered a medical explanation for my hyperactivity in the first days of treatment, though I think there were some purely psychological reasons for my agitation as well. The adrenaline flows when you know you are close to the edge. You want to make the most of your time. As my counts dropped, the adrenaline, real or imagined, waned. The steroids also stopped with the end of chemotherapy.

A few days after the chemo ended, I met Judy, Noah's friend, who conducted a private meditation session for Jen and me. Rather than relaxing, I found the experience taxing. It was hard to maintain that meditative state that's just a smidge above falling asleep. If Judy had allowed me to pass out, that would have been great, but that wasn't what she had in mind. Her goal was getting me to focus on my breathing, on feeling my abdomen rise and fall slowly. I knew that mastering the technique would help me to relax and to work through pain in the coming weeks and months, but I didn't have it in me. I canceled our second appointment, as exhaustion replaced my frustration about not being able to relax.

One person who wasn't slowing down at this time was my sister, Shana. Her personal life had become more of a concern to me once I learned that I had relapsed, since the next phase of my treatment would require her to donate stem cells, shown in previous tests to be a "perfect" replacement for my damaged bone marrow.

Doctors rate potential donors' stem cells on a six-point scale. The test gauges the likelihood that a donor's stem cells will graft to the host with few side effects. The stronger the match, the less the chance that the donor's cells will attack the host as a "foreign" body. Despite the test, cases where donor cells attacked were common, even among "perfect" matches. Shana's stem cells rated positively on all six counts.

My sister was thirty-two at the time, a few years older than me. She worked at our family's trading firm as its Head of Compliance, making sure everyone played by the rules. Besides being a single mom, she had an active social life and a rigorous yoga schedule. At my healthiest, I could never maintain Shana's schedule. She was rail thin and attractive and had little trouble meeting potential mates. Her longer relationships always seemed to be with previous boyfriends. No matter how difficult the breakup, Shana's beaus never disappeared for long.

In that summer of 2003, Shana was spending most weekends at the Hamptons beach house of her current boyfriend, Randy. Occasionally, Shana wouldn't stay at Randy's for the entire weekend, usually because a row had erupted between them. Although Randy never threatened Shana physically, if the two had a heated verbal spat, Shana wouldn't flinch at packing her bags and driving home to Manhattan at any hour of the night.

Normally I found Shana's dramas amusing, but that summer Jen and I were more frightened than amused by them; frightened because we now saw Shana as my lifeline. I tried to convey my unease to her without seeming like an overbearing parent. Jen seconded my feelings in a separate talk.

Shana, to Jen: "I know you think I'm reckless. But I would never do anything to put Roger in any jeopardy."

We couldn't do any more than voice our opinion. We searched for indirect ways influence her actions, asking the doctors if there were restrictions Shana needed to abide by to insure the stem cell donation would go smoothly.

Me: "Does she need to do anything in terms of eating, like maintain a minimum weight?"

Case manager: "No, she can pretty much be herself."

Me: "Does she need to stop smoking?"

"No. Smoking won't affect the harvest."

"Well, maybe you could tell her to stop, anyway."

In early August, the doctors asked Shana to give blood for a routine test to reconfirm that she was indeed a perfect match. The following day, Jen and I received a call from Dr. Roboz's assistant, asking us to contact Shana so that she could retake the test.

"Is something wrong?"

Nurse: "No. Everything is fine. We just want to double-check on something the computer noted. It was a slight abnormality, nothing to be concerned about, I assure you."

Shana submitted a second blood sample the following day. She was visiting me in my hospital room the following morning, along with my parents, when Dr. Roboz happened to come by and asked to speak privately with her in the hall.

Shana returned a few minutes later.

"Well, I'm pregnant!" Shana laughed nervously as she made her declaration to us.

"*What?*" our parents said in unison. I was floored, speechless.

"I guess it happened last weekend. They said it just barely showed up on the test."

Shana was referring to the hormone hCG, which is produced by the body when it detects impregnation.

Me: "Okay… What does this mean?"

Shana: "The stem cell harvest would probably damage the fetus."

Dr. Roboz, who had followed Shana back into the room, took over answering questions from there.

"Shana has to take Neupogen for her stem cells to circulate in the blood, where they can be harvested. It's not known what the effect of this would be on an unborn child, especially one so early in development, but it would probably be harmful."

I suppose I should have said, "I'm sorry," to my sister, but I wasn't sure of the appropriate response. Her face was difficult to read. Her tone suggested that she didn't see this new development as a dilemma. My transplant clearly was paramount.

Later the same morning, Jen called.

"How did Shana's retest go?"

Me: "I think you need to talk to her."

"Oh my god. She's pregnant."

Women's intuition, I guessed.

I was in a weakened state at that point, taking daily infusions of Abelcet, the anti-fungal drug that was so strong it required taking Demorol to inhibit rigors. The combination knocked me out for about four hours in the middle of the day.

Though I was outwardly somnambulant over the next few days, Jen could sense the anxiety I felt, if only because this was yet another complication with which I had to grapple.

In the days that followed, I never discussed the issue with my sister, other than obliquely, when we went over the technicalities of ending the pregnancy. The first time Shana took a "morning after" pill, it failed. A second attempt worked as expected. The immediate crisis passed, but indefinable feelings of hurt lingered on both sides.

It was again that time in the cycle of my treatment where my blood counts dropped to undetectable levels, and my "life force" shriveled as well. In those bleak days I did little and remembered even less. We all waited impatiently for the time when my body would summon the energy to rebuild itself.

. . .

A couple of weeks later, on August 14 at about 4 p.m., the lights went out. It was a sunny and hot day—more than 90 degrees outside, according to the weather report. (I hadn't been outside to feel the weather's intensity first-hand for weeks by then.)

Jen was with me in the hospital room. Her mom had just left to return home to Pomona, where Milo awaited his afternoon walk. Jen and I were playing Scrabble. The view outside my window, dominated by three hulking Con-Ed smokestacks painted with red stripes, suddenly became interesting. The power plant let out a groan like an eighteen-wheeler slamming its air brakes. We looked out to see a white plume rise from the stacks. Soon after, we heard the room's air conditioner stall.

Me: "Hey, look. The clock on the VCR is out."

Jen: "The bathroom light is out." (We'd always left that light on, for some reason.)

A hospital is a good place to be in a time of emergency. Still, as the temperature rose, we wished we could open the windows to let in a breeze from the river. Instead, the air in our room stagnated. A foul odor was mixed in when my chronic queasiness developed into a spell of nausea. Though the power was out, our telephone still worked. The institutional, touch-pad beige box was "old-school," powered solely by its landline. We called my dad's office, which had temporary back-up power in case of emergencies, to see what was going on. My cousin Mark told me that the traders heard reports of a lightning strike in Canada that had cut power up and down the East Coast, but no one was ruling out the possibility of terrorism. (We later learned the outage was caused by a series of foul-ups in Ohio. About fifty million people lost power as a result of them.)

With time on our hands, Jen and I called around to family and friends to check on their whereabouts. Cell phones were still operating. We located Jen's father driving east on Interstate 80, interrupting him as he listened to a book on tape.

Marty: "There's a blackout? It's news to me."

He assured us he had enough gas to get home. Lois, Jen's Mom, told us she had made it out of the hospital garage and saw street lights flicker, just as she jumped on the FDR. There was no sign of my mom for the moment, though she later turned up at her apartment on Park Avenue. Our friends Rich and Margie found each other as they walked home from their respective offices. Rich walked uptown from the Department of Health on Church Street, while Margie trudged cross-town and northward from 54th Street and Third Avenue. They met at 96th and Broadway and together climbed another hundred blocks to Washington Heights, where—surprise, surprise—they found their apartment was hot and dark.

Though we were warm, Jen and I did have it better than most everyone else in the city, since my hospital room was equipped with two outlets that ran on generator power.

Me: "So that's why those plugs glow red." (The rest of them were black.)

We used one plug to sustain my intravenous pump, which was always dripping fluid and medication into my body. The other outlet wasn't needed for anything critical, so we plugged in our mini-refrigerator/freezer, even though we were asked to conserve energy. This disobedience kept our stash of ice pops frozen. We were generous with our boodle, so the haggard nurses didn't complain.

One of the nurses on staff that night was Rita, who had admitted me to my hospital room on the first night I was diagnosed with leukemia. Though the blackout had occurred before Rita had left to come into work that evening, she donned her scrubs and drove from Bay Ridge, Brooklyn, to the hospital in Manhattan to report for her regular night shift. A policeman who was guiding traffic in the absence of streetlights stopped her.

"Only doctors are allowed to be on the road, for medical emergencies. "

Rita, to the policeman: "Ever been in a hospital? Who takes care of the patients, *doctors*?"

That was Rita, to a tee. She told us traffic was light once she got through the tunnel and onto the FDR Drive. We gave her a cherry ice-pop to keep cool. Occasionally, Jen and I unplugged our fridge to recharge the laptop computer. The computer also had a dedicated Internet connection that remained operable. That way we kept abreast of the blackout and Mayor Bloomberg's ever-lengthening deadline to restore power.

I sang to Jen: "Where were you when the lights went out? New York City."

Almost nobody knows the jingle. The infectious chorus, sung by the disco-era band The Trammps, had stuck in my head ever since I heard the song played live at a Hamptons hotspot in the late 1990s. The Trammps are better known by their mega-hit of the 1970s, "Disco Inferno." They could probably walk off any stage to cheers after singing just that one hit song, but the night that Jen and I saw them, they delved into their less-heralded set list, which included the aforementioned ditty, written as a reminiscence of the blackout of 1977.

At some point during the evening, definitely before sunset, we heard a knock on the door. It was Adam, to whom I'd lately given the moniker "Superdoc." Adam had hoofed up ten flights to see me, maintaining his record of visiting me in the hospital every day I was an in-patient and he was in the tri-state area. When the blackout hit, Adam had been intending to drive to his brother's house in Westport, Connecticut, where power still flowed. But his car was on a lift in a garage, and the garage couldn't lower it to ground level without power. Adam left our room around sunset, walking down the stairs in the dark.

Though I was getting treatment for a leukemia relapse, my hospital room was located in the spiffier bone marrow transplant unit. Larger rooms, like mine, had a pullout sofa bed for visitors. The night of the blackout was Jen's first hospital sleepover in almost a year. It was a hot night's sleep, at least temperature-wise.

We woke with the sunrise, as usual, not only because of the light, but because nurses made their usual rounds for blood samples and the like. Power was restored to the neighborhood around the hospital at about 10 a.m., when I noticed the VCR light blinking again. A few minutes later, the air conditioner hummed back to life.

The city's power-outage coincided with my own body's revival from a moribund state. The day of the blackout, the doctors told me my white blood count had risen from undetectable levels to 0.3, a small step on the way to normal, which is about 5.0. The doctors said I could stop taking Abelcet that day, and that I might be released from the hospital within a week. Then after a few weeks' rest, I could start treatment for my donor stem cell transplant.

The most important element in preparing for the transplant was that I would be handed off from Dr. Roboz to that of Dr. Tsiporah (pronounced "Sapora") Shore, who was a bone marrow transplant specialist. Dr. Roboz would still follow my case, but Dr. Shore would take primary responsibility from that point on. I'd met Dr. Shore on occasion during the previous year, but we hadn't formed a bond. A few days after I learned I was on the mend, Dr. Shore came by my hospital room to discuss what lay ahead.

She arrived unannounced. After making a brief introduction, Dr. Shore sat down with me to describe the transplant process. It would be different from my previous transplant, primarily because this time I would undergo total body irradiation to destroy my bone marrow, in addition to chemotherapy.

"You will stand in a room and a machine will fire beams at you for about fifteen minutes. There will be an intercom, and you can ask the radiologist to stop the session at any time, if you are uncomfortable. To distract you, there will be music playing."

"Do I get my choice of music?"

"I don't think so."

The radiation therapy would last for four days, twice a day.

"Most people don't feel side effects from the treatment. Maybe your cheeks will puff out, and you'll feel some "dry mouth." Some people feel fatigue. Once the radiation is complete, you will undergo the transplant."

Though that was a lot to process, I'd heard most of the details of the transplant procedure beforehand. I wanted to know more about the risks involved.

Me: "An allogeneic [donor] transplant is considered more dangerous than an autologous one, isn't it?"

"You're talking about the fatality rate?"

"Yes."

"It's about 20 percent."

"That's pretty risky."

"I suppose, but it's the best alternative we have."

"What about afterwards?"

"You will be very tired, as you know from your last transplant. You will also have to be careful because you will be immunosuppressed. You'll need to avoid infection at all cost and you will be on a restricted diet for six months—no fresh vegetables or uncooked foods."

"That's no fun."

"No, it isn't."

It went like that for a few more questions. Dr. Shore was straightforward and respectful, but the conversation lacked a personal connection. She did not let the conversation get beyond direct answers to specific questions. We skipped over the whole range of reactions I could have from the introduction of a foreign immune system into my body. She thought we should wait on that and cross that bridge when we got there. I didn't feel the warmth that Dr. Roboz exuded. I couldn't blame Dr. Shore. Each doctor had his or her own style.

When Dr. Roboz came by that afternoon to check in with me, I told her that I wasn't as comfortable with Dr. Shore as I was with her as my primary doctor.

Before addressing my concerns about Dr. Shore, Dr. Roboz asked about the situation with my sister, whether there had been any repercussions from the unexpected pregnancy. Dr. Roboz even managed to make a joke about what was a delicate situation.

"Have you put her in a habit, yet?" she asked, referring to the nun's costume.

"It's been relatively quiet since."

I had only mentioned Shana's surprise pregnancy to a few close friends and disclosed my distress about it only to Jen. The incident had caused me no physical harm, and my treatment had not been delayed. I had been focused on rebounding from my chemotherapy. Still, questions about the issue had swirled in my mind: Did I have a right to be upset? Wasn't it enough that Shana was saving my life by donating her cells? Should I be indignant she accidentally got pregnant? Did it matter whether her actions were reckless or if they were out of character?

I am still torn. Most transplant recipients never even learn the name of their donor. Because my sister was my donor, I knew a lot more than most. It was enough to have to worry about myself. Knowing my donor heightened my awareness of the fact that the stem cells I needed were out in the world, subject to all the risks inherent in daily life. Now I had to worry about every move those stem cells made as they rode around in her body.

As for my concerns about Dr. Shore, Dr. Roboz assured me that I was in good hands.

"Give her a chance. She will warm up. More importantly, she is a hawk and will have her finger on every facet of your transplant. Dr. Shore doesn't miss a trick."

That was comforting to hear. I resolved to ask Dr. Shore for another meeting, not so much to discuss my case, but just to get a better feel for her. Besides, Jen wasn't on hand for our initial consultation. Dr. Shore would have to go over everything again with Jen, regardless.

There was still time in our schedule for getting to know each other. I should have also suspected there would be delays and complications. By this point, it was almost as if they were obligatory.

LEUKEMIA FOR CHICKENS

19

The Winnipeg Healers

Never trust a cough. It's okay for a cough to live within you for a couple of weeks. But track closely your guest's activities and whereabouts. Consider its quirks. How does your cough sound? Like a bark or a bleat? Does it resonate with a peal or echo with a warble? From where does your cough emanate? Is it vocal or guttural? How do you feel when you cough? Does your chest thump or heave?

At what time of day are you most keenly aware of your insidious visitor? Does your cough talk about the weather? For example, would a sudden burst of air-conditioned mist cause it to grumble? Does your cough tickle you, or does it feel more like a prickly pear? Does your cough wear a coat? How thick a layer? (Yes, I am euphemizing phlegm here). Is your cough's sheath an ivory foam or more oily and vermillion? Finally, is your cough content with a single bellow, or must its rant persist?

Assume that any cough that comes to visit intends to stay; a cough will fight your attempts to uproot it. Though a cough surely resides in the lungs, it is almost impossible to pinpoint its exact position. The most advanced medical imager is powerless to map a cough's realm. Finding a cough's home base is akin to looking at road map of the entire United States to locate the house at 23 Palooka Street, Lincoln, Nebraska.

A cough, in truth, is not anything tangible. It is merely a signpost, the most easily observed residue left by a microscopic nit that lies deep within you. This nit may be a miniscule virus, bacterium, or fungus—something that is growing, spreading, clogging, and trailing detritus. Each cough you emit is an aggressive effort by your body to expunge this irritant.

Changes in your cough reflect developments in the battle between your immune system and that infiltrant. If your cough subsides, view that as a clear sign your body is triumphing over its foe. A cough that rises in clamor announces your challenger's ascendence. Heed the cough's call, and gird yourself with heavier armaments.

A cough is such a graphic and total indicator of the battle within your body that no physical examination would be complete without a doctor or nurse pressing a stethoscope against a patient's back. The doctor will listen for reverberations in a patient's lungs in at least three places. As the stethoscope touches skin, the doctor will call for the patient to take a deep breath. Should a cough intercede as the patient inhales, it's all the more helpful for the examiner to hear. The doctor will move his stethoscope to the patient's chest and listen in again. Breathe normally, a patient will be told at this point. To make contact between the stethoscope and the patient less jarring, a considerate doctor will huff a breath over the listening device's metal plate, warming it.

The patient may talk while a doctor listens via the stethoscope. The doctor's attentive stare deceives the patient into believing that he or she is listening to what is being said. Only after the doctor pulls away the stethoscope's earplugs and asks, "How are you feeling?" does the patient realize that the doctor has heard not a word. The doctor's intense focus on the sounds in the lungs is warranted for all the reasons mentioned above.

My doctors each made a mental note of the cough I developed just before I was released from the hospital in late August, 2003. The cough wasn't serious enough to keep me in the hospital. It was better for me to rest at home and gain strength for the few weeks until my second stem cell transplant.

Jen and I resolved to spend those last weeks of freedom in a feeding frenzy. Our goal was for me to add weight, but we also wanted to savor the taste of fine meals. One of the most dispiriting consequences of receiving a donor stem cell transplant was that once I completed the six-week treatment protocol, not only wouldn't I be allowed to eat uncooked food or fresh vegetables, but I wouldn't be able to eat any meal prepared outside the home for six months at least. My bone marrow transplant doctors demanded patients adhere to this restriction because the newly rebuilt immune systems created via stem cell transplants aren't strong enough initially to fight food-borne bacteria. I could only eat raw fruits and vegetables that had a "hard" rind. For example, apples were forbidden, oranges were not. Meat had to be thoroughly cooked. That meant sushi was out of the question, while a well-done cheeseburger was okay—no lettuce or tomato.

Eating at a restaurant was a no-no because it was impossible to know if someone sneezed within spitting distance of my plate before I was served. In short, I should get used to home-cooked meals. Though it wasn't the worst sentence one could imagine, New Yorkers tend to shudder at the thought of mastering kitchen skills. But because they are compelled to become proficient at cooking, more than a few leukemia patients I had met wound up pursuing culinary careers once they recovered from the illness.

My eating restrictions wouldn't start until I began radiation therapy in preparation for my stem cell transplant. That was a few weeks away. In the meantime, I ate as well as I could. Jen and I tried to make last-minute reservations at New York's top dining spots. Calling the restaurants ourselves, we found that reservations were not available. Undaunted, we called in chits we had spread among family and friends. They were happy to oblige. Our friend, Nancy, who worked at Tribeca Productions, Robert DeNiro's film company, scored us a table at the Japanese emporium, Nobu, an establishment in which DeNiro was an investor. My cousin, Mark, asked his college buddy, Jeff Wilpon, who was president of the New York Mets, to pull strings at Peter Luger's Steak House. A table for ten was summarily rustled up on two days' notice. We couldn't think of a connection that would help us procure a table at Babbo, a favorite of Italian gastronomes, but I couldn't pass up an opportunity for a last repast there. Jen and I decided we would stand by for a table. It is a little known fact that Babbo keeps its front tables available for patrons who arrive promptly at the restaurant's opening, 5:30 p.m. Babbo saves four two-seat tables for this purpose. Unfortunately, Jen and I were the fifth couple to arrive that evening, which meant we would have to wait until at least one couple finished eating before we could be seated. We decided it would be worth the wait and in the meantime distracted ourselves by figuring out why certain Hollywood celebrities, also dining at Babbo that evening, were eating together. For example: Mike Myers and Hillary Swank. We surmised that the two were connected via Swank's husband, Chad Lowe, whose brother Rob starred with Myers in "Austin Powers, International Man of Mystery."

Our wait for a table lasted longer than our ability to find ways to kill time as the first round of diners that were seated made friends with each other and sat chatting well past the time when they finished their meals. The maitre d' at Babbo refused to intercede. Jen and I finally sat down for dinner two-and-a-half hours after we arrived. The table next to ours still housed one of those lingering couples. The female diner tried to spark a conversation with us, but I was in no mood.

Female diner: "The people who sat here before you were so interesting."

Me: "I noticed you talked to them for a long time."

She sensed irritation in my voice and grumbled to her companion that I didn't seem nice.

Jen pleaded with me not discuss with the other diner the matter of our lengthy wait.

Me: "Since you chose to make conversation with us, I feel compelled to tell you that you should have wrapped up your meal by now."

"Excuse me?"

"You realize that other people are waiting for your table."

"It's my birthday."

"Everyone here is celebrating something special."

The couple left in a huff, with the female diner wishing me a "terrible meal" as she departed. While the tiff lessened my enjoyment of chef Batali's pumpkin *lune* (moon) ravioli, I felt a certain spiteful satisfaction knowing I had caused the other diner to leave with a bad taste in her mouth as well.

Those evenings out were tiring due to my weakened state, but I relished them. Mornings, however, were more difficult for me, punctuated as they were by worsening coughing fits. I reported to my doctors how my cough had developed and even submitted to a chest X-ray. Adam prescribed a "Z-Pak," a five-day regimen of the drug Zithromax, which fights some types of respiratory infections. My condition did not improve. The phlegm that I coughed up changed color from milky white to neon green, a sign that whatever was nesting in my lungs had managed to burrow deeper. On Monday of Labor Day weekend, I awoke short of breath. I twisted in bed, wondering what I should do next. As it was a holiday, no doctor's office was open. I rolled over, and woke Jen.

"I think I need to check into the hospital."

I expected her to resist, but she seemed resigned to the prospect, probably because she hadn't slept very well, a result of my loud coughing throughout the night. I didn't know if being in the hospital would help, but I knew I would feel more comfortable with the doctors closely watching me. I called Adam; he agreed that I should check myself in. He called the Emergency Room at NewYork-Presbyterian Hospital to see how long the wait was to be admitted. The ER was not busy, Adam reported back to us. "Not busy" still meant a few hours of waiting in the ER until I was moved to a room on 10 West, the bone marrow transplant unit.

The doctors started me on a series of "anti" medications, hoping that one of them would inhibit the growth of whatever virus/fungus/bacteria existed in my lungs. They ordered a CT-scan that would provide a more detailed view of my lungs' many pathways. The scan showed pathogens of some sort. The next step for the doctors was to devise some way of retrieving the intruder so it could be grown in a Petri dish, and then identified. If successful, the doctors would select a more targeted medication with which they could attack the microbe in my body. All this would take time; hopefully not too long, because the sooner I could start my transplant procedure, the better. No one expected that my latest remission from leukemia would last long, maybe two months. My last treatment was designed to be strong enough to put me in remission without weakening me so much that I wouldn't be up for my transplant. In addition, my transplant would be more likely to succeed if it began while I was still in remission.

But taking the first step in my transplant, destroying my existing immune system, was not advisable while it was clear that I had an infection in my body. Restoring my lungs to good working order had to take priority.

The doctors first ordered a bronchoscopy, a procedure by which fluid is coursed through the lungs and then retrieved in the hopes that the recovered fluid would contain a sample of my invader. A few days passed without anything growing in the Petri dish, so the doctors ordered a second procedure, called Video-Assisted Thoracic Surgery, or VATS. As the name implies, surgeons use an imaging device to get a rough idea of where they may find abnormal growth in the lungs. They then biopsy the lung tissue in those high-probability regions, place them in a Petri dish, and again, watch to see if anything grows. Nothing did.

I didn't tolerate these invasive procedures well. After the VATS, I spent two days in the Intensive Care unit, because the doctors were concerned I might have difficulty breathing. After I left the ICU, I still needed time to recover in my regular room. In the following week, as Jen and I watched the debut episodes of Ellen DeGeneres' new daytime talk show, my condition slowly improved. The doctors never did determine the nature of my lung infection, but the broad-based medications, including the high-powered Abelcet that I had taken since being admitted, lessened its severity and the resultant coughing fits. A week-and-a-half after I entered the hospital, the doctors said that I could go home. They added to my daily medication regimen high doses of Prednisone, an anti-inflammatory steroid. If my situation continued to improve, I could begin radiation therapy in a few weeks, I was told.

It was time for Jen and me to meet with Dr. Shore, my new doctor from the bone marrow transplant unit. We hoped that it would be a more personal encounter than my initial meeting had been. Because we spent so much time with our doctors, we found it awkward when we didn't discuss any topics other than those related to my illness.

The meeting was scheduled in early September, at her office. Jen and I didn't know much about Dr. Shore. We sensed that she was standoffish; though that was often the initial impression people had of her, it proved to be wrong. We had also heard that Dr. Shore was an observant Jew. This was true. Early in our meeting, the conversation turned to the upcoming Rosh Ha' Shana holiday. I described the camp-revival atmosphere at my parents' Temple on Long Island and how I felt it might be difficult for me to attend services there. She asked who the rabbi was. Carnie Rose, I replied.

"I know Carnie!" she exclaimed with a huge grin.

"You do?"

"His father was my rabbi in Winnipeg. I grew up with Carnie."

Put aside, momentarily, the coincidence that my spiritual guide and my Western medicinal healer both turn out to hail from the same cattle crossing on the far northern Canadian prairie. Let's marvel at the fact that I know something about Winnipeg. Besides having a memorable name, the city is familiar to me because of its former professional hockey team, the Jets. Growing up, I listened to radio broadcasts of New York Rangers games, among which were contests with Winnipeg's Jets. To pass time during commercials, I would look up information about the other teams' cities in the World Book Encyclopedia—the pre-Internet geek's guide to useless information. I found it easy to conjure an image of Winnipeg, which I learned was located due north of Fargo (that's Far-Go), North Dakota. Valid or not, I visualized modest skyscrapers disrupting a level, grey horizon. I had plenty of practice inventing pictures in my mind's eye as I tried to make sense of the verbal soup that was play-by-play radio coverage of the hockey matches: "Sal "Red-Light" Messina: "Andrechuk, cross-ice to Robitaille… VanBiesbrouck-save! Greschner clears the puck."

If you can make a picture out of that, creating a cityscape is a no-brainer. I assume Winnipeg chose their team's name, Jets, in an attempt to link the city with the jet age. The advent of jet travel surely reduced the city's sense of isolation. Alas, travel flows both to and fro. By the late 1990s, the Jets had moved to Phoenix. Rabbi Rose and Dr. Shore, unbeknownst to each other, each relocated, via a few stopover cities, to New York.

Dr. Shore's face had lit up at my mention of Carnie Rose. She recounted a few stories from their shared childhood. Once she established that bizarre connection with Jen and me, our conversation flowed freely. We traded jokes, then talked seriously about the upcoming transplant, tentatively scheduled for early October.

Dr. Shore told us not to be concerned that my sister's stem cells might not graft to my body. A sibling perfect match made the possibility of flat out rejection very unlikely. Of greater concern was whether, and to what degree, I would develop what is called graft vs. host disease, or GvHD as it is more commonly known. It occurs after a donor's cells establish themselves in a recipient. The new immune system will recognize that its host is a foreign body and it will likely go into attack mode. This aggressive reaction is welcome to some degree, because it helps fight residual leukemia in the body—they refer to this as the Graft vs. Leukemia effect. If the immune system becomes too aggressive, however, it will also fight good parts of the body. About a third of stem cell transplant patients experience a mild form of GvHD. Doctors try to limit the number of cases of moderate-to-severe GvHD by searching for donors who possess a similar immunologic profile, because such donors are less likely to stir up GvHD in their hosts. But some transplants provoke strong GvHD reactions regardless of whether they represent a close match.

Dr. Shore said I should be reassured that my sister represented a "perfect" match.

"I don't want to you start worrying about things that might go wrong. If something isn't working right, I will tell you. Trust me."

At this point, that was the best counsel I could hope to hear.

20

What, Me Worry?

Getting a handle on my lung infection pushed back the doctor's timetable to perform a stem cell transplant by a month at least. My infection had left my lungs swollen and irritated. For this the doctors proscribed anti-inflammatory steroids. Such steroids are not the kind used by athletes to build muscle. Those are anabolic steroids; what I was given were catabolic steroids, which work in the opposite fashion. That is, they break down tissue; thus, their effectiveness in reducing inflammation.

Catabolic steroids reproduce the chemicals that are naturally produced by the adrenal glands. In other words, they give you an artificial boost of corticosteroids, which act like adrenaline. When the body senses this high dose of corticosteroids, the adrenal glands shut down, and natural production of steroids is stunted. For this reason, a person must slowly wean him or herself off catabolic steroids. If a person quit cold turkey, the body would go into shock for lack of any steroid at all.

The doctors preferred that I rid myself of steroids before I began my stem cell transplant. They estimated it would take about three weeks for me to kick my steroid habit. It wasn't certain that I could wait that long to begin my transplant: With each passing week, I was pressing my luck, risking a relapse of leukemia.

Ideally, I knew I would want to go into my stem cell transplant leukemia-free, but I didn't much register the risk of a relapse. Rather, I felt lucky to be granted an additional few weeks of relative normalcy. Maybe I'd already internalized the advice given by Dr. Shore, which I interpreted as "Don't brood or read into things too much. I will tell you if something is wrong."

By offering to shoulder that burden, Dr. Shore enabled me to push thoughts about my illness to the back of my mind, though they never were far removed.

The break between my hospitalization for my lung infection and the time I began my stem cell transplant was one of the longest, most enjoyable periods I had spent since my first transplant in March. In the previous six months, I spent at least one night in the hospital every two weeks. Almost every time I left the hospital, I was anticipating when I would next return, whether it was for the catheter ablation to resolve my heart arrhythmia following my first transplant, or for my six high-dose injections of Interleukin-2, each separated by 10 days' rest. Then there was the chemotherapy after I relapsed during my final high-dose treatment in early August, culminating in my return within two weeks of being released to be treated for a lung infection.

Following that last hospitalization, three weeks of relative leisure awaited—barring something new coming out of the blue. I felt strangely liberated.

Steroids played a major part in my sunny outlook. I was literally hyped up. Just as I ran from activity to activity without much need to catch my breath, my mind raced from thought to thought, never pausing for reflection. My journal writings bore this out. Though prolific, my entries merely detailed the days' activities, without analysis. At least I was conscious of my lack of insight, writing in my journal at one point, "my body is leading my mind."

That was unfamiliar ground for me. I had always lived in my head, preoccupied with thoughts, and envying those who thought less and did more. Some of my favorite quotations ruefully acknowledged the advantage of ignorance as bliss. One favorite was John Lennon's "Living is easy with eyes closed." Another was Annie Savoy's, "The world is made for people who aren't cursed with self-awareness." (Annie Savoy was the lead female character in the movie *Bull Durham*.)

WHAT, ME WORRY?

I knew my steroid-induced, carefree state wouldn't last, but I made the most of its fleeting presence. I ate like a madman, though I couldn't gain much weight. My body burned through whatever calories I ingested. At restaurants, I would order two main dishes for dinner, then Jen and I would walk to the local bakery for a "magic" bar—consisting of coconut, sweetened condensed milk, chocolate chips and a graham cracker crust. I downed this dessert with a glass of whole milk. Nonetheless, my weight never topped 145 pounds. Granted, 145 pounds was the highest weight I'd achieved since falling ill, but pre-leukemia, I weighed in above 160 pounds. At low points during treatment I registered as little as 120.

With each passing day, I awoke earlier—rising at dawn, then before dawn. Jen and I filled our days doing errands. I optimistically bought a new fall wardrobe that I knew I wouldn't wear more than a few times in the coming months. We trekked to the 'burbs to see some friends. Other times friends visited us in our apartment.

One person I saw often was my neighbor, Monica. She was sweet, effervescent, and compassionate whenever I saw her. Monica went out of her way to make me feel good, once calling to ask if she could come by with hot chocolate from Starbucks. Lots of our neighbors made good will gestures, but Monica's small acts stood out. One morning I bumped into her on my way to the deli for an egg, cheese, and tomato bagel sandwich. She was fetching a morning coffee for herself (and the doorman, very likely).

Me: "Why don't you come to dinner with Jen and me? We're going to Lupa with Adam. You know Adam, my doctor. He's great. We have a reservation for three. I'm sure the table accommodates four. Come with us. It will be fun."

Monica: "I don't know. I don't look so good."

"C'mon. We'll laugh. It'll be a good time, guaranteed."

"Hmm… Okay. What time?"

"6:30. Jen and I eat early these days, but I eat a lot. It takes a while for me to finish. We'll call you around six and take a taxi together."

If Monica seemed unusually reluctant, it was understandable. Though I knew her as a friend and a fellow thirty-year-old, most everyone else knew Monica as the former President's mistress. Her notorious background made it difficult for her to meet people. If anyone could look beyond Monica's history and see her simply as a peer, that person would be Adam. I fear, however, that few will ever know Monica as anyone other than "that woman" with whom the President "did not" have sexual relations.

I called Adam and told him we had an unexpected guest for dinner. He was excited, as most people are when given the opportunity to meet a celebrity. We all met at the restaurant, a Roman-style *trattoria*. Nobody felt awkward and we chatted amiably through dinner. Monica made lighthearted references to her past only when it fit the conversation. I found her approach an effective way to disarm a potentially explosive topic. At one point Adam talked about his recent vacation, a wilderness adventure organized by Arthur Levitt, the former chairman of the Securities and Exchange Commission. Arthur was in his early seventies and had hosted this annual event for more than twenty years. Each year he assembled a guest list of twelve or so people—friends he knew from business, politics, and the arts—whose political leanings were varied enough to spark entertaining debates around the campfire. Each expedition included at least two outdoor guides and a doctor in case of an emergency. Adam, then forty, was the doctor-in-camp for the previous two trips, having taken over for a mentor who'd retired a couple of years back.

Monica said the trip sounded like fun, jokingly adding, "Could I be invited next year?" Adam unthinkingly responded that women were no longer invited, following a tryst between two guests that had led to a Beltway scandal.

You could almost hear Adam trying to stop his sentence mid-stream. Monica didn't skip a beat.

Monica: "Well, I don't see why he'd object to my coming along."

We laughed and remained at our table for almost three hours, making note of the long stares directed at us by other diners but paying them little heed. Monica told us later she'd go out with Adam on a date if he were interested. But she didn't sense much of a connection and Adam didn't call. We didn't ask.

A few days later, Jen and I celebrated Rosh Ha' Shana, the festival of the Jewish New Year, with our families. As the Jewish day begins with the evening hours, anticipating the darkness to come, so the Jewish New Year begins in autumn, time of the traditional harvest, when food is stored for the barren months ahead. On the eve of Rosh Ha'Shana, Jen and I drove with Milo to my parent's house on Long Island, where two chocolate Labs also lived. As usual our lanky Airedale terrier taunted the Labs, Auggie and Java, into chasing him around the back yard. Since Milo weighed just half of either Lab and they were known to play rough, Jen followed close behind, seeking to protect him. Milo looked like he could hold his own.

Marty, Jen's dad: "She's just like her mother."

I thought to myself, "Jen takes care of Milo like she takes care of me."

Shana and Rebecca also drove out for dinner, accompanied by Randy, still Shana's boyfriend. The three of them seemed comfortable and contented. I was reassured that Shana would come through as my transplant donor.

The following morning Jen and I attended services in the city. We went to a local temple, the Village Temple, which lived up to its namesake neighborhood's bohemian roots. The congregation came as they were, some dressed conservatively in suits, others wearing leather biker jackets. The cantor led sing-a-longs of familiar prayer chants, accompanied by an acoustic guitar. The rabbi added drama in her reading of the Torah—a retelling of the well-known, controversial story of when God commanded Abraham to sacrifice his son, Isaac, only to commute the sentence at the last possible moment—reciting each paragraph in Hebrew, then in English.

It was natural to reflect on the past year, a period that coincided closely with the duration of my illness. I'd survived the year. That was something for which to be thankful. Having survived, though, I'd never thought that I'd be fighting leukemia for so long. Still, next year at this time, I might be able to declare my leukemia behind me. My transplant would last about five weeks, and the average recovery period from a donor transplant was said to be six months at least. That left a season's worth of wiggle room for the unexpected.

After Rosh Ha'Shana, Jen and I still had a week of free time before I was scheduled to begin my transplant. That gave us a window to escape to our preferred retreat, Lake Placid, marking our fourth trip up there in fifteen months. We had postponed a visit planned for earlier that month because of my lung infection, but late September was a better time to travel north, in any event. The foliage would be beautiful this time of year. As the plans were last-minute, we scrambled to arrange lodging and a rental car. It was Saturday afternoon. We hoped to fly up to Lake Placid the following day. The Lake Placid Lodge had rooms available, but the Hertz rental desk at the airport was already closed and would remain so until Monday, the recording said. Each day Jen and I could spend out of the city would be precious; we didn't want to wait until Monday. I searched Saranac Lake Airport's Web site for a telephone number. It listed one for the "F.B.O."

Me: "Front Business Office?" (Actually it stands for fixed base operator, which is akin to general manager.)

I dialed the number and one Arthur Leavitt answered the phone, no relation to the Arthur who led the wilderness expeditions. This Arthur added an "a" to his surname. (Yes, I asked him).

I inquired of Arthur if he knew how we might contact the local operator of the Hertz franchise.

"Pat? He's at home today. Let me call him. Give me your number, and I'll call you back."

Five minutes later, Arthur called to tell us a car would be waiting for us when we arrived. Could we fax him a credit card and driver's license? Arthur didn't work for Hertz, but considering what he'd done for us already, how could we doubt his integrity at that point? We faxed him the information.

The flight into Saranac Lake only hinted at the crimson foliage below. On our last flight into the area, in January, the Adirondacks were whitewashed with snow. This aerial view was totally different. The mostly green trees were flecked with reds and yellows. Once we arrived, my sole concern was whether Jen and I would find enough ways to keep occupied in Lake Placid for longer than our typical weekend stay. I was, after all, hyped on steroids (probably not the only one to be so in this former Olympic village). After pacing Main Street twice in the first afternoon, we sought new ideas from the Lodge concierge. He had a few.

He sent us off on new trails that revealed huge boulders cupped with ancient roots, like fingers on a baseball. He recommended local (read: less touristy) restaurants that served everything from Tex-Mex to haute-French and Italian bistro specialties. And they were actually really good. Who knew? Each morning, I rose at dawn and wrote in my journal until seven o'clock, when the Lodge served breakfast on the veranda. Each night the cool air mixed with the relatively warm lake water, amassing a fog that nuzzled surrounding tree limbs and tucked itself under the leaves' summer-weight chlorophyll coat. As the morning sun rose, its rays vaporized the fog, revealing ever more leaves bearing their natural amber hue.

I watched this process from the lodge veranda each morning. As in the routine I had honed last January, I ordered a pancake or egg breakfast course as an accompaniment. Jen would join me a little later, and I would have a second, lighter breakfast with her at the table. We spent five days in Lake Placid that fall; by the end of our stay, we knew we were hooked long-term. Real estate brochures suddenly became interesting reading.

During one of our last dinners up north, Jen talked about how her close friend Elizabeth was having a rough time recently trying to make decisions about the direction of her life.

"Great," I responded, "and I'm dying of leukemia."

Jen's fork hit the plate.

"Do you really think that?"

"What? That I'm dying? No. I just say that. It's a pressure release."

"Well, don't. Don't scare me."

My cavalier statement hit her hard.

"I'm sorry. It's not how I feel. This transplant will be difficult, and I'm afraid."

I hadn't meant to belittle Elizabeth's problem, nor to make light of my own situation. I wasn't pessimistic, not then. Although we'd had a mountain of bad luck, everything had worked out so far. My whole life had been like that. Not to this degree, but after setbacks, I always managed to land on my feet. I couldn't look at things any other way.

We returned to New York City, and the next morning my body finally gave out. I slept until 10 a.m. As I untangled myself from the covers—you've heard this one before—I dislocated my shoulder, again. I was determined to return the shoulder to its proper position, and achieved my goal, with Jen's guidance. There was one final adrenaline rush, produced naturally this time around. I slept another six hours.

My good-luck month didn't really end until the following day, when I made my weekly visit to the doctor. A routine blood test revealed "blasts" in the blood stream. Leukemia. Though obviously disconcerting, there wasn't much we could do at that point. Radiation therapy was scheduled for the following Monday, four days away. Beginning treatment, we all hoped, would make things right, and we would just stick to our plans.

21

Buzzzzzz

How does it feel to have your body pelted by radiation? Not bad
enough, apparently. Dip a toe into a scalding-hot bath and the body
takes immediate evasive action. The leg reverses course, lurching out of
the water before the brain even registers pain. Absorb a deadly dose of
radiation, on the other hand, and the body makes nary a flinch; no
instinct exists to instruct people to automatically run for their lives.
Modern medicine compensates for this evolutionary shortcoming in
humans by decreeing that any exposure to high-dose radiation be
accompanied by an ear-splitting, atonal, alarm-clock-from-hell buzzing
sound.

Hearing this awful noise, a person would head instantly in the
opposite direction, slowing only as the sound receded. By creating this
buzz, doctors have come up with an effective device for protecting
innocent bystanders from the hazards of radiation. However, woe to
those who must withstand the clamor. Not only are they putting
themselves in mortal danger, they must suffer aurally as well. In
theory, radiation therapy could be as pleasant an experience as
reclining in a dentist's chair, a nose cone augmenting your oxygen
intake with sweet nitrous oxide, and soothing Musak playing almost too
low to hear. Instead, radiation therapy is as unpleasant to endure as it
is debilitating internally, as if to reinforce for the patient the trauma
that is being inflicted.

Rather than being seated, a radiation therapy patient stands vertically strapped to a flimsy metal apparatus. Supports are provided for the armpits and between the legs. A lead life preserver, shaped to match the contour of the lungs, hangs over the patient's aquamarine hospital gown. This custom-made cutout protects sensitive lung tissue from the kryptonite rays that eviscerate the marrow, liver and other vital organs.

The patient is perched on the metal contraption, while the center of the room houses the electron-beam transmitter, which most definitely must have once served as the inspiration for science-fiction artists looking to create a realistic space ship attack phaser. Or perhaps it's vice versa. Did retro cartoon-book drawings of inter-galactic space battles inspire makers of radiation therapy devices?

Given the '70s-era space-age motif of my surroundings, it was hardly a surprise to see that the sole decorative element, a border relief, was a map of the night sky. Lines connected significant dots that formed symbols of the zodiac. These were interspersed with whimsical drawings of "Ursa Major" and "Orion Slaying the Bull." I spent eight fifteen-minute sessions staring at those silly decorations, trying to block out that piercing buzz. Jazz music was piped in as a further distraction, but the fidelity was tinny, and the effort to mask the buzz seemed half-hearted at best. More encouraging were the occasional hoots and hollers I heard over the intercom that were being made by Jen and the technicians. They helped count down the minutes remaining for each session.

All that time I stood looking at those connect-the-dots constellations on the wall, I never wondered which was the astrological sign for Cancer? Whoever was responsible for decorating the hospital radiology unit must not have made the connection either. He or she would have to be a sadist to consciously place pictures of Cancer, something truly confounding to visualize, in the direct view of a patient undergoing radiation therapy. What the heck is Cancer, in astrological terms, anyway? A crab, apparently.

The radiation unit at NewYork-Presbyterian Hospital doesn't need to help patients visualize their disease, because a whole cottage industry exists to help us conjure images of the cancer within. If a patient can form a picture of his disease, so the New Age dogma goes, he or she can better focus mental energy on its eradication. I received as a gift one of those visualization tools as I entered the hospital for my second stem cell transplant. Unfortunately the audio-CD called upon imagery familiar to a wide audience, for purposes of commercial success, I assume, choosing scenes from light-saber battles such as those from *Star Wars*. I'm all in favor of mind-over-matter, but I think the inter-relation between the two is more complex than a silver screen battle between the forces of good and evil. That's not to say others can't find value in such techniques.

My four-day, twice-a-day, radiation therapy left few physical marks and caused minimal side effects, much as the doctors predicted. My skin became red and irritated, as if I'd received a mild sunburn. My saliva dried up, though some sores in my mouth actually healed because of the treatment. All of us knew things would get worse. That was the design. After radiation, the doctors ordered two days of chemotherapy to ensure killing off my existing bone marrow.

I was strong enough in this period to entertain guests. My friends Noah and Nancy came by the second afternoon of my radiation therapy, which coincided with Yom Kippur, the Day of Atonement in Jewish tradition. We recited prayers asking to be inscribed into the "Book of Life" for another year. Jews seek such repentance and renewal on an annual basis. For reference, we used a prayer book I'd borrowed from the Village Temple.

While I never pretended to be a religious scholar, I enjoyed leading Jen and my two friends in prayer. I did well in public school, but my Hebrew School teachers considered me a nuisance. After a long day of listening, I often became restless and disruptive. Still, I had paid attention in class enough to remember some major prayers from the high holidays, the general appellation for the ten-day period including Rosh Ha' Shana and Yom Kippur. I owe my memory of those prayers mostly to their familiar melodies. I also managed to recall a lot of the *Amidah*, a compilation of eighteen prayers recited out loud, and then in silence, during each service. Parroting this base of knowledge in my hospital room was sufficient to satisfy me spiritually.

I like the High Holidays because I associate them with fond memories. When I moved to Italy in 1998, the Rosh Ha' Shana holiday was just around the corner, as was the main temple in Milan, on Via

Guastalla. I walked alone from my apartment to the temple and sat in a pew in the central chapel. The prayer recitations were said in Aramaic. I was lost generally as to the progression of the service. Eventually the rabbis reached the moment when they removed the Torah scrolls from the Ark to be paraded among the parishioners. The congregation rose and shuffled to the edges of the pews to caress the ornate scroll covers on the sacred texts. To make a physical connection with the Torah, congregation members used either the fringes of their Tallit, the prayer shawl, or, lacking that accoutrement, a prayer book. As the scrolls made their way through the chapel, the rabbis chanted a melody also used by the congregation where I learned to pray.

I welled up with tears as I waited for my opportunity to touch the Torah. When the rabbis returned to the altar, we seated ourselves again in preparation for the Torah reading. I leaned over to a middle-aged man seated next me:

"Che bella. La stessa cosa e' repetuta dappertutto il mondo." (How beautiful. The same experience is repeated all over the world.)

Congregant: *"Dove mangerai dopo questo?"* (Where will you eat after this?) A typically Italian response.

"Non so." (I don't know.)

"Vieni con noi." (Come with us.)

We shared a long walk to his apartment. I learned his name was Franco. That day we began a lasting international friendship over a delicious brunch, prepared by his wife and his wife's sister, that concluded with an aperitif made from fermented rose petals. The concoction was homemade. They later introduced me to their nephews, Davide and Alberto, with whom I remain close friends to this day.

Following my two days of chemotherapy, my blood tests showed that my counts were in decline, as expected. The next thing the doctors needed to do was prepare Shana for her stem cell harvest. Jen offered to give her the daily shots of Neupogen she needed to stimulate stem cell production and get them circulating in her blood stream. This required Jen to leave my bedside earlier in the evening to get to Shana's apartment and administer the medication. Jen took to the task with her usual mix of nurturing and attention to detail, much as she tended to the proper care of my chest port, which still required fresh bandages every few days.

When Jen left early, I read chapters in *Dark Star Safari*, another non-fiction travel adventure by Paul Theroux. This one recounted his journey overland from Cairo, Egypt, to Cape Town, South Africa. It was a long, entertaining slog of a read. I had plenty of time on my hands to delve into Theroux's tales, which I particularly enjoyed because they were so far removed from my situation.

Shana came to the hospital to conduct her stem cell harvest on October 13, 2003. The doctors said that, because my counts were low and I was vulnerable to infection, I shouldn't visit her downstairs, nor leave my room in the Bone Marrow Transplant Unit on the tenth floor. Shana sat for her harvest on the third floor outpatient clinic. She had a sniffle at the time, so it was probably better that we didn't meet face-to-face. The harvest required that Shana be poked in each forearm with a large needle. It took about three hours to cycle Shana's blood through the aphaeresis machine, which filtered out the magic stem cells that would be inserted within me the following day. She seemed a little worn out from her cold, but otherwise expressed nothing but pride in being able to do this for her brother. The doctors complimented Shana on her large veins, she later told me over the phone. The following day, I would receive her stem cells and began the wait for her cells to graft in my marrow.

The day of Shana's stem cell collection also happened to be The Leukemia & Lymphoma Society's annual "Light the Night" walk, which is held in cities around the country. The New York walk goes to Brooklyn and back to Manhattan via the Brooklyn Bridge. Each participant carries a penlight that illuminates a red, helium-filled balloon. I'm told that the scene is dramatic, and the pictures I've seen are indeed pretty, though I've yet to walk in a "Light the Night" procession myself. I was represented in the walk by my family, Jen's family, and many friends. Having my stem cell transplant the next day was a poetic coincidence that made everyone feel warm-hearted.

I received many calls in my hospital room the following afternoon to congratulate me on my transplant, not that anyone believed all obstacles were behind me. It was still a significant milestone. The callers told me I was brave, that Jen was devoted and dedicated, and that our commitment to each other was inspiring. We'd heard these sentiments before, and they were welcome encouragement. But Jen and I knew that our strong front belied an shaky reality, rooted as it was in uncertain hopes for a brighter tomorrow. We never knew when the ground beneath us would crumble—and, in fact, for a little while at least in the weeks that followed, it all fell to pieces.

Roger and Milo, early 2004

Roger and Milo at Camp Little Pine, Lake Placid, June 2004

A home-cooked 31st for Roger, April 25, 2004

Roger and Dr. Shore on the BMT reunion cruise, July 2004

Peter and Roger in Nantucket, October 2004

Roger and "The Gates," Central Park, February 2005

Roger in his new apartment, May 2005

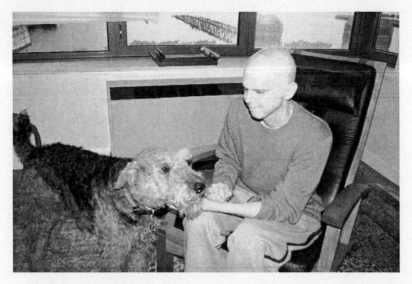

Roger and Milo at home, May 2005

Marion and Roger in British Columbia, July 2005

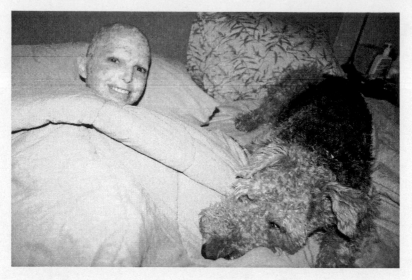

Roger and Milo keeping warm in bed, November 2005

Marion, Roger, Lois and Marty at Rebecca's 6th birthday party,
January 2006

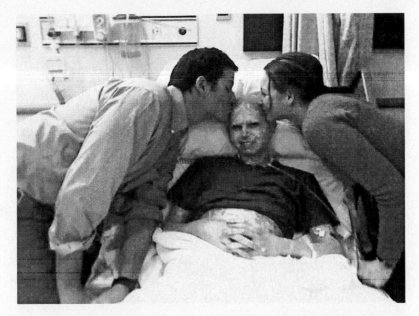

Noah, Roger and Jen in the hospital, April 2006

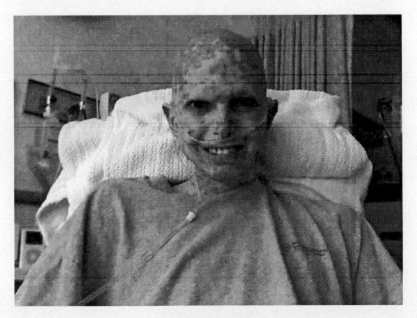

Roger sitting up in a chair in the hospital, April 2006

LEUKEMIA FOR CHICKENS

Part III:
Chronically Yours

22

The Beetle Begets the Rabbit

My second stem cell transplant became complicated when I came down with sepsis, an infection of the immune system that pervades the entire body. My sepsis infection arrived when I was at the most vulnerable stage of my transplant procedure: the period after the doctors had destroyed my body's natural ability to fight infections and after they had transfused me with the donor stem cells that would eventually constitute my new immune defenses—but before those cells had taken position in my marrow and matured into a functioning defense corps.

The process of rebuilding an immune system via a stem cell transplant takes about seven to ten days. To prevent infection in the interim, the doctors fed me a preventive dose of antibiotics and food that carried a low risk of harboring microbes. Doctors typically hold off on prescribing patients more potent medications until there is a sense that something is amiss.

Sepsis is difficult to treat because it does not lodge in any single place and is difficult to identify and target with drugs. Even with a healthy immune system, sepsis can cause widespread inflammation and lead to organ failure.

The first symptom of sepsis that I reported to my doctors, that I had "unusually cloudy vision," was vague. Yet very soon after I made that report, I was transferred from my isolation room in the Bone

Marrow Transplant Unit to the even-more-sterile Medical Intensive Care Unit five floors below, where I could be monitored more closely.

Just a few hours passed between my initial report to the doctors and my transfer, but my condition declined rapidly during that time. After the doctors departed, I ate bits of my breakfast: the usual cold cereal, warm oatmeal, banana and hard-boiled egg. Then I rose from bed and entered my private bathroom, rolling with me my ever-dripping IV pole, to wash myself down with a damp towel. That mild activity made me short of breath, par for the course at this phase of my treatment because I could not produce blood cells of any kind—red, white or otherwise. Every few days I received transfusions of red blood cells, which circulate oxygen, and of platelets, which clot blood in the event of a wound. Those transfusions kept me functioning at a low level. As for infection-fighting white blood cells, patients must do without them to the best of their ability. When my donor stem cells eventually grafted, my immune-defense capabilities would be restored.

I finished my wash-down and as I returned to my bed, my vision went from a cloudy haze to a dense fog. Everything became a shade of grey, with a bright spot at the center of my viewing field. It was the morning sun. It was a good thing that I was connected to my IV-pole, since I used it for support until tipping myself onto my mattress. I had just enough presence of mind to press the nurse call button.

"I feel weak. Please send a nurse."

A nurse arrived within minutes and did what all nurses do when they encounter a sick patient: she jabbed my ear with a digital thermometer. It beeped instantly and registered a temperature of more than 101.5 degrees Fahrenheit, at which point the medical handbook calls for blood cultures to be taken. The sample was extracted directly from a vein, not from my chest port. A vein sample, or needle prick, is preferred because it shows if an infection is in the patient's body, rather than in the port.

Blood cultures are grown in a Petri dish, and it takes time to yield results. The doctors just assumed my condition was bad enough to remand me to Intensive Care immediately, without a specific diagnosis. The diagnosis of sepsis came the following day.

Intensive Care is an odd-duck hospital unit, starting with the fact that the sound heard most frequently is a quacking akin to what one hears when looking up at a migrating flock. This squawking noise is unmistakable and intentionally intrusive because it is the call of a ventilator's alarm function, something that requires a nurse's immediate attention. Also, patient rooms in Intensive Care have no bathroom. Rarely do patients leave their beds. A flexible plastic bag mounted bedside collects urine via a catheter that goes you know where. Feces are deposited in a bedpan, or if a patient lacks the ability to wait for a bedpan to be placed, in a plastic bag pre-attached to his or her rear quarters with an adhesive donut. Given the complex contours of peoples' behinds, this latter solution is often inefficient. Good thing there are so many competent nurses in Intensive Care.

The nursing staff in Intensive Care is generally a hospital's best. Each is assigned no more than a few patients, compared with eight or ten patients in other units. Though they have fewer patients for whom to care, Intensive Care nurses have the most difficult workload, because they take responsibility for most every need of their patients. In Intensive Care, even bathing is done in bed. To keep patients warm while wet, the nurse activates heat lamps, like those found at hot entrée counters. Employing a trade skill, the nursing staff rolls patients left, then right, then left, as they apply fresh, dry sheets to the mattress. Patients in Intensive Care who have cognitive abilities would likely go crazy with boredom were it not for television. Even with that diversion, many still do.

My stay in Intensive Care was brief, just three days. Whatever powerful antibiotics the doctors administered, they managed to subdue my sepsis. I regained some strength and begged my doctors to return me to my corner room in the bone marrow transplant unit. To prove myself worthy, I made half a lap of the Intensive Care ward, after which the doctors agreed to return me to my room, 247-A on 10 West, the following day.

Though I was feeling better, everyone around me was finding their nerves fraying. I had spent almost a month this time in the hospital, mostly in my room in a bit of a fog, undergoing my second stem cell transplant. Everyone else had paced these same hospital halls for almost a year, without cease. Even my doctors, who had more than just my troubles to consider, started to lose it.

Dr. Roboz, my leukemia doctor who although no longer officially responsible for my care still kept close tabs on my progress, heard a story that the nurses in the bone marrow transplant unit had complained about my father. What Dr. Roboz heard had left her irate, but it turned out that the story had been mangled horribly as it was passed through the grapevine. What had really happened was quite funny.

My father had continued to leave a large bag of bagels for the nurses and aides every morning that I had been in the hospital. One morning that week, a nurse's aide came into my hospital room and held up a bialy to my father.

"What's this?" she asked him.

She had never seen a bagel that didn't have a hole in it. My father, a devout fan, explained that it was a bialy, a cousin of the bagel. It was made with eggs and was quite tasty. She should try one.

The aide said she already had tried it and agreed it was tasty. She politely asked my dad to include more of those onion-flavored treats in his daily dozen. My father was delighted to have spread the bialy gospel.

When Dr. Roboz heard the story, it wasn't put so sweetly. She was told that one of the aides had complained to my father about the selection of bagels and made specific requests for a different assortment than he had been bringing. The doctors responded by reprimanding the nurses and aides, telling them that they should just be thankful for whatever he brought. Dr. Roboz told my father that he should bring lumps of coal instead of bagels the following week. My father explained the conversation and assured everyone that he found the bialy appreciation endearing. Everything was smoothed over.

It takes a long time before such a relationship can develop between hospital staff, patients and visitors. My family tried to hone hospital visits to a science. Other than maintaining a schedule of "who would be where and at what time," we never figured out how to make everyone comfortable, including me. I found the schedule exhausting because I was "on call," so to speak, from 8 a.m. to 8 p.m., give or take an hour. Everyone felt helpless, but, wanting to be of use, they decided that simply having someone in the hospital room with me at all times might be worth something. It did help to have someone there when nurses couldn't be tracked down, but tensions often rose when a new party would arrive and the person already there would wonder whether it was appropriate to stay. Jen and I tried to explain that room 247-A wasn't just my hospital room, it was also our home for now. We needed time alone together. Beyond that, I needed time alone—by myself—too.

At about the four-week mark, my donor stem cells grafted and my counts slowly rose. Dr. Schuster, the head of the bone marrow transplant unit, surprised me one morning by handing me a folded Post-It note. I opened it and read out loud, "November 4." This was my scheduled release date.

I like it when people set dates as goals. But I understand why many are reluctant to do so, because the disappointment can be crushing if the preset goal is not met.

Dr. Schuster: "We'd like to send you home by then. But, remember, lots of patients come back to the hospital in a few weeks if they develop GvHD."

As I've explained, GvHD, the side effect of a donor stem cell transplant, occurs when your new immune system discovers that you are not the person you used to be. The immune system cries out "I want mommy!" and lashes out at its new host with guns blazing. Most allogeneic transplant recipients get some form of GvHD, but the range of severity is wide. Patients take a host of immunosuppressants in an attempt to keep the effects at bay. The hope, long-term, is that GvHD will "burn itself out" and that doctors will be able reduce the suppressive-drug load before debilitating side effects of the drugs occur.

That process takes time and is a principal reason why recovery from a donor stem cell transplant generally takes longer than recovery from an autologous one in which you receive your own cells back, thereby avoiding any rejection issues.

My personal bout with GvHD didn't take weeks or months to appear. It arrived almost as soon as my immune system kicked back into action. As the calendar turned towards November 2003, marking almost a month since I had begun my transplant procedure, I noticed I had newly developed diarrhea. I reported the runs to my doctors but did so dismissively, wanting to will this new wrinkle into non-existence. Though my runs persisted, my family and I all acted as if I were going home in a couple of days anyway. Jen and my parents packed my clothes and food, reducing in-room supplies to a minimum. The day before my scheduled leave date, I started to roll up the posters that adorned the mud-yellow walls of my hospital room: pictures of Lake Placid; a larger-than-life photo of Milo on the living room chaise; and an 8" x 10" of my cousin Ariel, bald from her own chemo, wearing boxing gloves and a big smile.

Late that afternoon, Adam made one of his regular visits. He asked me how I was feeling. I told him about my distressing bowel situation as I peeled sticky Fun-Tac off the backs of posters before rolling them into transport tubes.

"You realize you're not going to go home tomorrow."

"I guess. Maybe later this week. This will pass."

Clinging to my denial.

"I just don't want you to be disappointed when you find you have to stay. You know you can't go home feeling like this."

I acknowledged his point. He was right, I said, thanks for being honest. Adam left smiling.

Missing a date that had been set for me to leave affected everyone in the group. Before I entered the hospital, my parents had penciled in a trip to Florida for a business roundtable that my father was expected to attend. The trip was scheduled for the weekend following my anticipated release. The trip could have been canceled, but my parents hadn't done so. They probably hoped that not canceling showed an optimism that everything would turn out okay and I would be able leave the hospital as planned. We all needed a break from each other by then, in any event.

My condition grew worse as my scheduled release day arrived, and then passed. I developed a skin rash, from which the doctors took a biopsy that would confirm whether the cell formation suggested GvHD. My parents' trip was looming, and my father asked me if mom and he should stay in New York.

Me: "No, you should go."

There was nothing more they could do, I said, continuing to deny my worsening situation. It was true that there was little my parents could do for my physical state. What I didn't get was that if they stayed behind, they could help carry some of the load borne by people outside of the hospital staff, like Jen.

Jen saw clearly that I was deteriorating mentally. She told my parents that it was not the time for them to leave. Since my parents hadn't developed as close a relationship with Dr. Shore as Jen and I had, they sought counsel from Dr. Roboz instead.

Dr. Roboz assured my parents that I would be okay under the doctors' supervision and that it was okay for them to leave for a few days. They could always fly back sooner than planned if something changed. My parents left for Florida, and my condition continued to deteriorate, both physically and mentally. Thirty-six hours later, Jen summoned my parents back to New York.

At the time I was unaware of this jockeying, which played itself out in hospital hallways, waiting rooms, and over the phone. All I knew was that my father came to see me one morning at 6 a.m. and asked how I was doing. I was surprised but happy that he had returned, not capable of understanding the background machinations, which were only related to me after my condition improved.

Meantime, while I lay semi-conscious, emotions among my family were seething. Jen was angry because my parents had chosen to leave at a critical moment, against her wishes. Everyone felt helpless and unable to provide support. In retrospect, I marvel more at Jen's endurance in standing vigil than I question my parents' gasp for air.

One reason that I knew things were getting worse was that I overheard the doctors discussing a new blood count they were watching closely in my daily tests. That latest "hot number" was my bilirubin, a liver enzyme that rises in value when the liver isn't functioning properly. A normal measure of bilirubin is about 1.0 on whatever scale doctors employ. In early November, my bilirubin rose to about seven. Many people know bilirubin rises in newborns as high as 15, but in adults anything above even half of that level can be life-threatening.

My hospital stay stretched into its fifth week, and I grew depressed about my static surroundings. Jen asked my friend Noah to visit and try to soothe me. Noah sat beside me, patted my back, and listened as I rambled about how restless I felt. As I spoke, I ripped apart pages from a magazine called *Bell' Italia*. Its thick-stock, laminated pages made good fodder for tearing into smaller and smaller squares. Other times, I punched pillows to beat out excess energy. A hospital psychiatrist also came by daily to talk to me about how I felt.

"Do you want to hurt yourself?"

"No."

"Why not?"

"That would be pointless."

Thus it was determined that, although depressed, I didn't need to be moved to the locked psychiatric ward and put on around-the-clock suicide watch. The psych unit was one of only three hospital floors I'd yet to visit since being diagnosed with leukemia. In total, the Greenberg Pavilion had eleven floors. Number nine housed the hospital's ventilation units and was also used to store broken beds and old medical equipment. I had been on seven, the maternity ward, as an outpatient when our friends Lauren and Tom had their first son, Ben. It was joyful, but difficult, visiting them in the hospital: Lauren and Tom had just started dating a few weeks before the night I first met Jen, and yet here we were years later, unable to ignore what radically different paths our lives had taken.

In place of twenty-four hour supervision, the doctors prescribed Haldol for me, a potent anti-psychotic drug. That put me to sleep, which was my preferred coping mechanism during that time, in any event. Contributing to my depression was the fact that I was too restless to sleep. After I went on Haldol—and later Zyprexa and Trazidone, two other anti-depressives—I don't recall much of what transpired in the following week. I remember my therapist, to whom I'd been talking for the past three years, came by to say hello and offer support. She woke me up, and I asked her why she had come to see me in the middle of the night. It was actually 4 p.m.

Another night, after all my visitors had left, a nurse stopped in to check my blood pressure and heart rate, something that was done every six hours, around the clock. We talked briefly, and I learned she was French-Guyanese. She wore a large gold cross and asked if she could say a prayer for me. I assumed she meant in her church, and I said yes, please do. She placed her hand on my leg, closed her eyes, and for about a minute sang a lovely hymn that I assumed was French in language and Catholic in spirit.

Short of that pleasing respite, my battle with GvHD, confirmed by the skin biopsy, was harrowing and lasted almost two weeks. Then, for whatever reason—the mix of medications, time, burnout, what-have-you—my bilirubin stopped rising. It peaked somewhere around 8.0 and then slowly receded. I gained some strength again. Others told me my jaundice had also faded. I got over a hump mentally, and was able once again to see over the horizon.

The doctors presented me with a new release date: November 25—three weeks after my initial release date, seven weeks after I began treatment for my second stem cell transplant, and almost exactly a year from the day that I was first diagnosed with leukemia. I would make that date. Unlike 2002, in 2003 I would eat a Thanksgiving dinner at home, at a table in my apartment. What a year.

· · ·

My second transplant experience—my whole leukemia battle, in fact—recalls for me the masterful advertising campaign developed for Volkswagen's Beetle—the most successful, beloved car in history. The Beetle is considered the archetypical product sold using modern marketing techniques. That is, the car's endearing flaws were presented as being as important from a marketing perspective as were its merits. Through cramped, it had a cute shape. The engineering was oddball, with a motor placed in the back of the car, behind the rear wheels. No matter. The Beetle's idiosyncrasies made it that much more alluring.

VW moved more than twenty-one million Beetles off dealer lots over three decades. Better cars came and went, but none sold as well as the Beetle. Late in its run, Beetle marketers created a keen ad for their still-hot product: on a plain white backdrop, a silhouette of the Beetle's classic double-egg shape. Beneath it, black text asked, "How long can we keep giving you this line?"

Forever, it seemed, at the time. But affection fades when people decide the object of their affections lacks substance. The Beetle's flaws began to grate, with familiarity and the passage of time.

All but die-hard aficionados grew weary of the long-term relationship. And so VW retired the Beetle after thirty years of putting it on the market annually with minimal changes, starting during the War in the 1940s. Its successor arrived in 1974 and was radically different. Soft curves had frozen into squared edges; engineers moved the engine to the front bay, where it was more accessible and efficient. The new model was spacious and comfortable.

U.S. marketers of the Beetle understood the shift in the public's priorities and adapted the successor accordingly. They created a fresh sales pitch that was attuned to the virtues of the new car. Nostalgia wouldn't do. This daring new automobile wouldn't, couldn't, be loved like the old Beetle. There would be no *Herbie, The Love Bug* edition. The new car, which VW named the "Golf" in Europe, was hard-nosed, grown-up. Its greatest selling point, plain and simple, was this: it was better.

As was I, finally, after a year of fighting leukemia. For that battle, I had armed myself with what I hoped was an endearing, can-do spirit. The strategy worked, but the emotional rollercoaster on which it placed me had taken its toll. And on my supporters, since rooting for an underdog can provide great thrills, but banking on a winner is much easier on the psyche. My better self, my healed self, might not be as lovable as my original self—leukemia had chiseled too many hard lines in me for me to maintain a soft-edged façade—but it would earn the respect of its peers for its newfound durability and sensibility.

The clever marketers at VW must have viewed the challenge of selling the new Beetle to America in a similar fashion. The first thing they did was get rid of its bland "Golf" appellation, choosing instead, brilliantly, the "Rabbit."

The Rabbit. A leap forward. (My words, not theirs.)

And while leaps forward may be courageous, they come with caveats—the most notorious being, "Look first."

23

Grates and Stones
May Break My Bones

After spending those seven weeks in the hospital receiving my stem cell transplant, going home didn't feel as I'd expected it would, because my home didn't seem the same to me. Even my couch seemed lumpy. But the couch hadn't changed its form while I was in the hospital. It was my rear that had lost cushioning, a result of me sitting on my backside for weeks on end, as well as having lost significant weight again.

It wasn't just my couch that felt different. Our whole apartment seemed out of proportion. Before I entered the hospital, I considered the distance between my couch and the refrigerator a mere sidestep, if I thought about it at all. Now the path included a distinct right, then a left, and another left. In the hospital I had everything I needed to survive within arm's reach. Anything beyond that could be brought to me by a guest or by a nurse on call. I was rarely alone.

In my apartment, I needed to make a concerted effort just to grab a bottle of water from the fridge. The task involved thought, planning, and a summoning of will in order to be executed. Often I would decide that maybe I wasn't so thirsty after all. Better I should watch that show Jen had "TiVo-ed" the previous evening. Our cable TV provider had installed a digital video recorder in my absence. All that I needed to do to watch the show that had been recorded was to press a few buttons on the TV remote. Even that task seemed hard. So many Chiclet-colored keys on that silvery candy bar! As I studied the remote, the word *telecommando* popped into my head. That's "TV remote" translated into Italian. Apparently my brain now registered the TV remote as some kind of foreign object.

The world hadn't changed much since I'd last encountered it. Yet in less than two months I'd lost a sense of everything around me. At least I found a way to understand my feeling of alienation. I recognized it as being akin to the reaction I had seen in some movies of felons who are released from jail. Specifically, I thought about Morgan Freeman in *The Shawshank Redemption*. In that movie, when Red, Freeman's character, was released, the film showed scenes of him starting again to go about daily tasks in the outside world. The camera framed Red's face; his look was troubled. He was baffled by his surroundings, which appeared ordinary to the audience.

Like Red, who had spent years in jail, I, too, had become "institutionalized," though admittedly not to such a degree. I had become dependent on others to complete the activities necessary for daily life. I couldn't just reassume my old responsibilities without taking time to reorient myself. Everything that I was feeling warned me that I should be measured in my actions. But I was impatient, and rushed headlong into the world. My lack of caution had predictable consequences, bad ones.

My first misstep, literally, came in December, less than two weeks after I was released from the hospital. To get me moving faster, Jen and I decided to buy an elliptical training machine. This device would help me build my stamina safely. We reasoned that a treadmill was dangerous, because I would need to lift my legs from the running strip. On an elliptical machine, my feet would rotate but never leave their position in the stirrups. In retrospect, musing over an exercise machine at this stage of my recovery was pure delusion. The reality was that walking the hallways was probably challenge enough for me.

On our first visit to the fitness equipment store, I tried to test one elliptical model, but, fearful that I would fall over, I was unable to maneuver myself into the stirrups. Jen and I left the store, vowing to return the following week. On our second visit to the fitness store, I didn't even make it to the front door. When I stepped out of the back seat of the car onto the curb, I slipped on a mound of shoveled ice. As I fell, I caught my pinky in a storm grate.

Before Jen could lift me from the sidewalk, I glanced at my finger's awkward position, wedged between the bars of the grate. It wasn't natural. I probably had broken a bone. Shit. As Jen lifted me, she screamed that I should have waited for her to assist me out of the car. I could have really hurt myself, perhaps broken my hip. As it was, something in my body probably was in need of repair. We went immediately to Adam's office. A nurse took an X-ray of my hand. A physical examination suggested no other areas of my body had been affected, that I had broken only my pinky. Nothing terrible, said Adam, who fitted me with a foam splint and sent me home.

"Just take it easy there, big guy. Stick to the pavement, and stay off the exercise machines for now."

As a precaution, Adam sent my X-ray to a hand surgeon for a second opinion. That doctor was less sanguine about my fracture. By his reckoning, it was one of those rare breaks in a finger that would actually require surgery. He would need to insert a pin into my finger to steady the bone and reset it, so that it would heal properly. If I didn't undergo surgery, my little finger would likely remain permanently crooked and inept, the doctor said, preventing me from making a tight fist or holding a pen. As if surgery weren't enough of a hardship, for three weeks after the operation I would have to wear a plaster cast as protection. Dr. Nolan made a cup formation with his hand to guesstimate the thickness of the cast. I judged it as about the size of a caveman's club.

Me: "Not so small."

Dr. Nolan: "Casts are not something I receive compliments about very often."

After my cast was removed, I would undergo six weeks of hand therapy to rebuild the muscles that had atrophied while I was in the cast.

I needed the surgery. All the doctors agreed. I had it done the next week.

Stupid friggin' elliptical machine. I guessed I would chalk up that blunder as yet another instance in which Roger makes life more difficult than it need be. Like the time when I was thirteen: I walked off a plane that was about to depart, and the plane left for Florida without me. Why did I get off the plane, leaving my friend Russell behind? To buy a magazine, of course.

Me, to mom on the phone: "But the stewardess said it was okay to go get a magazine."

Mom: "She thought you meant a magazine from the front of the plane, not the newsstand."

Moron. I begged my way on to another flight that took off six hours after my originally scheduled flight. My parents' friends drove back to the Florida airport a second time to retrieve me.

Or there was that time in Italy when I borrowed my landlord's Nissan Sentra, only to have to abandon the car in a mud flat in some nameless valley in Chianti.

Giulio, my landlord: "You thought that was a road? The farmer who towed my car out with his tractor said he hadn't seen a person drive down that trail since the War." (He was referring to the Second World War).

I have many such stories in my past. Sure, those goofball foibles of mine caused aggravation when they happened, but the anger of the aggrieved parties dissipated with every opportunity they had to recount another "Roger" tale. Everyone would have a good belly laugh at my expense. Because my sorry antics rarely caused long-term damage, they would often endear me to people. Did it matter if the emotion they felt was akin to pity? Well, yes, if I wanted to be treated like an adult rather than a child.

I was at a strange point in my life to feel a need to stake a claim to independence. I was as helpless to survive on my own at that moment as at any time since I was a toddler. And the fallout that could result from a mere pinky break proved that I couldn't laugh my troubles away so easily anymore. I would learn from my missteps, though not immediately. My leukemia may have been in remission, but nothing doctors prescribed could save me from self-inflicted wounds. A person has to cure that ailment on his or her own. I finally got the message three weeks later, after I made my next misstep.

Me, to the heavens: "I hear you, now: 'Look before you leap'."

As December 2003 snowballed into frigid January 2004, the frosty temperatures took nobody by surprise. The weather forecasters were right on the money. They had accurately predicted record cold, and the Polar Express descended from Canada on schedule.

Me, to Jen: "We need to get out of here. My bones will shatter in this weather."

Jen: "Where to? You can't fly."

Me: "We can go if we take a small plane. I'll ask my dad if we can go to the house in Palm Beach."

"That's crazy."

"Crazier than being cooped up here, where it's too cold to move? It'll be okay. My dad will go for it. He wants us to be able to get away."

"I don't think I can take care of you down there by myself. My mom needs to come with us, at least."

Jen's mom, Lois, had recently retired from teaching in the New York City school system after twenty-five years. Her schedule was open for the time being. Jen's dad was in North Carolina on business. He could meet us in Florida that weekend. My parents planned to come down to Palm Beach the following weekend. There would be space for all of us, in any event.

Me: "It's fine with me if your mom comes."

Jen: "What about Milo?"

"Let's take him, too. Let's just get out of here."

Jen was sold.

To be honest, neither Jen nor I are big fans of Palm Beach. It's a great place to visit, or even to live, if your wish is not be perturbed. The manicured landscapes are immaculate and the conversation drifts toward sleepy platitudes about inconsequential topics—inconsistent golf swings, fickle weather, and the like. Thus Palm Beach is flattened emotionally, much as the region's contoured geography is smoothed over by Florida's uniformly rectilinear byways.

Jen and I put together our itinerary in twenty-four hours. Jen, Lois, Milo and I flew via Cessna Excel Jet to Palm Beach International Airport and drove ten minutes to my parents' house, located on the barrier island off Florida's coast. We arrived just after sundown, January 6.

I was still wearing my pinky cast, which I'd dubbed my brontosaurus bone, because it looked to me like a shank that Fred Flintstone might eat for dinner. When we arrived at my parents' house, I was eager to show Milo his vacation home. Too eager; I grabbed Milo's leash, something I hadn't done since leaving the hospital, and walked him through the glass-paned front door.

"Look at your living room. So much space, Milo."

The front door closed back on itself. Jen knocked on the door to be let in. Milo looked back, seeing Mommy with Grandmommy behind her. He lunged for the door.

I tried to let go of his leash, but the hand-loop couldn't slip over the fat end of my cast.

Jen (watching helplessly as I am felled like a tree): "Oh, no."

Ker-smack!

Milo's rush to the door yanked me down to the cement-floored hallway of my parents' vacation home.

Oh, yes. And shit! That hurt. You Dumbass.

It was fortunate for us, at that most unfortunate moment, that the person responsible for maintaining the house, Cheryl, was present. She gave us directions to the nearest hospital, Good Samaritan, which was across the Intra-coastal Waterway in West Palm Beach, about fifteen minutes away.

As far as hospitals go, Good Samaritan had the spit and polish, as well as the efficiency, one would expect in an upscale, suburban community like West Palm Beach. While New York is presumed to have the best medical care—the best of everything, in fact—its actual facilities rarely match the physical sheen of other hospitals around the country. I probably was in as good hands in Palm Beach as anywhere. The area is full of retirement-age people. Broken hips are as common as a case of the flu. The doctor on call said I had an "impaction" fracture of my hip, based on the X-ray he took. I translated the rest of his diagnosis as: "This sucks, and it hurts. But there's probably nothing anyone can do about it but let it heal."

I would be able to move around with the assistance of a walker, then later, a cane. Jen and I talked with another doctor in Palm Beach and a specialist in New York as well. The initial diagnosis became the consensus. At least my hip wasn't going to turn out like my pinky and require surgery. Still, the healing process was no picnic. Jen and I stretched our long weekend in Palm Beach to eleven days. That was the time it took for me to become mobile enough to board even a private plane back to New York.

Word of my bonehead maneuver traveled fast. Of course the story of my fall got garbled in the retelling, making me look like an even bigger fool.

Dr. Roboz, over the phone: "I heard you fell off a *skateboard*?! What were you thinking? You can barely walk."

Me: "I didn't say to your assistant, 'I fell off a skateboard.' I said, 'I fell onto a stone floor.' Was the phone connection that bad?"

"Oh. Well, how did that happen?"

"Milo knocked me over."

"I don't want to know any more. Just get better, and get home."

"I know. I feel like a jerk as it is. Not that I mind lying here on this veranda. I just wish Jen's father didn't need to walk me here from the den."

After breaking my pinky and my hip, I finally understood that my desire to return to normal exceeded my ability to do so. I curtailed my ambitions in the months that followed, applying "look before you leap" to every aspect of my recovery. In the process of taking a more careful approach to my recovery, I didn't anticipate that my difficulties might increase, regardless. As I did less, I experienced fewer mishaps, but I sensed I wasn't keeping on top of new complications that arose and made returning to normal more difficult.

Prednisone's deleterious side effects weren't limited to weak bones. My continued use of the drug also cut my enzyme production, as predicted. In March, an endocrinologist told me that I was temporarily diabetic, meaning that I had high levels of sugar in my blood, because my pancreas wasn't producing enough natural insulin. I would need to monitor my carbohydrate intake and give myself insulin shots to keep my blood sugar level in normal range, which was around 100.

A high blood sugar level would make me fatigued, while a low blood sugar level would cause cold sweats and shakes. The latter symptoms, which resulted from accidentally overdosing on insulin, occurred rarely, but were the more debilitating of the two.

Even before I was classified as temporarily diabetic, I had been spending an inordinate amount of time thinking about my food intake. I needed to eat a lot to reclaim lost pounds. In early 2004 I was lucky to weigh in at 135 pounds, more than twenty-five pounds below my pre-morbid weight. While I needed to pack in as much food as possible, my eating options were still limited to cooked foods and dry or baked goods, with a few exceptions. And still, the doctors said that it wasn't safe for me to eat in restaurants.

As Dr. Shore colorfully put it, "The busboy could have sneezed on that plate right before he put it in front of you."

To that burden I would now add being diabetic, monitoring my carbohydrates, measuring my blood-sugar level using a finger stick, and then giving myself a shot of insulin so that my level remained within normal range.

I wasn't alone in my eating-awareness campaigns. Jen watched over my eating like a hawk. Not that she had to conduct covert investigations to know what I ate. Jen prepared half of my meals, if not more.

She might have made every one—a lame hip made it difficult for me to remain standing and prepare food—had Jen and I not received a godsend of a gift from my Uncle Bernie and Aunt Ruth. When we returned to New York, we were given the use of a personal chef, Diana, who was employed by an elderly man named Norman, a dear and generous friend of my aunt and uncle.

Diana cooked for us four, sometimes five nights a week. She normally worked in Norman's New York City apartment, even though he spent most of his time on a boat in Florida and hadn't been back in three years. She had been cooking for other family members and his staff, until we came along. Diana packed our meals in Tupperware and brought them to our apartment for us to reheat in a microwave.

This luxury-beyond-compare provided an essential break for Jen and me. Most importantly, Diana's cooking took some of the burden off Jen. Also, with Jen not catering to my every need, I could delude myself into believing I was at least somewhat capable of living independently—with Jen's assistance. If I hadn't been able to believe I had some independence, I would have felt like the helpless child that, in truth, I was at that point. Such a dynamic could have wrecked our marriage. Diana's assistance helped me to see myself as Jen's husband, not her dependent, and to feel that we, as a couple, could survive independent of our friends and family—even as her services to us proved the fallacy of that notion. At a minimum, Diana made delicious meals and was a cheerful person to have around.

From watching my food intake to considering every step I took, my life became premeditated in the extreme. I was meticulously conscious of my actions in whatever moment I existed. For example, I mapped the day so that I was never more than three hours from a meal.

After a couple of bad breaks to start the year, I adjusted to maintaining a schedule, and my recovery proceeded steadily, if slowly. If there was disappointment in my decision to focus intensely on the present, it centered on this: that amorphous date I'd flagged in my mental calendar, sometime in late spring or early summer. That date I'd circled in red with the word "normalcy" written inside. That date faded farther into the future.

LEUKEMIA FOR CHICKENS

24

Dare I Eat a Peach?

For every precaution I took to protect my health, my efforts amounted to a fraction of the work required. Preparing dinner wasn't as simple as having someone chop me a salad, and our chef-on-loan, Diana, had to quickly learn the rules. Likewise, when the doctors told me I shouldn't be around plants because the soil might contain bacteria that could lead to an infection, Jen and I removed our plants from the windowsill in our apartment. But we didn't want to just throw them away. My restrictions were expected to last only about six months so we asked our neighbors to serve as foster parents for our three large plants until I healed.

No doctor had to tell me I needed to hone my skills of persuasion to facilitate my recovery; yet what I found was that I required the helping hand of others to carry out almost every task in my daily schedule. The role I needed others to play was significant, and many of the people—from neighbors to shopkeepers—whom I asked for assistance had little reason, other than sympathy, to help me. I did what I could to convince people that I wasn't as great a burden as I really was. I worked on this as much I worked on finding ways to help myself.

Put in the proper context, my requests for assistance were well-received. Most people were happy to oblige, as long as I didn't ask any single person for assistance too often. I risked crossing that line only with a few close friends and family members. In particular, I asked a lot of Jen.

I had too much pride to tell all the people around me that their efforts were so vital because I was weak and frail. To deflect my guilt for having to ask so many favors, I often qualified my requests with the exculpatory phrase, "Sorry. It's doctors' orders." I played the term "doctors' orders" like a trump card whenever I sensed any resistance to my instructions. It worked like a charm.

If only I cowed before my doctors' orders to the degree everyone around me did. I was always looking for ways to circumvent my restrictions. I knew they were designed to keep me healthy, but they often denied me the ability to enjoy some of life's simplest pleasures. What was more frustrating was the fact that enjoying those pleasures had served as an incentive for me to fight my leukemia. On occasion, I broke the rules outright. More than once, I ate a slice of pizza from the pizza parlor—a serious infraction in my doctors' eyes. I couldn't resist the temptation to bite into a cheesy, greasy slice. Especially when that pleasure called out to me from every street corner.

My doctors' orders put restrictions on many different aspects of my life. I couldn't enter crowded rooms, like movie theaters or sports arenas, because those places were bound to contain one person or another who had a cold that could be transmitted to me. If I wanted to see a movie, it would have to be at a weekday matinee of a film that had been in theaters for a few weeks at least so that attendance would likely be light. My doctors also instructed me to avoid small children because their noses were always running. I couldn't ride buses or subways. And of course, I couldn't eat out at restaurants, as the food couldn't be trusted to be sanitary.

In addition to cooked foods and fruits with a hard rind, most pre-packaged foods—cookies, pretzels, canned corn, etc.—were also permitted. For that reason, I often snacked on cold cereal and cut bananas. To satisfy my salad craving, Jen would make a bowl of artichoke hearts, avocado, and hearts of palm for me. Our neighbor, Julie, who had also had a stem cell transplant and was familiar with my restrictions, dropped off a homemade banana bread shortly after I came home from the hospital.

I also ate a lot of cheese to help with weight gain. Any cheese I ate needed to be pasteurized. That wasn't a significant constraint, although gorgonzola, among some other gourmet cheeses, wasn't allowed. There were a few strange prohibitions on the doctors' list, including miso, a fermented soybean derivative. Fermentation requires bacteria, I learned. I couldn't eat honey either. Apparently honey can carry bacteria as well. In some cases, my restrictions were similar to ones that my female friends followed while they were pregnant—only quirkier.

Occasionally Jen threw in an eating restriction of her own, on top of what my doctors' forbade. In early 2004, Jen didn't want me to eat beef—raw or cooked. She put that rule in place after hearing a news report that a steer out west was found rubbing himself oddly against a tree. That future sirloin steak was diagnosed with "Mad Cow disease," the mysterious ailment that was linked to a few dozen human deaths in England in the 1990s. Since she was the one doing most of the shopping and cooking, I soon became a connoisseur of lamb varietals, including rack, shoulder, and top loin.

My eating restrictions were expected to remain in place for at least six months following my stem cell transplant in late 2003. The doctors didn't offer a precise date for when they would be lifted since that would depend on when I stopped taking immune-suppressive medications.

I believed my doctors when they told me that I would be free of my restrictions in half a year, even though virtually nothing about my battle against leukemia had so far conformed to the experience of the average patient. But for me to think that the restrictions would last longer than six months would have been needlessly depressing.

It was bad enough that my sister's donated immune system was doing its job too well, fighting not only my leukemia, but many healthy body parts, starting with my liver. The most serious consequence was that I was drained of energy. Later bouts hurt my gastro-intestinal tract, lungs and skin. The medication I took to suppress my immune system's fighting ways simultaneously limited my ability to stave off infection. My systemic weakness, both internal and external, was what prompted my doctors to set such strict limits on my actions.

For the most part, I did follow my doctors' orders closely. I was scared enough for my health not to regard them casually. When I didn't follow their orders to the letter, I justified my actions as still following the "spirit" of the rules. For example, I rationalized that a pizza oven was so hot it would kill any bacteria, so eating a slice was reasonably safe, if not completely so.

I also made quite a game of figuring out ways to expand my eating options within the limits of my restrictions. If my restrictions were a list of "don'ts" (i.e. don't eat raw meat), I thought about "do's." For example, did a runny poached egg qualify as cooked? Is smoked salmon considered cooked? If the answer to both questions was "yes," then *voila!* Eggs Florentine was back on the menu. (I knew the dish's other key ingredients—sautéed spinach and toasted muffins—passed muster. And I figured I could concoct a safe version of hollandaise sauce as well.)

The game, however, wasn't as simple as just convincing me that it was okay to eat something. I had to get Jen on my side. If my interpretations of my eating restrictions constituted a form of "judicial activism," then Jen's philosophy fell into the category of "strict construction." Jen feared my efforts to expand the scope of the rules risked heading down a slippery slope where I might deem almost anything permissible to eat. Jen had good reason to keep me on a tight leash. After all, if I fell ill in an attempt to satisfy a fleeting craving, she would also suffer consequences.

When Jen and I reached an impasse as to what fit within my eating restrictions, we knew better than to fight over it. Instead, we turned to Dr. Shore for an objective ruling, since her Bone Marrow Transplant unit had devised the restrictions. Did she really have in her head the specific answers she gave us to our arcane food inquiries? It wasn't likely. It was more probable that she just permitted me to eat something that was off the chart but relatively safe from time to time— throwing me a life preserver, in effect, when I appeared desperate.

I won the case in favor of Eggs Florentine. I lost many others, including one where I tried to convince Dr. Shore that a cucumber rind was indeed hard, longing to eat the crisp green flesh within. I missed biting into fresh food items like cucumbers. When all of the ingredients in a meal have to be cooked, it's hard to replicate that taste and texture.

If it seems odd to put so much energy into fighting to eat a cucumber, consider that eating was one of the few pleasures available to me at that time. I posed new food questions to Dr. Shore almost every week when I went to the hospital for my checkup. At each visit, a nurse drew blood that was analyzed to measure my progress. Knowing I would suffer a weekly "pin prick"—a euphemism uttered by all phlebotomists just before they insert their needle—made me less than enthusiastic about my weekly checkup. In addition, I was often anxious about the results of my tests, which were available about twenty minutes after I gave blood. It was those tests that had provided the first sign of my relapse in 2003. After my second transplant, some other tests showed "poor counts," which made the wait for the following week's results nerve-wracking. None ever suggested a relapse, however. Eventually, I stopped asking for the actual results of the tests, instructing Dr. Shore to alert me only if the trend of my results had changed direction.

In addition to the prospect of Dr. Shore adding new foods to my diet, I had another reason to look forward to my weekly checkup. Afterwards, I was allowed to eat in the hospital cafeteria. That might not seem like something to celebrate to most people, but the hospital cafeteria was the only venue where I was allowed to "eat out," since the food there was prepared to a high standard of cleanliness. I could eat from the cafeteria whatever I pleased, as long as I stayed within my restrictions.

Each week, Jen and I took the elevator down to the basement level, where the windowless, fluorescent-lit cafeteria was housed. The cafeteria was somewhere between an institutional food outlet and a contemporary food court. There were food items under hot lamps sitting next to counters staffed by chefs ready to prepare orders. I scoured the options available to find some heretofore forbidden menu item.

I knew the self-service salad and pasta bars were off-limits. It was okay, on the other hand, to order food from the deli counter. There, I could request a turkey and cheese sandwich without lettuce or tomato. A side of pickles was also okay under my restrictions, I learned, because the pickling process eliminated the risk.

But what about that Sushi Guy to the left of the deli stand? Sure, I knew raw sushi was a no-no. But some sushi is cooked, I reasoned, like crab, eel, and shrimp, for example.

Me, to Jen: "Maybe Shore will go for it."

Jen: "No way."

A week later, Dr. Shore ruled in my favor. It was my biggest victory yet, even if she had some caveats.

Dr. Shore: "[Sushi Guy] needs to prepare the rolls in front of you. You need to tell him to wash his knife beforehand. And make sure that your food doesn't touch any raw fish."

As usual, Jen and I went straight from Dr. Shore's third-floor clinic to the hospital cafeteria. I would have run if I could have. This time, I approached the sushi counter and greeted the sushi chef.

"Can I ask you a favor? It's a little unusual, I know. But it's doctor's orders."

The chef smiled. His English wasn't terrific, but he made it clear he wanted to help. Jen and I repeated our order a few times to make sure Sushi Guy understood my situation. Sushi Guy then prepared for me maki rolls of cooked crab and eel, as well as three pieces of shrimp sushi. One of my biggest cravings had been sated.

Thereafter, I returned to Sushi Guy for lunch whenever I had a doctor's appointment in the hospital—sometimes twice a week or more, and sometimes when I was just in the neighborhood. I became a regular. Soon I would approach Sushi Guy's counter, and he would call out my order to me in advance:

"One California roll, no cucumber. One eel-avocado roll. Three piece shrimp sushi. No wasabi. No problem."

One day, I ate my sushi lunch at one of the tables near the front entrance to the hospital. I was interrupted by a fellow leukemia patient who was under the same eating restrictions as I was.

Leslie: "You're eating sushi?"

Me: "It's okay, It's all cooked. Dr. Shore approved it."

"I've got to get in on this."

A month later, Jen ran into Sushi Guy in the hospital lobby. I was upstairs for my checkup at the time. Jen said, "hello" and Sushi Guy said, "goodbye."

Jen: "What do you mean?"

Sushi Guy explained that he had lost his station to a competitor who offered the hospital a bigger profit.

"Maybe next year," Sushi Guy said.

He paused, leaned into Jen, and added, "They use frozen shrimp." He shook his head.

A "Go Sushi" franchise moved into Sushi Guy's station that day. Service was never the same.

• • •

The temptation to break my restrictions was ever present. In our apartment, where I spent most of my time during my recovery, Jen kept a bowl on the dining room table filled with fresh fruit. Each week, Jen stocked the bowl with nectarines, apples, oranges, peaches and bananas, depending on what was in season. The selection in the bowl wasn't entirely forbidden to me since I could eat bananas and oranges. But dare I indulge in that juicy peach?

The peach in our fruit basket sang to me a siren's song that recalled my favorite poem: "The Love Song of J. Alfred Prufrock," by T.S. Eliot. To say that I have a favorite poem is to say that I don't know much about poetry. Ask me which is my favorite car, a topic in which I consider myself expert, and I wouldn't be able to give a straight answer. I would need to inquire first, "A car for what purpose? Do you mean my favorite two-seater for going to the beach, or my top carryall to transport a family to a mountain getaway? Are we talking contemporary cars or classic models?"

Likewise, if someone were to ask me which is the best movie of all time, I would need to ask for specificity: "Do you mean my favorite action flick, or comedy?" The two genres are different enough as to be incomparable, kind of like apples and oranges.

Few are the poems I have read that aren't among those selected for *Norton's Anthology*, a reference book of poetry that I was given when I took an English literature class in my senior year of high school. My limited base of knowledge gives me the confidence to proclaim a hands-down favorite: That is, "Prufrock."

In Eliot's poem, Prufrock laments not indulging in life's richness, because he fears that reality will fall short of his dreams. Thus he lives on the margins, experiencing few highs and lows. Late in the poem, he asks, "Do I dare to eat a peach?"

In early 2004, I found Prufrock's fear of eating fruit amusingly literal. His larger conundrum also mirrored my dilemma: What price indulgence? Prufrock feared stepping out of his normal routine – a life measured in "coffee spoons," as Eliot puts it. My fear was for my health. Many people would say that the risk posed to Prufrock paled in comparison. I can see our plights as equal.

Though my restrictions—that is, my doctors' orders—were devised to protect me, they weren't foolproof. Were I to forego the peach, I might have a better chance of staying healthy, yet I might yet fall ill for one reason or another. Restraining myself offered no guarantees and I wouldn't savor the peach's juicy sweetness.

Prufrock, as well, knows he is vulnerable regardless of his action or inaction:

I have seen the moment of my greatness flicker,
And I have seen the eternal Footman hold my coat, and snicker.

The question for Prufrock, and for me, was this: What if the peach weren't so great after all? Where would I be then? Maybe it was better to savor the temptation rather than the taste.

I never ate any of those peaches in the fruit basket. I owed my restraint less to self-discipline than to my doctors' decision to ease my restrictions over time. By spring of 2004, I was taking lower doses of immunosuppressants than earlier that year. This gave the doctors comfort enough to allow me a few extra liberties. Many of these new privileges came in the form of rulings by Dr. Shore, such as the decision in April to let me sip champagne and eat caviar on my birthday.

By Memorial Day, I was feeling relatively solid. I had recovered from my hip injury in January and was walking without a cane. Jen and I looked at the calendar and saw a window open for us to leave New

York City and take refuge in Lake Placid. We rented a house and planned to stay for six weeks. That getaway, our longest period outside Manhattan in years, went surprisingly well, health-wise. We took Milo, who loved the outdoors. The owner of the house initially said "no pets allowed," but relented after I told him that Milo was vital to my recovery—another twist on that old "doctors' orders" routine. We also assured him that Milo was house-broken and would not mistake the many tree trunks decorating the Adirondack-style home for real ones that he would mark outdoors. Milo was a true city dog and preferred marking car tires to tree trunks any day.

     Jen and I knew we couldn't stay up north for six weeks straight without returning to the City to see my doctors. We traveled back home a few times during that six-week stretch. Dr. Shore added to our excitement of going away by lifting the restriction that forbade us from eating in restaurants. All that was required was that we meet in advance with the chefs and counsel them on my eating restrictions. Dr. Shore reasoned that the small-scale operations in Lake Placid would pay closer attention to my requirements than the typical New York City eatery.

     Thus, Jen and I ventured back into the world of waiters and tables for the first time in six months, following the steps we took first with Sushi Guy in the hospital. I printed up 3" x 5" cards with my eating rules to hand out to chefs in local restaurants so they wouldn't have to rely on memory to keep them straight. Invariably our initial discussions about my eating restrictions led to a broader recounting of my struggles with leukemia. Soon enough Jen and I made friends with several of the restaurateurs who enjoyed the challenge of specially preparing meals for me and kept my card tacked up in their kitchens. Getting to know the locals was as enjoyable as exploring the mountains and wilderness around us.

     We had already known that Lake Placid's restaurants are surprisingly varied and upscale. We ended up being regulars at five local restaurants. Since two of the eateries had separate menus for their bar and dining room, we had a total of seven eating options available to us—more than enough to keep us happy. We were lucky that we were there in early summer, when the local shopkeepers had time to indulge us. The summer "busy season" didn't begin until the Fourth of July, which happened to be our last weekend at Camp Little Pine, our Lake Placid home away from home.

Summer ended early that year for many people in the Northeast. The weather turned misty and cool in August, feeling more like October. As metaphor would have it, my health deteriorated late in the summer season. My immune system acted up as I tried yet again to wean myself from immune-suppressive drugs. That August flare-up marked my third failed attempt to reduce my immune-suppressive medications below a certain threshold. Each time I tried to reduce my intake of Prednisone below 10 milligrams a day, my immune system attacked some part of my body that was heretofore healthy.

That third attack hurt my bladder, irritating its lining and causing me to urinate frequently. At my worst, I felt pressure to go to the bathroom every twenty minutes, day and night. To remedy the condition, the doctors raised my steroid dosage. That weakened my immune system, though it eased my bladder condition. It also pushed back by months the date by which I hoped to rid myself of steroids.

After three attempts to wean me off of immune-suppressive medications, my graft-vs-host disease was not "burning itself out," as my doctors had anticipated. They officially declared my GvHD condition "chronic." Though just a subtle change in nomenclature, appending the word "chronic" to the disease caused quite a paradigm shift.

In one sense, I could declare my recovery from leukemia over. I viewed "recovery" as a period in which I would progress from a state of sickness to normalcy, which I vaguely defined as something akin to how I lived my life before I was diagnosed with cancer. I viewed the period from the end of my second stem cell transplant until that August, a little less than a year's time, as my recovery period. Now that my condition was declared chronic, I could no longer expect to heal in a linear fashion. My progress would be cyclical, ebbing and flowing depending on the acrimony between my immune system and other parts of my body. The best I could hope for was that my peak moments would raise me higher than my troughs would sink me.

My recovery had fallen short of my hopes and expectations. I did not have the strength to consider returning to a "nine-to-five" job. My doctors still directed me as to what was safe for me to do. I would be less than independent for a while longer—perhaps a year, if not more.

If there was any solace to be found—other than the fact that the alternative to being chronic was even worse—Jen and I could console ourselves with the fact that we were not alone in this purgatory. The experience was common enough among stem cell transplant recipients that the Leukemia & Lymphoma Society had created a public service announcement to educate patients. They called it, "The New Normal," the title of a video that offered suggestions as to how best to manage this difficult time. I didn't watch "The New Normal." I unfairly assumed that anything that was mass-produced wouldn't speak to my personal concerns.

Dr. Shore, for her part, made it easier for Jen and me to accept my "new normal" by allowing us to continue the practice of eating out in select restaurants, so long as the restaurants accommodated my restrictions. Living in the West Village, a small town of sorts in the middle of the big city, it wasn't hard to find that kind of restaurant.

We chose about five places that were small enough that we could get to know the staff and ask them to modify their menu offerings to suit me. The restaurants covered a range of Continental and Mediterranean cuisines. Asian restaurants remained elusive because of the scale of their operations, language barriers and ubiquitous presence of miso. As in Lake Placid, we formed bonds with the local proprietors. We enjoyed forming relationships with the chefs and staff as much as we relished the meals we were served.

I coped with my limited options by making the most of them. I had more trouble being optimistic for the future, optimism being something I would need to persevere through the more difficult periods that I knew would lie ahead. The notion of normalcy that I had held previously had faded so far into the future that it seemed beyond my reach. If a better tomorrow was no longer within my grasp, would I find the drive to move forward at all?

LEUKEMIA FOR CHICKENS

25

Living Under the Decree

When Jews talk about Rosh Ha'Shana and Yom Kippur, two holidays that fall between early September and early October, the discussion usually has nothing to do with religion. What conversation inevitably revolves around is when they begin. The discussion is common enough that it has developed its own shorthand: the holidays are either "early" or "late."

The holidays are "early" if they begin any time in September, because that disrupts the beginning of the school year. The High Holidays are considered "late" whenever they fall in October, because that means services conflict with baseball playoffs. And since the holidays are "early" in September and "late" in October, they are never "on time."

The fuss about timing seems strange when one considers that Rosh Ha'Shana commemorates the start of the Jewish New Year. (Yom Kippur is celebrated ten days later.) It would be reasonable to assume that the start of a new year would be a constant, not a variable. It is a constant on the Jewish calendar, at least, which differs from the Gregorian calendar used by most Western nations. As far as the Jewish calendar is concerned, the start date of Rosh Ha'Shana is always *Tishrei 1*.

The months of the Jewish calendar are roughly based on the twenty-eight day lunar cycle. The difference in time between lunar months and a solar year is resolved by adding leap months. The arrival of the New Year can catch even Orthodox Jews unawares; it is not intuitive for anyone.

Many Jews only go to temple during the High Holidays, despite the fact that Rosh Ha'Shana and Yom Kippur are not the holiest days of the year, according to the Torah. That honor belongs to the Sabbath, which occurs every seventh day and the observation of which is among the Ten Commandments. Forgive me if I find it hard to accept that fifty-two days out of every year should be considered the holiest of holy days. I don't believe that holiness should be so easy to come by. Apparently many other Jews agree.

No doubt people discuss such minutiae around the High Holidays because they seem to need a little levity. According to tradition, the purpose of the two holidays is deadly serious. On Rosh Ha' Shana, the Jewish community gathers in temples around the world to confess the sins that were committed in the previous year. Jews repent and ask God to provide them with another year of life. On Yom Kippur, the Torah tells us that God gives his decree, and the fate of the Jewish community is sealed for the year to come.

Pretty grim stuff. Yet the High Holidays are the only events in the Jewish calendar that are certain to pack every synagogue. Many charge a premium for tickets to attend Rosh Ha'Shana and Yom Kippur services. Clearly the acts of confession and redemption resonate among the Jewish people; that and the fact that many synagogues also serve as a social vortex for their community. For many, prayers and preening go hand-in-hand.

The proceedings of the services have changed since I was a child and attended my parents' conservative temple on Long Island. In those days the High Holidays loomed over the fall like a dark cloud. Services seemed to drag on for an eternity. Congregants sang dour chants that repeatedly asked for forgiveness and requested inscription into the "Book of Life." At the end of the official services, additional prayers were made in honor of loved ones who had passed on. Lastly, a "martyrology" service was held, recognizing the acts of heroic Jews who died for the right to practice their faith.

When I was a child, the rabbis and elders in my community were often survivors of the Holocaust. Their Jewish identity was intertwined with the suffering they experienced and witnessed. During the past decade, I have witnessed a new generation of American-born rabbis take control of congregations. The temple I attended in my youth, which formerly allowed no musical accompaniment, added violinists on Yom Kippur. A new cantor introduced melodies that enlivened communal prayers. The rabbi moved his altar from the front of the main sanctuary to a more central location, amongst congregants.

Older members complain that the changes have made services "campy," especially since young Rabbi Rose took over. I find that the changes have merely made services more enjoyable, or at least bearable over long stretches.

Tradition hasn't been cast aside wholesale. Many congregations recite the same prayers as always, even as the message of the prayers conflicts with contemporary notions of the role God plays. The prayers speak of a God who determines the fate of every Jew. Many modern congregations do not ascribe to the notion that God plays an active role in their lives.

The paradox posed by such mixing was evident at the temple where Jen and I decided to attend High Holiday services in September 2004. That year was the third year that we had chosen to commemorate the High Holidays separate from our families. Whenever I attended services at my parents' synagogue, I couldn't help but feel like that bored child of my youth. For the past two years Jen and I had attended services given by the Village Temple, which is located in our neighborhood. As one might surmise, the swollen crowd during the High Holidays was too big for their synagogue and services were held in an auditorium at Cooper Union, a few blocks across town. A female rabbi, Chava Koster, guided the service, mixing traditional chants with high-minded contemporary sermons. The proceedings seemed progressive, even as they retained traditions which I found comforting. Jen and I also liked the diversity of the congregation, which matched what we saw in our neighborhood.

In 2004, the High Holidays marked the one-year anniversary of my second stem cell transplant. Any anniversary gives a person a reason to reflect on what has happened in the past year. This anniversary of my stem cell transplant was no different. I had experienced a lot in that period. Some good, some bad. The year had been so tumultuous that I was happy simply to repeat something that I had done in the previous year—that is, attend services at the Village Temple.

A year earlier, Jen and I were at the evening service of Yom Kippur—the day when, according to tradition, God seals the fate of every Jew for the year to come. The following day, I began total-body radiation therapy for my stem cell transplant. Both Jen and I believed that attending the nighttime service was worthwhile, even if I had to report to the hospital at 6 a.m. the following day. Doing so grounded us and helped us brace ourselves for the difficult period that lay ahead. Superstition played a role, too. How could we not pray for my survival on a day when every Jew prays for survival?

For the first morning of Rosh Ha'Shana 2004, Jen and I arrived at services around 10 a.m., an hour after they had already begun. As was typical for that day, the congregation sang the special prayers written for Rosh Ha'Shana prior to the reading of the Torah. One of those prayers was the *Unatenah Tokef.* The hymn was one of those dark and foreboding prayers that troubles many Jews who prefer to think of God as a benevolent force—or at least one that doesn't dole out punishment or perform miracles.

Here is an excerpt:

We shall ascribe holiness to this day.
For it is awesome and terrible.

In truth You are the judge,
The exhorter, the all-knowing, the witness,
He who inscribes and seals,
Remembering all that is forgotten.

Who shall reach the end of his days and who shall not

But repentance, prayer and righteousness avert the severity of the decree.

Following the recitation of the prayer, the rabbi assumed the podium and asked the audience rhetorically. "What are we to make of this 'awesome and terrible' day?"

The *Unatenah Tokef* would be all hellfire and brimstone, were it not for the fact that "repentance, prayer and righteousness can avert the severity of the decree."

It was that final sentence that kept the prayer palatable enough to be included on this day, according to Rabbi Koster.

It was clear to me at that moment that Rabbi Koster was about to make one of those seemingly impromptu mini-sermons that rabbis offer during services to make the proceedings more relevant to the audience. Her speech would explain why she thought the *Unatenah Tokef* had merit and deserved to be included in the service.

I enjoy these philosophical asides, unlike the many temple-goers who resent them for lengthening an already long service.

Rabbi Koster began her speech by talking about the people whom she had met during the previous year who were not lucky enough to be written into that year's "Book of Life." Many had died of illness.

I listened closer as I heard Rabbi Koster speak of the fate of the ill. I had not sought out spiritual guidance as a way to understand and cope with my own illness, unlike my father, who began attending Sabbath services regularly after I was diagnosed with leukemia. He joined temples in Manhattan and Palm Beach, in addition to his home temple in Old Westbury, so, regardless of where he was, he wouldn't have to miss Saturday morning services. He was usually in the company of men many years older than he. He admitted to sleeping through portions of the services, but still found solace in the act of attending. He must have felt as if one of the few things he could do for me was pray. We had exhausted lots of other options, so in many ways there was a reasoning to his actions.

I was open to ideas that would reinforce the ones that had kept my spirits afloat so far. Although I had put my faith and hopes in a better tomorrow, I was forced to put my energy into more earthly efforts. While my father looked to a higher power to change the pattern of my days for the better, I struggled daily to put weight on my slight frame, strengthen my atrophied muscles, and swallow dozens of pills for problems I couldn't even see or feel. As Sisyphean as my routine felt, my doctors had prescribed it and it gave me purpose. As long as I kept working at it, I maintained hope that things had to eventually improve.

As we marked the passing of another year, I was confronted with dreams I had postponed and would have to postpone again: small things, like being able to go for a jog, and big things, like being able to start a family. If tomorrow didn't turn out better, I had little to rely on. The strength it took to get through each day, much less each week, was starting to wear me down. At that time, I sensed the tomorrow for which I'd hoped was fading into the distance.

The rabbi continued her speech, saying that she prayed for the health of the sick people she met, even though she did not believe that prayer alone would alter their fate. Why, then, did she pray? The answer for Rabbi Koster lay in the final sentence of the *Unatenah Tokef*: that "repentance, prayer and righteousness can avert the severity of the decree." I liked how Rabbi Koster used a neutral phrase—"the decree"—as a substitute for a harsher word like "death."

Rabbi Koster said she could not change "the decree" that was every person's fate. Not only was it beyond her prayers, it was beyond the power of the God in whom she believed, for "the decree is the decree." It did not matter whether one was good or bad. Sooner or later we all would face "the decree."

So what should we make of our sometimes grim fate, the rabbi rhetorically asked? Her answer was that we must show that our actions make us humble. In repentance, we ask others to forgive us. In prayer, we acknowledge that we are not so important that our survival is paramount. And in righteousness, we give back to the community that nurtured us.

Though we cannot change the severity of the decree, the rabbi said, we can change our understanding of, and reaction to, that decree. With humility, we can recognize that none of us is eternal. But our contributions to the world live beyond us, she concluded.

The rabbi's admonishment to be humble gave me strength. But it also gave me a pass—I didn't have to worry all through my days that I wasn't doing enough for my survival. She helped me understand that I could not vanquish every foe. No one can. It would be enough simply to try. That lesson was, for me, a confirmation of the way I chose to be. Her sermon did not make living easier, but it made me believe the time that I would live could be rich in value. It was up to me to make it so. In addition to nourishment and healing, I might now seek out joy in my days.

I found in Rabbi Koster's sermon another reason to continue to pursue my unfulfilled dreams. I already knew that my will was strong. Two years of fighting leukemia had proven that. Now, with Rabbi Koster's help, I could accept the fact that, as strong as I believed my foundation to be, sooner or later, I would face the decree. Everyone does, regardless of how hard they fight.

Jen and I left services that morning before they ended. I didn't have the strength to sit through the entire proceedings. I did, thanks to Rabbi Koster, have the strength to not worry whether I would be inscribed into the "Book of Life."

But when, ten days later, Yom Kippur rolled around, I still prayed that God would make it so. I hadn't given up my physical fight, nor did I write off the impending decree. Yet whether or not it helped, I felt that praying for my survival was the right thing to do.

LEUKEMIA FOR CHICKENS

Part IV:
Epilogue

LEUKEMIA FOR CHICKENS

26

One Year Down

October 25, 2004

Marking the first anniversary of my transplant represented a milestone in my recovery. One year of survival from cancer was not much of a milestone in anyone's book except my own. A year didn't signify the end of anything. Although I was relieved to have made it through with mostly self-inflicted setbacks, issues were lurking on the horizon and every fix had its own related issues to deal with as well. I was careful not to take my present state for granted. I was also cognizant of the fact that any feeling of completion would be pushed back at this point.

Only ten days after this anniversary I felt sick. It was a conventional kind of sick, complete with a head cold, weakness, and shivering. But for me, it was unusual. I hadn't felt sick like that for almost a year, since my last stay in the hospital for my transplant.

These cold-like symptoms didn't seem worrisome at first. To make myself feel better, I took a hot shower in the hope that I would sweat out what ailed me. I steamed up the bathroom and festered there, getting a little dizzy in the process. When I came out of the shower, I dressed and tried to eat a turkey-and-cheese sandwich that Jen had prepared. The sandwich went down slowly. I took my temperature, and it read 100.3 degrees. That was 0.2 degree below the official threshold at which I was supposed to call my doctor. I wavered about calling, not wanting to disrupt my plans for the rest of the day.

Jen: "Roger, if you feel this bad, we need to call the doctor."

"Can I just nap for an hour first and see what happens?"

"No. You have to call."

Ring.

"Hi. It's Roger Madoff. I know I'm supposed to be in for my weekly checkup tomorrow, but I started feeling run-down today. I took my temperature and it was 100 point 3. Do you think I need to come in?"

Melissa, the doctor's assistant: "What are your other symptoms?"

"Weakness, chills, typical stuff."

"Let me ask her." A few moments pass. "You should come in."

"Now?"

"Whenever you can."

"Okay. See you soon."

Click.

"She says we should come in."

Jen: "Should we pack a bag in case you're staying overnight?"

"No. Worst case, you'll bring stuff for me tomorrow. We haven't stayed overnight in almost a year. I don't see why we'll have to now."

"I'm sorry, Roger. I bet you caught the cold I had last weekend."

"That's silly. You've been sick before without me catching it. And if it is your cold, I'll get over it soon, like you did. With me, they just have to be more careful."

I half-slept my way to the hospital in a cab. We met with Dr. Shore, who performed a standard physical examination on me. Apparently, my temperature had risen to 39.1 degrees Celsius, or 102.4 degrees Fahrenheit, in the short period of time since Jen and I had left our apartment. Dr. Shore next ordered a chest X-ray. She also called the infectious disease team to consult on whether I should be admitted to the hospital.

Dr. Shore: "The infectious disease team thinks it's too dangerous for you to be on the outside, if this turns out to be a pneumonia. You'll have to go to 10 West. The good news is I'm on call this week, so I'll be seeing you."

Dr. Shore's casual use of the word "pneumonia" didn't worry Jen or me terribly. After fighting leukemia for almost two years, we had both learned that horrific sounding words often describe generic conditions. For example: pneumonia refers to any type of lower-lung infection. Bronchitis, on the other hand, refers to an upper-respiratory infection. The severity of the condition would be left to whatever adjective the doctors chose to append. For example: acute, severe, slight, etc.

Regardless, infections need to be treated, and any infection that I contracted was going to be watched like a hawk by Dr. Shore. My immune system was still weak because it was being suppressed so it didn't fight every organ in my body as I suffered with GvHD. The doctors had expected the back-and-forth fighting between my immune system and my body to "burn out," but the process was taking longer for me than for other patients.

Jen and I made our way to the X-ray lab. I presented Dr. Shore's order to the radiology unit. While I waited to be scanned, Jen walked back to the admitting office, where she secured a private room for me. Within an hour I arrived at my room on 10 West. Though I had walked those halls for weeks at a time while receiving my two stem cell transplants, my return to 10 West unsettled me. I recognized the faces of several nurses on the floor. They offered me a wary smile, as if to combine two thoughts in a single expression, which I translated as "good to see you," and "please don't tell me you've relapsed."

I rattled off a list of deflecting responses as I wheeled past them in a chair on the way to my room:

"I'm not really here. This is a body double."

"I wanted to stay in a hotel for a few nights, and this was the only place deemed sanitary by my doctors."

And finally, stealing a phrase recently popularized by the Homeland Security Department, "Exercising an overabundance of caution, the doctors decided it was best for me that I spend some time in a secure environment."

As soon as I situated myself in my room, I was reminded of the minute inanities of hospital procedure that I had come to take for granted during previous visits. A nurse whom I hadn't met before came in with a list of papers that she needed to fill out in order to admit me officially.

Nurse: "Do you have any previous medical conditions?"

Me: "If you look under hospital ID 299-7511, you'll find quite a story. What part should I summarize?"

"I'll get it. List of medications?"

"Again, lengthy. I've already gone through this with Dr. Shore in the clinic. We should be covered."

"No allergies?"

"No."

"Family history of serious illness?"

"What kind? Forget it. My father had bladder cancer. That should be enough. Can you please also put down that I am temporarily diabetic, because my steroid medication suppresses my insulin? I will need regular insulin shots."

And so it went. My room, No. 252, faced west, overlooking a rock-strewn roof that the staff of 10 West referred to euphemistically as "Pebble Beach." Though it was accessible through my hospital room window, patients were not allowed to venture onto Pebble Beach, originally conceived as a landing pad for Medi-Vac helicopters, but no longer used for that purpose. Looking beyond the patio deck, I noticed some changes in the skyline since my last admission. Construction had progressed on Memorial-Sloan Kettering's new medical tower. The metal scaffold was complete. Workers had begun to sheathe the edifice in glass.

A nurse's aide entered the room to take my blood pressure and check the level of oxygen in my blood. The 'pulse-ox' meter, as I called it, showed I was breathing at 80 percent capacity. Normal was 95-100 percent. Clearly concerned, the nurse exited and returned with a nasal canula, or breathing tube, like one sees attached to any television show character that is sick. She positioned one end below my nostrils, threaded the tubes behind my ears and connected the other end to a port on the wall. That nasal canula was the good kind of nose tube, unlike an NG tube. Instead of continuing down my throat into my stomach, with a nasal canula, the port on the wall pumped oxygen through the tube. Water vapor was added to the mix to keep my nose moisturized. The mist also provided a bit of atmosphere, as the device produced a sound akin to a babbling brook. I imagined the water trickling from my bedside down to Pebble Beach. Western medicine meets Feng Shui.

Jen and I had a few moments to rest before we called our respective families to alert them that I was back in the hospital. My mom, dad, and sister all came by around 5 p.m.—work-world quitting time. Seeing them enter, I had ugly memories of longer stays that I did not wish to repeat. It showed on my face.

Shana: "You don't want us to stay. That's okay. I understand."

"I just don't want this to be a big deal. It shouldn't be. And if it is, I'll deal with that mentally later. Sorry."

After a short recap of what brought me to the hospital and what the doctors knew so far, my family departed. Jen stayed behind with me. A "fellow" from the bone marrow transplant unit visited my room. (A fellow is defined as someone who has finished his or her residency and specializes in a specific field of research but is not yet a staff doctor.) The fellow said he had reviewed the X-ray of my chest. He saw nothing unusual. However, he thought it best that I undergo a CT scan, because the picture taken by that device would provide the doctors with a more detailed view. Given my weak breathing, it was worth investigating my illness further. Something obviously wasn't working properly. The scan would be conducted later that day, he said.

Me: "You mean sometime in the middle of the night."

Fellow: "True. Probably not until then. This means, of course, you can't eat or drink anything after midnight."

Jen had ordered in a pizza for dinner from John's on 64th street. After dinner, Jen and I watched sitcom reruns, which flowed into World Series baseball, at which point Jen departed for the night.

Jen: "Big hug." She made a circle with her arms, showing affection without risking a transfer of germs.

Jen: "Grrr," imitating a squeezing hug sound.

Me: "Love you." I blew a meek kiss.

Late that night, a phlebotomist came by to insert a temporary IV into my arm. Nurses would use the IV port to administer fluids and medication. Temporary IVs don't allow nurses to draw blood. Whenever doctors requested that I give blood—something that occurred at least once a day—it required a separate poke in the arm. I also gave a urine sample and coughed up some "sputum," or mucous, that I spat into a sterile cup.

The antibiotic infusions finished around midnight. Not feeling sleepy, I flipped through the hospital TV's limited viewing choices, landing on CNN's continuing coverage of Election 2004, which finally put me to sleep. Around 4 a.m., I awoke and called the nurse in to my room to ask if she had heard anything about my CT scan. The nurse said, "no."

I told her that I planned to eat at 9 a.m. that morning, fast-for-the-CT scan be damned. It was more important that I not lose more weight.

Me: "If they want to do a scan on an empty stomach, they need to do it before then."

I wasn't sure if being petulant would move me forward in line, but I had learned from my frequent hospital stays that remaining silent wouldn't help my cause either. However, the radiology lab called the nurses' station at 6 a.m. to instruct them that my scan was booked for 6:30 a.m. A person from the intra-hospital transport unit wheeled me down to the radiology unit, where a technician perched me in front of the donut-shaped CT scanner. I was passed back and forth through the donut hole a few times, as a mechanical voice instructed me to "Hold your breath... breathe," over and over.

Within a half hour I had returned 10 West. It was too late to fall back to sleep. I killed time watching TV until my dad arrived an hour later with his usual delivery of a dozen bagels, decaf iced coffee, and the day's newspapers. Though our morning ritual had been on hiatus for many months, we easily fell back into our routine. I knew my dad enjoyed these quiet times to talk sports and business. Our morning chats would never have happened had I not been stricken with leukemia and been bed-ridden in a hospital. It was one of those strange positive by-products of being ill.

Early that morning, Dr. Roboz dropped in to say hello.

"I saw your name on the admission sheet, and I almost turned white. And when I saw the leftover bagels at the nurses' station, I knew it was true: You're back. But you're okay, right?"

"I guess so. I'm telling everyone I'm not really here. What you're seeing is actually a hologram."

"Sounds like you're in good hands, and everything is under control."

Dr. Shore rounded with her interns later that morning. She told me that my CT scan showed "nodules" in my lungs. I had learned early on that nodules were ill-defined clumps of something or other. The mass could be bacterial or fungal in nature. Or the lumps could be the result of inflammation from a virus. They were not tumors. Dr. Shore said that the antibiotics I had taken the previous night might treat the nodules. Further tests were required. Dr. Shore needed to talk to the pulmonary unit about the best way to take a sample of those nodules from my lungs.

There was a selection of procedures the doctors could perform to extract tissue. The least invasive, and thus preferred, method was via a needle biopsy, in which a doctor would insert a needle through my backside into my lung. The doctor would use CT scanner to guide him in locating nodules. Samples drawn from my lung would then be grown in a Petri dish. I could remain awake for the procedure.

Me: "I'm guessing we won't be able to do this today. I just ate breakfast."

Dr. Shore: "Probably not. You look like you're feeling better, though."

"I am. My fever is down, pulse-ox up." I gave a thumbs-up.

"Well, sit tight. We'll let you know."

There was a hitch, of course. Only one doctor on staff at NewYork-Presbyterian Hospital was qualified to perform needle biopsies. That doctor was on vacation for the week. A second doctor who was qualified to perform the biopsies had died a few weeks prior to my admission in the hospital. Worse, no qualified doctor was available at Memorial-Sloan Kettering, the hospital across the street.

A doctor from the pulmonary unit, someone not qualified to do the biopsy, proposed performing the more-invasive procedure, a bronchoscopy, sending fluid up my nostril and down into my lungs. The fluid would then be retrieved and tested to see if anything had grown yet. The bronchoscopy procedure was uncomfortable. It required mild sedation. I had undergone a bronchoscopy once before during my recovery. It was not an experience I wanted to repeat.

Worst of all, neither option had more than a fifty percent chance of being successful in determining what matter the nodule consisted of. All of the doctors agreed on that.

While the pulmonologist and I mulled over the idea of a bronchoscopy, Dr. Shore entered and said she didn't like idea. She told me, as well as the pulmonologist in the room, that she had located a lung biopsy specialist in Great Neck, on Long Island. That doctor might be available to conduct a needle biopsy tomorrow. The pulmonologist left in a huff, exposing a level of intra-hospital political infighting rarely witnessed by patients. Dr. Shore shrugged off the incident and said she would let me know early the following morning if I would be taking a little road trip.

"So don't eat again after midnight in case we need to get you out there tomorrow."

Dr. Shore then added, almost as an afterthought: "I need to tell you that the main risk of a needle biopsy is that your lung could collapse. It's not likely to happen, of course. If your lung does collapse, we'll make arrangements for you to get back here."

It was yet another situation where I needed to remind myself that the word "collapse" was unusually graphic, while the actual condition was not nearly as severe as the term suggested. Never mind the gory image in my head.

That night, a phlebotomist came to replace my temporary IV port, which had ruptured its vein, causing swelling and leaving in its wake a deep purple bruise on my forearm. The nurse poked my arm twice without finding a "good" vein. The third prick went in smoothly, though I felt a sting when another nurse began to administer antibiotics. The following morning, I received yet another prick, when a nurse came by to take blood for daily labs. The nurse noted that my blood pressure was low.

"It's often low when I first wake up."

The nurse nodded, departed the room, and returned a few minutes later with a large bag of saline solution.

"The doctor has ordered a bolus of saline to be given at 500 milliliters an hour."

"That seems fast. I don't think this IV can take it."

I knew from previous experience that saline normally flows through an IV at about a quarter of that rate.

"I can start it at half that (250 milligrams per hour) if you want."

"Can't I just drink a bottle of water? I can put down 500 milliliters in 10 minutes. If it's just about hydration, what's the difference?"

"This is what the doctor ordered."

I acquiesced. The nurse snaked the tube leading from the bag of saline through the IV pump and into my temporary IV. The vein infiltrated, that is blew open, in less than a minute.

An alarm sounded on the IV pump as the flow of saline stopped. I pressed the red Nurse Call button and let my beeping pump speak for me.

"As you can hear, the IV's out."

Nurse: "I'll leave a note for the IV team to get you a new IV."

"Don't bother. They'll probably send me to Great Neck before that happens."

At 8:45 a.m., I received my first indication that I would, in fact, venture to Great Neck: A nurse practitioner, a senior-level nurse, entered my room and asked if I possessed a copy of my insurance card.

"No. It's with Jen, but there should be a policy number on file."

"You haven't eaten yet today, have you?"

"No."

Dr. Shore entered my room 15 minutes later.

"Could you be in Great Neck by 10:30?"

"Well, Jen's still home; I just spoke to her. It would be a stretch for her to get from downtown to here and then to get to Great Neck by 10:30. But my dad, the Bagel Man, should be by any minute."

As if on cue, my dad entered, sporting a plastic bag that held within it a dozen bagels in his left hand. Under his right arm, there were copies of the *Times*, *Post* and *Journal*.

Dr. Shore: "We need you to take him to Great Neck. And then we need you to bring the specimens back, whether or not your son has to stay there longer. We need to have the specimens in the lab as soon as possible."

Dad didn't miss a beat. I could even see him smile as he received his instructions, excited by the challenge. He called Mom to turn the car around. Mom had dropped dad at the hospital. Dad headed to the entrance to meet Mom, who would take a taxi home to their apartment, while Dad would drive me to Great Neck. Meantime, I dressed for my trip, and Dr. Shore returned with further instructions.

"We told you about the lung collapse issue. If it does happen, the doctors will call for an ambulance to take you to North Shore Hospital, which is the closest hospital. We have spoken with people there, and they will bring you from that hospital back to here. But it's not likely to happen, of course."

Dr. Shore handed me copies of the previous day's CT scan for the biopsy specialist to reference. I met Dad at the entrance to the hospital and directed him to take the Tunnel and Expressway. He countered, saying that taking the Drive and the Triboro would be better. He was right. We hit almost no traffic, while it took Jen, following the Tunnel-Expressway route that I had favored, more than an hour to reach the clinic in Great Neck.

At the doctor's office, the manager greeted us warmly. She recognized my last name because, coincidentally, she had been one of my mom's bridesmaids at my parent's wedding more than thirty-five years earlier. The manager introduced my father and me to the biopsy doctor, who had already reviewed the scans that were given to me by Dr. Shore. Because of the location of the nodules in my lungs, the doctor estimated the risk of a lung collapse at 25 percent. The chance of extracting valuable tissue was just 50 percent, he added. That made the procedure more risky and less promising than Dr. Shore had led me to believe. I asked the doctor to call Dr. Shore and run his estimates of success and failure by her.

"If she is comfortable, I am comfortable."

Dr. Shore said she was comfortable.

"Go for it," she told me.

Though I was nervous about the odds that my lung might collapse, the biopsy went smoothly. As I rested in the operating room, the doctor handed samples to my father to take back to New York-

Presbyterian Hospital. The samples were placed in sterile cups and fastened into a cardboard box that had been used to serve morning coffee earlier that day.

Doctor: "Don't spill."

Jen and I stayed behind for an hour at the clinic. The doctor performed a final scan of my lungs to verify that the procedure hadn't resulted in my lung being punctured. On the way home, we stopped in nearby Little Neck at Slims' Bagels, one of my dad's preferred bagel bakeries. I introduced myself to one of the bakers, Yuri, who had heard about my struggles against leukemia from my father's many visits and from Dr. Schuster, the head of the transplant team, who also stopped by daily for bagels en route to the hospital.

Jen and I ate a bagel lunch in our car. A thin line of autumn-tinged trees blocked our view of the Long Island Expressway. I noted how it felt better to eat in a car than in my hospital room, which was far more spacious, but oh-so-sterile.

I returned to NewYork-Presbyterian Hospital for another night's observation before being released the following day, a Thursday. Now that my fever had disappeared and I no longer had trouble breathing, the doctors said I could await the results of the biopsy at home.

Two days later, while visiting Jen's grandpa in the suburbs, I received a call from my dad, who told me that my mom had entered the hospital late that night with terrible cramps. She had a blockage in her intestines, my dad said. The doctors inserted one of those dreaded NG tubes down her throat to clear a pathway. They were waiting for a bowel movement to occur before they could release her.

If the blockage did not resolve itself before Monday, the doctors might decide to operate. Mom was not happy, Dad said. The following day, over my mom's objections, Jen and I drove to North Shore Hospital, where she was being treated. My mom was the first ailing person I had visited in a hospital since my own ordeal had begun two years earlier. Jen and I stayed beside her for a little while and ran an crrand for my father. As we returned to the city, I received a call from my father that Mom had passed gas. The doctors were now optimistic that the blockage would clear on its own.

LEUKEMIA FOR CHICKENS

Mom was released from the hospital that Monday. Sometimes I wonder what healthy people, who don't have to spend huge portions of their lives in hospitals, do with so much free time on their hands.

27

Two Years Down

I now understand that milestones are not just windows of opportunity but portholes into the abyss. This road has been a lesson in managing expectations, as I have had no idea what lies around the next bend. To survive, I have shortened my perspective on life and redefined my notions of progress and victory. Even for those smaller rewards, I require greater assistance than I could have imagined as my recovery goes forward. I couldn't fathom the support I would need to persevere, or the sense of dependency on others, especially Jen, that I would develop.

I have come to believe that all actions are partly rooted in self-interest. My apologies to the true altruists, whose selfless acts are exceptional. Most people's kind acts help both those in need and those who have the ability and desire to give. This is not to say I am a complete cynic. In fact, the acts of charity I have received while I have battled leukemia have helped me persevere. Indeed, I feel guilt that I have taken more than I have given. But it makes me feel better to believe that in their giving to me, they also are giving to themselves.

So what have I done with this excess generosity? I have used it as fuel to battle onward. And so I don't disappoint those who are giving so much, I have adopted a hero persona for my supporters.

Me, to the assembled crowd: "I can do it."

And the throng roars back, "He can do it!"

Thus I am spurred onward in my fight against an unfathomable foe.

My hero portrayal appealed to many, but that larger-than-life figure seduced no one more than it seduced me. I had the power to become a Superhero, or so I thought. Thus I pressed onward in my battle against leukemia.

Some people might have chosen simply to try to recover from their illness and get on with their lives. I knew that to overcome my particular disease, I would need major support from others. I feared their support might fade over time, unless the idea of my recovery inspired them as well. Thus I would maintain an army for my battle.

From the first diagnosis on, I struck a tone of defiance and perseverance.

Assembled: "He's so brave."

Later, when I thought I had a moment of relative quiet and could reflect on my journey, I inscribed my hero-self to the page, ensuring the posterity of this image.

Assembled: "He's more real than ever now."

If the support I received helped me to recover better, quicker, and faster, great. But what if my recovery turned out to be harder than any of us anticipated? I would need the support of others even more. And I would have less and less energy to rally them to my cause.

Although the past year had been somewhat tumultuous, by fall 2004, I had recovered enough to have some free time and ample energy to gather my thoughts. After completing a physical endurance test, it was time to conduct "brain rehab." I enrolled in Marion Landew's weekly writing course at New York University, "Writing your Memoirs." At New School University I learned the ins-and-outs of Photoshop, the picture-editing software program. I also located a private Italian language tutor with whom I chatted for an hour each week.

I didn't expect the foreseeable future to fit a memoirist's caricature. I wouldn't be rising slowly from bed to don a velvet robe and brew coffee to sip later at my typewriter, I wouldn't be reclining in a leather chair to muse about my experiences, taking breaks to thoughtfully rub my chin while tamping my pipe tobacco. No, if I wasn't going to one class or another, I was visiting various doctors to deal with some new ailment or another that had emerged in the aftermath of my transplant. I ended up squeezing writing in between maladies that were caused by GvHD, even though my leukemia was officially in remission.

After my "slight" pneumonia in October, in November I had the feeling that was I losing my balance. An orthopedist told me that the steroids I had been taking for more than a year had caused necrosis of my joints, leaving them brittle and prone to injury. He told me I needed to replace my right knee as well as my left hip. I replaced the knee in mid-December; the hip is pending.

In February 2005, between physical therapy appointments to break in my new knee, I began weekly phlebotomy treatments. That is, doctors leeched from me a pint of blood, then threw the bag in the medical waste bin—a barbaric but effective way to drain me of excess iron, itself a consequence of my having received so many transfusions over the course of my treatment. After each phlebotomy treatment, a nurse injected Procrit to hike my red-blood cell count sufficiently to withstand the following week's yield.

In March 2005, a nagging rash on my forearm flared into a full-body phenomenon, yet another iteration of my chronic GvHD. My severe reaction prompted the hospital to order its first photo-phoresis machine, a tool used in other stem cell transplant centers around the nation to mitigate the effects of GvHD. It didn't hurt that my charitable parents put in calls to procure the machine.

Each session of photo-phoresis takes about three hours. Sessions can be conducted multiple times each week, depending on a patient's stamina. Sitting in a pseudo-La-Z-Boy for six hours each week leaves you restless and sore. Fortunately, while you're sitting in that chair you hang out with Manny, the nurse who runs the machine and is one of the most interesting people you could be stuck with. Manny could regale patients with stories about traveling the world playing basketball on a unicycle and about his current pursuit of the Japanese martial art of Akido, in which he competes the world over. To extract blood to be entered through the machine, Manny inserted a needle into a "good" vein in my arm. The machine extracted five to ten percent of my blood at each sitting, cycling it through a centrifuge and separating out white cells. The white cells were mixed with a drug made from the active ingredient found in Nile River grass. The machine snaked the mixture through a clear plastic tube and baked it on all sides with ultra-violet light. It then returned the sun-treated white cells to me. According to the pharmaceutical rep who trained Manny to use the machine, the process is Western medicine's adaptation of an Egyptian hieroglyph that depicts lepers eating weeds and lying in the sun to heal wounds on their skin. Honest.

Photo-phoresis did help my rash somewhat, but it wore me down physically.

In April 2005, I underwent two surgeries to remove cataracts, another side effect of long-term steroid use. On my off week, we moved around the corner to a new apartment. Perhaps it is more accurate to say that from my perspective, our apartment was transferred to a new, improved receptacle around the corner, because I left my old apartment at 11 a.m. on Tuesday for writing class and a phlebotomy session and returned seven hours later to a new home. Jen and her parents pulled off quite the magic trick.

Having so many other issues with which to contend, it would have been reasonable to put aside artistic pursuits to focus on more pressing problems. But I continued to use any spare time to write, viewing it as a refuge from everything going on around me. Between September and April, I cobbled together and spell-checked 200 double-spaced pages of what I referred to initially as "an experiment in narrative" or "a way to help me understand what I've been through." A few months into the process, feeling confident about my work so far, I told my friends officially that I was writing a story about my experience.

By the end of the spring semester, I declared my offering worthy of being called a book—something that I wanted others beyond my close relations to read. I viewed the 200-page mark as an achievement equivalent to when a jockey reaches the fifth-sixths furlong in a horse race. At that point, the jockey makes his (or her) final left turn and can glimpse the finish line.

Race announcer, voice rising in pitch: "And down the stretch they come!"

I, too, looked ahead upon reaching this point and envisioned my own finish line, perhaps six-weeks hence. I was feeling ever more the fatigue that I had pushed aside just to reach that present mark. As a reward to myself, I sent my four closest friends from college the first five chapters, which I had written in September. Oh, and I also told them I would not be able to go to Duke's Class of 1995 10-year reunion that coming weekend. I simply did not have the energy.

That same week, following a Tuesday phlebotomy, Dr. Shore, still the doctor monitoring me on a weekly basis, called to tell me I was anemic.

"Don't do anything that you don't have to."

Me: "Like go to North Carolina for a reunion."

"Right. Nothing like that. Get some rest."

I took her advice and settled on our newly delivered couch in our new apartment. In a day I felt a sniffle, then a cough. By Wednesday, I knew I would be checking into the hospital, fearing and anticipating that I would be diagnosed with my second pneumonia in six months.

I would not take this setback lightly. I saw finally that I needed to slow down, relax. I was not Superman, but a regular guy trying to recover from leukemia. I entered the hospital and was assigned to the same corner room where I had spent seven consecutive weeks receiving my second stem cell transplant.

I was chilled by the room's sameness, save its empty wall space. As I gasped for breath through an oxygen mask, I wondered how I had convinced myself that I could pull all this off. I'd only made it this far by nursing myself with a steady dose of painkillers like Percocet and Oxycontin. I took them first in January to dull my knee pain after surgery, and then again in March to ease the chafing pain caused by my body rash.

To think that up until the day before I checked into the hospital, a Tuesday, Jen and I had planned to host Passover Seder for twenty people that Saturday evening in our new apartment.

I had clearly hit a wall, but the momentum I'd instilled in my supporters was still going strong. I had only myself to blame. I insisted for so long that everyone should "bring it on." I could take it.

Dr. Roboz came by to visit.

"You look okay. Maybe we could send you home for Saturday [Passover] with an oxygen tank."

Not this time. In the hospital, I would hide.

Even after two years in recovery, I had pushed celebration too soon. It's difficult to explain that celebration can be taxing. In any event, rather than allowing me a quiet stay in the hospital, with the best of intentions my supporters brought a three-ring Seder circus to my room.

Assembled: "We brought chicken soup. And chopped liver. And gefilte fish."

Friends whom we had invited to our apartment for Passover called in, enabling me to share aurally in their traditional feast.

"We're calling you from our makeshift Seder at the hotel conference room. We miss you."

Me, through an oxygen mask: "Thank you. Thank you all."

I hung up, and I cried. On Sunday, I barely rose out of bed, sleeping most of the day in order to regain strength—for Monday.

Assembled: "It's your birthday!"

Hugs, kisses, smiles, and presents. A homemade lobster roll to eat on my hospital tray. Scooby-Doo Dunce Caps, courtesy of Diana, our cheery chef.

Assembled: "So sorry you have to celebrate in the hospital."

Me, bitter and demoralized after so much struggle: "Why remind me of it then?"

Jen presented me with her delicious homemade carrot cake with cream-cheese topping.

Jen: "It's from *Cooking Light*. But I took out the 'light'."

Exaggerated laughter.

Me: Cough. Cough.

Nervous silence all around as I breathe deep and slowly to stop the coughing.

Me: "No. It's good. Laughing makes me cough. Coughing brings up mucous. Laughter is strong medicine, if you can hack it." Cough.

Assembled, relieved: "He's okay!"

A bronchoscopy and a lung needle biopsy later, the doctors and pathologists pronounced that I would, in fact, be okay. For the time being, however, I needed intravenous antibiotics and anti-fungal medications. I also needed to reduce the swelling in my lungs that had been caused by those infections. I would likely stay in the hospital for two weeks before returning to my ever-more-furnished, beautiful new apartment. There I could watch Milo splayed comfortably on our Oriental rug. Out the window, I would see trees bloom in Hudson River Park. Jen and I would soon invite everyone over either for lunch or dinner so we could all share our new haven together.

It is my vain regret that my recovery will most likely provide more satisfaction to me personally than it will offer an opportunity for others to celebrate my heroic feat. I wish I could deliver a smashing sixth-consecutive Tour de France-type victory to my loyal supporters. Their efforts on my behalf warrant a triumph at least that exuberant. Unfortunately, all I can offer is a meritorious "also finished the race," worthy of no more than a polite round of applause from those who hung on to watch someone other than the champion complete his journey.

But wait. Could I perhaps find a second wind halfway down the backstretch? To reduce inflammation in my lungs, the doctors ordered that I take a megadose of Prednisone. I've come up with a new way to help people understand what it feels like to be on Prednisone: Remember as a kid when you went to the zoo and visited the chimpanzees? You saw signs hanging from cage walls telling onlookers that the DNA of chimpanzees and humans is ninety-five percent the same. Those monkeys in there were our closest extant evolutionary relatives.

You watch them in their cage and try to imagine their human counterparts: in the navel-picker you see the introvert; the lip jabber is the class clown; and that one petting her child, the soothing maternal figure. Up in front of this crowd is a gaggle of screeching chimps who don't remind you of any humans you've seen outside of Mardi Gras or Carnevale. They bounce from branch to branch to branch, leap to a steel rib of the cage, and use a free hand to hurl feces at onlookers: on a megadose of Prednisone, those lunatics are your spiritual kin.

The Prednisone did its trick and I was sent home. This stay at the hospital scared me into reprioritizing. I managed to continue my writing, which was nearly completed, but strictly limited any other activities I deemed strenuous. Only the most important social activities made my roster: the annual benefit dinner of the Leukemia & Lymphoma Society in May; Jen's friend-from-work's wedding in June;

the Bone Marrow Transplant Unit's Reunion Cruise in July. I even cut down on plans with my family, to their very vocal dismay. Jen went on her own to our friends' children's birthday parties, her 10-year Cornell reunion, and some dinners with friends we'd put off for months.

I cut down on my activity in part to prepare for a trip in late July that I couldn't miss. Jen's brother, Evan, was getting married at the home of his fiancée, Jasmin, in Hills, British Columbia—a town of just eighty people located in the mountains halfway between Vancouver and Calgary. Such a long trip to such a remote location was clearly pushing my limits, but we made every effort to ease the strain. My Canadian-born doctor enthusiastically set me up with emergency contacts in Vancouver, which lessened my anxiety about being across the continent from NewYork-Presbyterian Hospital.

Even with all our preparation, the travel was taxing. Good thing there was nowhere to go once we arrived. I lazily sat beside "the cleanest lake in British Columbia" staring at mountain scenery, realizing what good medicine fresh air can be. It was reassuring to be able to sleep through a night at Jasmin's family's back-country ski lodge, located a short drive 3,000 feet up a logging trail, from the only road in town. I managed to give a toast at the wedding and even wiggle my withered hips as the wedding band played a "house-funk" version of the theme from *Knight Rider*. Despite my efforts to rest whenever possible, I was exhausted and changed my plans to leave a day early.

The trip was refreshing but the benefits didn't provide any respite from my ongoing health issues. My weight dropped regardless of my efforts to keep eating. The photo-phoresis produced only a partial response in my skin condition and Dr. Shore called off the experiment. My skin had changed, but it was debatable whether it was actually better. Instead of scaly and flaky, it was like a suit that was several sizes too small. I was shedding layers of skin each week and chafing soon caused sores in the most painful of places on my body. Getting through the day had become unbearable, and by mid-August I admitted myself to the hospital because my depression had reached an all-time low. I didn't have the strength or the will to function on the outside. Although Dr. Shore still had treatment options on her list, none of them jumped out as the one to bet on next. For the first time in almost three years, we sought out a second opinion.

My cousin Andy was amazingly healthy, but had maintained relationships with doctors all over the country who were doing research related to his lymphoma. He pushed us to talk to a group at the Fred Hutchinson Cancer Research Center in Seattle. The "Hutch" is considered the Mecca of the transplant world because it pioneered much of the research and practice in the field. Mary Flowers is the head of their Long-Term Follow-Up group and was believed to have seen more GvHD cases than anyone. After Andy placed a few strategic calls, she agreed to squeeze us into her schedule a week later. Jen and I made our second grueling trip out to the Pacific Northwest in just two months.

Over three days in Seattle, we met a host of doctors who deconstructed my disease and gave us a summary of their findings before we returned to New York. Their findings were a mix of reassuring and disheartening news. Dr. Flowers had seen cases like mine before, though not many. And while the details may have differed, the team at the Hutch considered the treatment I received in New York to be the standard of care. She told me that my GvHD was among the most severe cases, but it was possible to outlast it. I just had to make it to the point where my body and my immune system learned to tolerate one another. On average, this can take from three to five years. Much of this was not a newsflash to Jen and me; it was obvious from what we had been through already that we were working against the odds. With heavy hearts, we swallowed their diagnosis and returned to New York the next day.

My daily goal had to be to keep on truckin'. It would be easier to give in, retreat, plead for mercy. But I had fought hard to get to this point. I had to reconcile myself to the fact that there are forces beyond my control, and yet I had to continue to work as if there weren't.

Maybe I was turning a blind eye to the reality of my struggle, but I knew I would resume living my life as fully as possible. I would try to find richness in every day I had in front of me. I had always tried to live this way and I would reserve my strength for the moments that mattered, regardless of how small they were and how often they came.

A Note from Jen

Summer 2006

Over the course of the fall of 2005, Roger's GvHD became increasingly worse. His skin became tight, thin and ulcerated, to a point where he began taking methadone to manage his chronic pain.

Roger's joints continued to fail him as well and, unfit to undergo surgery for his broken hip, he was forced to begin using a wheelchair whenever he left home.

Almost immediately following the completion of this manuscript in August, Roger's eyesight deteriorated significantly, a result of the continued use of steroids to treat his GvHD. Retina, cornea and eye inflammation specialists were unable to offer him solutions and he was left unable to read.

In December, Roger was hospitalized for two weeks with severe depression. After upping his psychiatric medications, Dr. Shore and Dr. Flowers searched relentlessly for novel treatments for what they categorized as one of the most severe cases of GvHD they had ever seen. At their direction, he underwent Total Lymphoid Irradiation and low-dose chemotherapy treatment using Cytoxan. These offered slight relief from his discomfort and bought his doctors time to think of next steps. Roger's spirits were lifted and he maintained the hopefulness that had always characterized his fight.

In mid-March 2006, Roger was again hospitalized, this time for a cough and a suspicious-looking wound on his lower leg. Within hours of being admitted, Roger required a nasal canula to maintain a sufficient level of oxygen in his blood. It was soon discovered that the wound on his leg was the source of a fungal infection that had spread throughout his body. Dr. Shore surmised that this was most probably at the root of his cough, causing a fungal pneumonia in his lungs, the most feared infection in the immunosuppressed. As dismal as the prognosis was, Roger vowed to fight on, determined to get out of bed and eventually leave the hospital.

Dr. Shore consulted with a team of surgeons from the Burn Unit, who performed an extensive surgery to remove much of the tissue from the lower part of his right leg, hoping to rid his body of the source of his infection. After surgery, Roger's breathing became increasingly labored. His pulmonologists stepped up the level of supplemental oxygen he was receiving by giving him a facemask. As we dealt with the probability that it was unlikely he would ever be strong enough again to breathe on his own, Roger and I made the most difficult decision yet—to order that his doctors Do Not Intubate—also known as a DNI. The DNI would prevent him from being attached to a respirator in a state of unconsciousness for the remainder of his life. As hopeful and positive as Roger remained, what he had fought so hard for was not that existence.

On Friday night, April 14th, gasping for breath, Roger asked for morphine to calm his panic and slow down his lungs. He had come to accept what seemed inevitable. Dr. Shore came by to check on him as she was leaving the hospital. Roger asked her for nothing more than a hug, and gathered the strength to say "Thank you" as they embraced. She wept, sensing this might be their last visit together.

Less than twenty-four hours after starting the drip, on April 15th, surrounded by his family keeping vigil at his bedside, Roger passed away, peacefully and on his own terms.

Appendix

Acknowledgments

Roger cherished the relationships that made his life so rich and he made a habit of thanking people for their help and encouragement. Since he never imagined publishing this memoir posthumously, on his behalf, I would like to thank the leagues of supporters who kept Roger and me afloat and filled the pages of his life and this book. They include, but surely are not limited to, family, friends, doctors, nurses, teachers and editors. We thank you and know you will keep Roger's spirit and love in your hearts, always.

Our thanks especially to our family: Marion, Peter, Shana, Rebecca, Eric, Lois, Marty, Grandpa Lee, Evan, Jasmin, Andy, Debbie, Mark, Stephanie, Bernie, Ruth, Charlie, Carolyn and Ariel.

And to our physicians, nurses, Weill Cornell staff, friends and teachers: Tsiporah Shore, Adam Stracher, Gail Roboz, Dean Gotto, Eric Feldman, Michael Schuster, Abe Sanders, Jon Harpel, Lynne Strassfeld, Jessy Ryan, Sandy Allen-Bard, Bita Jalilizenali, Scott Possley, Susan Karch, Linda Halpern, Rebecca Belin, Jamie Johnston-Renwick, Pat Gutter, Michael Sellers, Mary Flowers, Nancy Curcio, Larry Dyche, Noah Hendler and Nancy Lefkowitz, Rich Murphy and Margie Menza, Russell and Elyse Klein, Lauren and Tom Rotko, Stacy and Eric Poritzky, Ben Maxymuk, Jorge Baron and Tyler Crone, Justin Nelson, Andy Frankenberger, Davide and Alberto Goldstaub, Giulio Curiel and Lunella Rivetti, Diana Newsom, Julie Lerner, Monica Lewinsky, Elizabeth Leff, Alyse Kramarow and Brian Saed, Jen and Richie Strassler, Dena Berman, Rabbi Carnie Rose, Stephen Piorkowski and Marion Landew.

To a friend and advocate of Roger's work, Ruth Charny.

To Roger's dedicated editor, Nancy Hardin.

And lastly, to Milo.

We are grateful to all those who continue to help find cures for leukemia and lymphoma by supporting the Leukemia & Lymphoma Society, the Gift of Life Bone Marrow Foundation, the Lymphoma Research Foundation, Weill Cornell Medical Center and the hospitals that provide care, treatment and research for patients and their families.

With love,
Jen

LEUKEMIA FOR CHICKENS

Resources

The Leukemia & Lymphoma Society
New York City chapter
475 Park Avenue South, 8th Floor
New York, NY 10016
(212) 448-9206
www.lls.org

The Gift of Life Bone Marrow Foundation
The Roger Madoff Marrow Donor Recruitment Program
7700 Congress Avenue, Suite 2201
Boca Raton, FL 33487
Toll Free: (800) 9-MARROW
www.giftoflife.org

New York-Presbyterian Hospital
Weill Cornell Medical Center
Leukemia and Bone Marrow Failure Program
525 East 68th Street, 3rd Floor Payson Pavillion
New York, NY 10021
(212) 746-6736
www.med.cornell.edu

Fred Hutchinson Cancer Research Center
1100 Fairview Avenue North
Seattle, WA 98109
(206) 667-5000
www.fhcrc.org

The Lymphoma Research Foundation
111 Broadway, 19th Floor
New York, NY 10006
(212) 349-2910
Toll Free: (800) 235-6848
www.lymphoma.org

LEUKEMIA FOR CHICKENS

Notes to Jen

LEUKEMIA FOR CHICKENS

May 20, 2006

Dear Jen,

I wanted to thank you so much for the pictures and the letter that you sent me. I have been thinking about you but have consciously avoided calling you to give you some space away from the whole medical system to regroup. Despite your and my experience, the majority of society goes through life without spending time in a hospital. Nevertheless, I think of you frequently and wonder how you are doing. It must be like your whole world is upside down to go from a 100% devoted wife and caregiver to someone whose role is somewhat undefined and remains for you to recreate. You were his #1 advocate and his most fierce protector. Now you must channel that energy into the development of a new existence for yourself. I have no doubt that it is exceedingly difficult *and* that you will do it in a stellar way. Part of the reason that you will have the strength to move forward is the example that Roger left for you and for all of us.

Roger was one of those patients who changed my life. Every once in a while, you meet an individual who presents a perspective that makes you sit up and take note. Roger did that for me. He challenged me as a person and as a physician, not in a negative way, but in a way that led me to grow positively. I appreciated that.

I love the pictures that you sent me. Roger was always Roger, no matter what he looked like externally. In both pictures, he was smiling and had the ability to enjoy life despite difficult circumstances. In the *Pirkei Avot, Chapter 4, Mishnah 1*, it is said: *"Who is rich? He who is satisfied with his position."* So many of us strive to live by these words and falter, but Roger absolutely knew how to do this with the joy to capture the moment.

I miss our weekly visits, our chats, our friendship. Perhaps some would say that I have allowed the patient-doctor relationship to get too personal, but I'm glad that I did. It was so worth it!

At this point, all I can say is to give yourself plenty of time. You will find the path that is right for you. A part of Roger lives on in the people he loved, as they internalized his approach to life. Keep in touch when you feel that the time is right. I would like that.

Sincerely,

Tsiporah Shore, MD
Associate Director, Bone Marrow and Stem Cell Transplantation
New York Presbyterian Hospital/Weill Cornell Medical Center

June 23, 2006

Dear Jen,

I just wanted to say hello and let you know how much admiration I have for you, even more so after reading Roger's memoir, which I just finished now... What a wonderful book... I could not stop reading it.

Thank you so much for the privilege of having me read it. I wish English was my first language to convey more eloquently how much the book touched me. Roger's expression of love for you and for life is marvelously expressed in this book. The sociological, philosophical, religious and contemporaneous aspects of life brought to this book by his (and your) struggles to better understand human suffering, life and death, and love, are deeply inspiring and educational.

The love, strength and humbleness that Roger and you have for life, and each other, were immediately felt by everyone privileged to have known you both. It was like that upon being in close contact with you we got "infected" immediately by the wonderful bug called respect, admiration and humbleness that you both carry in your hearts, to make this world a better place today.

Roger certainly did not just pass through this life - he has touched those in his path in a significant way, so that we all carry a little bit of him (and you) forever in our hearts and minds.

Take care.

Mary Evelyn D. Flowers, MD
Director, Clinical Long Term Follow-up
Fred Hutchinson Cancer Research Center

June 27, 2006

Dear Jennifer,

It has now been a little over two months since Roger's death – I am sorry that it's taken me this long to finally sit down and put my thoughts in a letter to you. I have thought of Roger and you very often over the past few months.

For me, Roger was at the same time the easiest and the most difficult patient to care for. The easiest for the obvious reasons – he was so intelligent and knowledgeable about his disease (and so much more!); he was kind and compassionate always, often forgiving of us for our shortcomings in caring for him; he was strong and motivated, with an amazing inner strength. The most difficult, as well, for the fact that we all cared so deeply and personally for him. I can say that I felt for him (and for you) as though you were (and are) part of my own family. I admired Roger so much and was pulling for him until the end. He was a remarkable man.

And it is also clear what a remarkable woman you are. In more ways that we can enumerate, Roger was not lucky. But he was lucky to have had you as a wife and a life partner. Your devotion to Roger was unfailing. You were always there for him and always real to him. You carried Roger, your family, and us as caregivers with your strength. In knowing that, it must still continue to be enormously difficult each day for you, as Roger's death was so recent and his presence is still so near.
I have to hope that you know you gave it your all, your 100%. I have hopes, too, in looking forward for you, Jennifer – for a bright, happy, fulfilled and peaceful future. And please don't take this sentiment the wrong way – Roger will always be remembered and with you I am certain, but I guess it's just my way of caring for and relating so profoundly to you.

I continue to think of you both, and your families, often. I would like to remain in touch, if okay by you.

My deepest sympathies and much love to you.

Lynne Strasfeld, MD
Assistant Professor of Medicine
Division of Infectious Diseases
Oregon Health & Science University
(Formerly of NewYork-Presbyterian Hospital/Weill Cornell Medical Center)

May 2006

FINDING INISFREE

Roger looked up at me over the oxygen mask, his eyes drawn wide by the sores stretching his face. He lifted a hand for me to take.

"I'm glad you're here," Jen had said before I'd entered his room. "They've taken him off a lot of the medication. He's very lucid, but he's depressed and scared. Maybe he can get some of that out to you."

Roger and Jen had been referred to me for couples therapy six months earlier. They were both 32, together ten years. Three years before that, Roger had been diagnosed with leukemia. A bone marrow transplant had left him cancer-free, but his prognosis for surviving the rejection response was becoming increasingly pessimistic. The couple would frequently argue, sometimes harshly, over Roger's desire to be independent and Jen's fierce insistence on managing his care.

When they first came to my office, Roger, bent and thin, shuffled through the door on a walker. He acknowledged me from under a baseball cap pulled low over his light-sensitive eyes. When he removed it, I saw that his face was covered with scabs, his bald head mottled in odd colors. It was an effort for him to make himself comfortable on the sofa. Jen let him struggle; at the time, it was hard for me to tell if it was out of respect or neglect.

Jen spoke first, asking how much of her husband's medical situation had been explained to me. I shared what I had been told, being careful not to paint too negative a picture. Then Roger spoke. His calm, thoughtful voice provided a stark contrast to his physical appearance and demeanor. He seemed remarkably free of resentment about his condition. As he told me about the ways in which leukemia was shrinking his world, he would occasionally smile faintly and absentmindedly stroke a missing eyebrow. Soon Jen and Roger both were telling me of the irritations that put them, like any other couple, at odds with one another.

Their next two appointments were cancelled because of Roger's medical needs and the difficulty he had in traveling. I realized that their inability to keep to scheduled office visits might disrupt the continuity needed in therapy. Their apartment was on my way home, so I offered to see them there. They were surprised but pleased, and gratefully accepted my offer.

So began the fall and winter of our work together. On my first visit to their home, I noticed their framed wedding picture. Roger, vibrant, handsome, held Jen firmly to his side. They were the same age as my youngest son. I was struck once again by the cruelty of their lot.

Jen's smile was quick and easy, but her eyes seemed weary with apprehension. During my visits, she would bring me a large cup of instant coffee and Milo, their Airedale, would stand behind his gate and watch us. I would remind them that their situation was exceptional, pointing out that the tensions between them were magnified by their fear of losing one another: for Jen, that Roger might die; for Roger, that Jen might walk away.

Roger had gained the reputation with his doctors of being an inveterate fighter, and the couple showed little inclination to consider the very real possibility that Roger might not survive. I avoided challenging their denial, and soon fell into it myself, despite the fact that Roger, try as he might, could not seem to gain the weight he needed. Gradually, I fell in love with them, as a father loves his children—not always the best thing to do in my trade. Perhaps I sensed the treatment would be brief; perhaps I was awed by their courage.

Roger's hospitalizations became more frequent and, as the rains of April came, his therapist called to tell me that his current stay was likely to be his last. And so, on that day, I went to see them in the hospital. I brought with me the unnerving conviction that I needed to do something to prepare them for Roger's dying.

Death is not familiar to me. My parents died quickly, and far away from me. I, myself, am hopelessly hypochondriacal, and a new ache can sometimes throw me into a panic about my own mortality. I've read a lot of the psychology literature about therapeutic work with the dying, but it always seemed too formulaic to be helpful. I felt hopelessly ill-equipped to help Roger and Jen on that day.

The hospital is old and large and Byzantine. I wound my way through long corridors to Roger's area. Through the door of his room, I could see a man putting ointment on Roger's feet. Gray-haired and distinguished-looking, he might have been one of the doctors but for his jeans and his weary look. Jen waved me in and introduced me. He was Roger's father, a man renowned on Wall Street. Apologizing for not taking my hand, he rose to let us have the room to ourselves. He looked as if he would give all he owned to keep his son.

Jen asked me to see Roger alone. I made my way to his bed, my uncertain steps reminded me of the day Roger first entered my office. I sat awkwardly on the arm of a chair and half-lay beside him. A light behind his bed was blinding and I had to keep shifting in order to be near enough to hear him through his mask. His words were muffled, hollow, like bubbles rising from the depths of his illness. Between labored breaths, he told me he was growing weary, he didn't know if he could continue to fight. But each time he tried to tell Jen how he felt, he was stopped by the fear he saw in her eyes. "You seem much more worried about Jen than about yourself," I told him, amazed that someone in such pain could be so attentive to another.

As I listened to Roger, I realized that for them to accept Roger's illness meant giving up. The very determination that had led them to battle it so heroically was now denying them an opportunity for rest and openness with one another. Finally I asked Roger, "Life shouldn't only be about fighting, should it?"

Roger lay quiet for a minute, and then asked me to bring Jen in. After sitting down, she immediately began discussing his medications. I interrupted to tell her that Roger was having a hard time talking to her, that he was worried that she might not be able to go on without him.

"I can't even think about that, Roger, but I don't want to stop you from talking to me," she said.

"Jen, you've taken a lot from me," he began.

"Roger, I . . ." she interrupted, but almost reflexively I reached to stop her.

"Just listen," I said.

"Jen," he continued, "You are my soul."

With this, I left them together, found my way back through the long corridors and stepped out into the pouring rain. A poem by Yeats, "The Lake Isle at Innisfree," was drifting through my thoughts:

And I shall have some peace there, for peace comes dropping slow
Dropping from the veils of the morning to where the cricket sings.

Two days later, Jen called me early in the morning to tell me that Roger had died peacefully the night before, with her beside him. Despite her grief, she thanked me profusely for the talk I had had with Roger, saying it had calmed him, helped him to reach a different place. I felt the urge to tell her that I hadn't done anything; or, at least, that I hadn't known what I was doing.

Instead, I just listened.

Larry Dyche, ACSW
Albert Einstein College of Medicine

LEUKEMIA FOR CHICKENS

In Remembrance of Roger

Many groups and individuals have made meaningful tributes to Roger's memory. These are just a few examples of memorials established on his behalf, all of which would make him proud.

The Madoff family, Duke University's *Chronicle* and *Bloomberg News* have collaborated in establishing The Roger Madoff Scholarship. Each summer, in Roger's honor, an outstanding student journalist at *The Chronicle* will be awarded an internship at *Bloomberg News* in New York City. To learn more about the scholarship, please contact Jonathan Angier, general manager of *The Chronicle*, 103 West Union Building, Duke University, Durham, NC 27708.

• • •

The High Peaks area of the Adirondacks was a treasured refuge for Roger. The Madoff family and the Adirondack Mountain Club have dedicated "Roger's Outlook," a viewing platform on Heart Lake, in his memory. Heart Lake is located in the Adirondak Loj recreation area, five miles south of Lake Placid. For information about visiting or to make a donation towards the preservation of the Adirondack Park, contact the Adirondack Mountain Club at www.adk.org.

Roger and Jen's niece, Rebecca, at Heart Lake, September 2006

LEUKEMIA FOR CHICKENS